Published by Concordia Publishing House

and Fortress Press in 55 volumes.

General Editors are Jaroslav Pelikan (for vols. 1-30)

and Helmut T. Lehmann (for vols. 31-55).

LUTHER'S WORKS

VOLUME 39

Church and Ministry

I

EDITED BY

ERIC W. GRITSCH

GENERAL EDITOR

HELMUT T. LEHMANN

FORTRESS PRESS / PHILADELPHIA

Library of Congress Catalog Card Number 55-9893

ISBN 0-8006-0339-7

Printed in the United States of America *1-339*

GENERAL EDITORS' PREFACE

The first editions of Luther's collected works appeared in the sixteenth century, and so did the first efforts to make him "speak English." In America serious attempts in these directions were made for the first time in the nineteenth century. The Saint Louis edition of Luther was the first endeavor on American soil to publish a collected edition of his works, and the Henkel Press in Newmarket, Virginia, was the first to publish some of Luther's writings in an English translation. During the first decade of the twentieth century, J. N. Lenker produced translations of Luther's sermons and commentaries in thirteen volumes. A few years later the first of the six volumes in the Philadelphia (or Holman) edition of the *Works of Martin Luther* appeared. But a growing recognition of the need for more of Luther's works in English has resulted in this American edition of Luther's works.

The edition is intended primarily for the reader whose knowledge of late medieval Latin and sixteenth-century German is too small to permit him to work with Luther in the original languages. Those who can will continue to read Luther in his original words as these have been assembled in the monumental Weimar edition (*D. Martin Luthers Werke*. Kritische Gesamtausgabe; Weimar, 1883-). Its texts and helps have formed a basis for this edition, though in certain places we have felt constrained to depart from its readings and findings. We have tried throughout to translate Luther as he thought translating should be done. That is, we have striven for faithfulness on the basis of the best lexicographical materials available. But where literal accuracy and clarity have conflicted, it is clarity that we have preferred, so that sometimes paraphrase seemed more faithful than literal fidelity. We have proceeded in a similar way in the matter of Bible versions, translating Luther's translations. Where this could be done by the use of an existing English version—King James, Douay, or Revised Standard—we have done so. Where it could not, we have supplied our own. To indicate this in each specific instance would have been pedantic; to adopt a uniform procedure would have been artificial—especially in view of Luther's own inconsistency in this regard. In each volume the translator will be responsible primarily for matters of text and language, while the responsibility of the editor will extend principally to the historical and theological matters reflected in the introductions and notes.

Although the edition as planned will include fifty-five volumes, Luther's writings are not being translated in their entirety. Nor should they be. As he was the first to insist, much of what he wrote and said was not that important. Thus the edition is a selection of works that have proved their importance for the faith, life, and history of the Christian church. The first thirty volumes contain Luther's expositions of various biblical books, while the remaining volumes include what are usually called his "Reformation writings" and other occasional pieces. The final volume of the set will be an index volume; in addition to an index of quotations, proper names, and topics, and a list of corrections and changes, it will contain a glossary of many of the technical terms that recur in Luther's works and that cannot be defined each time they appear. Obviously Luther cannot be forced into any neat set of rubrics. He can provide his reader with bits of autobiography or with political observations as he expounds a psalm, and he can speak tenderly about the meaning of the faith in the midst of polemics against his opponents. It is the hope of publishers, editors, and translators that through this edition the message of Luther's faith will speak more clearly to the modern church.

J.P.
H.T.L.

CONTENTS

ABBREVIATIONS

BG – *Luthers Werke für das Christliche Haus,* edited by Georg Buchwald *et al.*, 4th edition (Leipzig, 1924).

CIC – *Corpus Iuris Canonici,* edited by E. Friedberg (Graz, 1955).

CL – *Luthers Werke in Auswahl,* edited by Otto Clemen *et al.* (Bonn, 1912-1933; Berlin, 1955-1956).

CR – *Corpus Reformatorum,* edited by C. G. Bretschneider and H. E. Bindseil (Halle/Saale, 1834-1860).

DRTA. JR – *Deutsche Reichstagsakten unter Kaiser Karl V,* edited by Historische Kommission bei der Bayrischen Akademie der Wissenschaften (Gotha, 1893-).

EA – *D. Martin Luthers sämmtliche Werke* (Frankfurt and Erlangen, 1826-1857).

LW – American Edition of *Luther's Works* (Philadelphia and St. Louis, 1955-).

MA^3 – *Martin Luther.* Ausgewählte Werke (3rd ed., München, 1948-).

MPL – *Patrologia, Series Latina,* 221 vols. in 222, edited by J. P. Migne (Paris, 1844-1904).

NCE – *The New Catholic Encyclopedia* (15 vols.; McGraw Hill Book Company, 1967).

PE – *Works of Martin Luther.* Philadelphia Edition (Philadelphia, 1915-1943).

PNF – *The Nicene and Post-Nicene Fathers of the Christian Church.* First Series: edited by Philip Schaff (New York, 1886-1900).

PNF[2] — *The Nicene and Post-Nicene Fathers of the Christian Church.* Second Series: edited by Philip Schaff and H. Wace (New York, 1886-1900).

RGG — *Die Religion in Geschichte und Gegenwart* (3rd ed.; 6 vols.; Tübingen, 1957-1962).

St. L. — *D. Martin Luthers sämmtliche Schriften,* edited by Johann Georg Walch. Edited and published in modern German, 23 vols. in 25 (2nd ed.; St. Louis, 1880-1910).

SW — *Selected Writings of Martin Luther* (Philadelphia, 1967).

WA — *D. Martin Luthers Werke.* Kritische Gesamtausgabe (Weimar, 1883-).

WA, Br — *D. Martin Luthers Werke.* Briefwechsel (Weimar, 1930-).

WA, DB — *D. Martin Luthers Werke.* Deutsche Bibel (Weimar, 1906-1961).

WA, TR — *D. Martin Luthers Werke.* Tischreden (Weimar, 1912-1921).

INTRODUCTION TO
Church and Ministry

Luther's understanding of church and ministry is deeply imbedded in a dialectic characteristic of his theology as a whole: a childlike faith clinging to the word of God and a theological sagacity tracking down the weakness of the word of man. "Thank God," Luther wrote in the *Smalcald Articles* of 1537—his theological testament in the face of threatening divisions in his own camp—"a seven-year-old child knows what the church is, namely, holy believers and sheep who hear the voice of their Shepherd [John 10:3]. So children pray, 'I believe in one holy Christian church.' Its holiness does not consist of surplices, tonsures, albs, or other ceremonies of theirs [the papists] which they have invented over and above the Holy Scriptures, but it consists of the Word of God and true faith."[1]

Obviously such a simple definition of the church sufficed neither for Luther's own time nor for subsequent Protestant generations, as Luther's ecclesiological treatises and innumerable "Lutheran" theological studies clearly demonstrate. As Heinrich Bornkamm put it, "It cannot be denied that theological research has always viewed this seven-year-old child with some envy or perhaps with a bit of doubt."[2] Moreover, Luther research itself has produced so many studies, particularly in the past twenty-five years,[3] that it is probably true to say more has been written about Luther than about any other person except Jesus Christ.[4] And yet Luther's definition of the church in the *Smalcald Articles* discloses the center from which his theological reflections radiate: the word of God.

[1] Theodore G. Tappert (ed.), *The Book of Concord* (Philadelphia: Fortress Press, 1959), p. 315.

[2] Martin H. Bertram (trans.), Heinrich Bornkamm, *Luther's World of Thought* (St. Louis: Concordia Publishing House, 1958), p. 134.

[3] Cf. "Luther Research Since 1945," *The Lutheran World,* XIII (1966). This issue can serve as a guide for further reading in Luther's ecclesiology.

[4] The statement is attributed to Albert Hyma. Cf. Lewis W. Spitz, "Luther's Ecclesiology and His Concept of the Prince as *Notbischof,*" *Church History,* XXII (1953), 136.

True faith, he insisted, rests on the word, that is, God's self-disclosure in Jesus of Nazareth, in whom "the word became flesh and dwelt among us."[5] Thus Luther did not begin his drive for church reform on the basis of a pious individualism born in the agony of a selfish urge to be saved from doubt and inner turmoil (*Anfechtung*). Rather, Luther urged ecclesiastical renewal on the basis of a clear conception of the church derived from intensive scholarly study and existential appropriation of the word of God in Holy Scripture. "Where the word is, there is faith; and where faith is, there is the true church."[6] Karl Holl[7] has shown that Luther arrived at his new understanding of the church even before 1517, through his lectures on the Psalms (1513-1515). Ernst Kinder[8] and Heiko Oberman[9] have drawn attention to the influence St. Augustine and late medieval strands of theology had on Luther's ecclesiology and doctrine of justification. The thesis is therefore warranted that Luther already had formulated his ecclesiological principles at the beginning of his career as Professor of Biblical Theology at the University of Wittenberg in 1512. "It is due to this fact that, later, when Luther, as the leader of the Reformation, had to serve as the guide, interpreter, and defender of evangelical Christianity, his views, proposals, and criticisms always showed a remarkable fundamental consistency in spite of the fact that the pressure of

[5] For a systematic study of the concept of the word in Luther, cf. Joseph Sittler, *The Doctrine of the Word in the Structure of Lutheran Theology* ("The Knubel-Miller Foundation Lectures" [Philadelphia: Muhlenberg Press, 1948]), pp. 14-27.

[6] Cf. *Resolution Concerning the Lutheran Thesis XIII on the Power of the Pope (Resolutio Lutheriana Super Propositione Sua Decima Tertia de Potestate Papae),* 1519. *WA* 2, 208.

[7] Cf. Karl Holl, "Die Entstehung von Luthers Kirchenbegriff," in *Gesammelte Aufsätze zur Kirchengeschichte* (6th ed.; 3 vols.; Tübingen, 1928-1932), I, 288-325. Cf. also the critique of Hans J. Iwand, "Zur Entstehung von Luthers Kirchenbegriff," in Wilhelm Schneemelcher (ed.), *Festschrift für Günther Dehn* (Neukirchen, 1957), pp. 145-166.

[8] Cf. Ernst Kinder, "Gottesreich und Weltreich bei Augustinus und Luther. Erwägungen zu einer Vergleichung der 'Zwei-Reiche' Lehre Augustins und Luthers," in Friedrich Hübner (ed.), *Gedenkschrift für D. Werner Elert* (Berlin, 1955), pp. 24-42.

[9] Cf. Heiko Oberman, " 'Iustitia Christi' and 'Iustitia Dei': Luther and the Scholastic Doctrines of Justification," *The Harvard Theological Review,* LIX (1966), 1-26. Cf. also by the same author, "Simul gemitus et raptus: Luther und die Mystik," in Ivar Asheim (ed.), *The Church, Mysticism, Sanctification and the Natural in Luther's Thought* (Philadelphia: Fortress Press, 1967), pp. 20-59.

the demands that were made on him impelled him to improvise most of his writings and to address them more or less spontaneously to the issues at hand."[10]

Luther's basic definition of the church is derived from the biblical teaching about the "people of God" and the confession of the Apostles' Creed, "I believe in the communion of saints." Thus Luther emphasized the noninstitutional character of the church—he disliked the word "church" (*Kirche*) and preferred terms such as "community" (*Gemeinde*), "congregation" (*Gemeine*), and "assembly" (*Sammlung*)[11]—as seen in the interaction of the persons who are living members of the body of Christ. The communion of saints is both a hidden (*absconditus*) community (in the sense of Paul's statement in I Cor. 2:7-15) and a visible (*sichtbar*) fellowship.[12] It must be hidden because faith is "the conviction of things not seen" (Heb. 11:1); it is never completely realized on earth in either its universal or its congregational extension, since God has reserved the complete realization of faith to the Last Day. The true nature of the church, therefore, is not fully revealed, just as God was not fully disclosed even on the cross of Jesus, and has remained a hidden God (*deus absconditus*). On the other hand, the church can be recognized through concrete signs such as the preaching of the word, the distribution of the sacraments, the confession of faith, and even the ban.[13] Luther maintained this dialectic between the hidden church and visible fellowship with a fundamental consistency throughout his writings, even though he directed his attention more and more to the church in this world.[14] Thus he could say, on the one hand—using a daring image—that "God does not want the world to know when he sleeps with his bride";[15] and on the

[10] Wilhelm Pauck, *The Heritage of the Reformation* (2nd ed. rev.; Glencoe, Ill.: The Free Press of Glencoe, 1961), p. 31.

[11] On Luther's various translations of the Greek *ecclesia*, cf. *ibid.*, p. 32.

[12] On the significant problem of the relationship between "hidden" and "visible" church, cf. Ferdinand Kattenbusch, *Die Doppelschichtigkeit in Luthers Kirchenbegriff* (Gotha, 1928).

[13] Cf. *A Sermon on the Ban*, 1520, below, pp. 5-22. On Luther's concept of the ban, cf. Herbert J. A. Bauman (trans.), Hans-Werner Gensichen, *We Condemn* (St. Louis: Concordia Publishing House, 1967), Part II.

[14] Cf. Gerhard Müller, "Ekklesiologie und Kirchenrecht beim jungen Luther," *Neue Zeitschrift für systematische Theologie und Religionsphilosophie*, VII (1968), 128.

[15] In a sermon on Luke 19:1-10, preached in 1527. Cf. *WA* 17^{II}, 501.

other hand, that "the assembly of the church is visible for the sake of the confession of faith" (Rom. 10:10).[16]

When Luther elaborated his basic definition of the church as the communion of saints, he stressed the fellowship into which Christians are called by the Holy Spirit. Accordingly, the church consists of people who are incorporated into Christ and each other like the ingredients of a cake: none is for himself, but instead each is blended with the others in the fellowship of love.[17] Luther himself depended on the "consolation of the brethren" (*consolatio fratrum*) whenever he suffered inner turmoil and temptation—especially in the year 1527, when he was plagued by illness, the loss of friends, and various other forms of *Anfechtung*.[18] Communion meant true communication to Luther, through word and sacrament, in the giving of oneself to Christ and to one's neighbor. Just as Christ emptied himself for the world on the cross (Phil. 2:5-11), so the Christian is to empty himself to his neighbor in love. And yet Luther did not present an idealistic or perfectionistic picture of the church. He had a sense for the historicity of the people of God, for the trials and tribulations of the men of God, be they Old Testament prophets, New Testament apostles, or medieval clerics. The communion of saints is at the same time the communion of sinners who have to bear each other's burdens. Luther's theology of the cross here extends into his ecclesiology: just as Christ renewed mankind through his death, so, too, the Christian must become a "Christ" to a fallen world. Thus Luther emphasized the Christian's responsibility not to run away from the church when it is in trouble, but to stay and work for its renewal.[19]

Luther's commitment to church reform in "spirit and structure"[20] was based on his understanding of the word of God as the continuing force with which God accomplishes his mission of salvation in the world. His return to the biblical understanding of community—nourished particularly by his intensive study of the

---

[16] Thesis 27 of a disputation held on February 3, 1542, at the promotion of John Machabeus Scotus. Cf. *WA* 39^{II}, 161.

[17] In a sermon preached on Maundy Thursday, 1523. Cf. *WA* 12, 487-488.

[18] Cf. Luther's correspondence of 1527. *WA*, Br 4; Preserved Smith (ed.), *Luther's Correspondence and Other Contemporary Letters* (2 vols.; Philadelphia: The Lutheran Publication Society, 1913), II, 389-428.

[19] Gf. *Lectures on Galatians*, 1519. *LW* 27, 392.

[20] Cf. Jaroslav Pelikan, *Spirit Versus Structure: Luther and the Institutional Church* (New York: Harper and Row, 1968).

Old Testament[21]—gave him a sense of the church's historical continuity.[22] He concluded that the church of his own time had fallen away from true obedience to the word of God; the papacy and hierarchy of Rome had gone beyond the proper limits of tradition, even if they did defend their existence in the name of an authentic tradition. Consequently, Luther's dialectic between the hidden and visible church soon drove him to the question of whether or not the Roman church was a true or a false church. His studies in the history of the church, especially the problem of the origin of papal authority—so vehemently debated at the Leipzig Debate in 1519—provided him with convincing evidence that the Roman church could no longer claim to be the true church. On the contrary, Luther argued, those who are evangelical (*evangelisch*) are "the true, ancient church, one body and one communion of saints with the holy, universal, Christian church."[23] Yet Luther did not teach absolute biblicism in the sense of anti-traditionalism.[24] When sacramentarian groups argued against infant baptism and the doctrine of the real presence in the Lord's Supper on the basis of Scripture, Luther emphasized the validity of ecclesiastical tradition. "It is dangerous and terrible," he wrote in 1532 to Duke Albrecht of Prussia, who had complained about the infiltration of Dutch and Schwenckfeldian radicals into his territory, "to hear or to believe anything contrary to common witness, faith, and doctrine which the entire holy Christian church has maintained throughout the world from the beginning until now—for more than fifteen hundred years."[25] On the other hand, when the papacy claimed to be the only interpreter of Scripture on the basis of a long-standing ecclesiastical tradition, Luther insisted on having Scripture be the standard of what can and cannot claim to be good tradition in the church.[26] Such seemingly contradictory statements grew out of Luther's fundamental conviction that the word of God could never be identified completely either with the biblical text or with ecclesi-

[21] Cf. Eric W. and Ruth C. Gritsch (trans.), Victor I. Gruhn (ed.), Heinrich Bornkamm, *Luther and the Old Testament* (Philadelphia: Fortress Press, 1969).

[22] Cf. Wilhelm Maurer, "Luthers Anschauungen über die Kontinuität der Kirche," in Asheim (ed.), *op. cit.*, pp. 95-121.

[23] Cf. *Against Hanswurst*, 1539. *LW* 41, 199.

[24] Cf. Robert C. Schultz (trans.), Paul Althaus, *The Theology of Martin Luther* (Philadelphia: Fortress Press, 1966), p. 335.

[25] Cf. *WA* 30^{III}, 552.

[26] Cf. Althaus, *op. cit.*, p. 335.

astical tradition. He simply followed his conviction, grounded in the depth of Pauline theology (Gal. 1:10), that "it is far safer to ascribe too much to God than to men."[27] Just as the word of God and the word of men are not identical as long as man lives within the boundaries of history, so, too, the true church and the empirical church are not the same. Luther maintained that there are some points at which both churches testify to each other: in the gospel, the sacraments, the keys, etc.[28] He refused to dissolve this paradoxical dialectic through the Aristotelian logic permeating the theology of his time. To him, the church is neither an invisible Platonic reality nor an unchanging institution. Rather, like the individual Christian, the church is continually struggling and constantly recreated and sustained by the word of God. "It is not in the stage of having become but of becoming" (*Sie steht nicht im Gewordensein, sondern im Werden*).[29] That is why Luther was angered by the ecclesiastical positivism of the Roman church and the enthusiastic (*schwärmerisch*) spiritualism of radical reformers such as Thomas Münzer.[30]

Luther's definition of the church as the communion of saints is the basis for his definition of ministry. In his early studies of the New Testament he already discovered that the saints of the church live on earth rather than in heaven. "The living saints are your neighbors—the naked, the hungry, the thirsty, the poor, those who have wives and children, those who live in shame. Direct your help to them."[31] Thus Luther opposed the nonpersonal, materialistic definition of sainthood in scholastic theology and the related doctrine of the treasury of merits formulated in the thirteenth century[32]—according to which the ordinary Christian could receive indulgences by investing moral efforts and even financial means in the sainthood of those who had preceded him and had done more than was required by the law of God. Luther substituted service (*Dienst*) for merit (*Verdienst*). Just as Christ carried the burden of men, giving them *his* righteousness, so one Christian is to carry

[27] Cf. *Lectures on Galatians*, 1535. *LW* 26, 66.

[28] Cf. especially *On the Councils and the Church*, 1539. *LW* 41, 148-178.

[29] Cf. Bornkamm, *op. cit.*, p. 149.

[30] Cf. my book, *Reformer Without a Church: The Life and Thought of Thomas Muentzer, 1488[?]-1525* (Philadelphia: Fortress Press, 1967).

[31] Sermon preached on November 2, 1522. Cf. *WA* 10^{III}, 408.

[32] Cf. Thesis 58 in the *Ninety-five Theses*. *LW* 31, 20-21 and 30.

the burden of the other. To be a priest means to intercede for the other before God, to proclaim the word of forgiveness, to hold the power of the keys, to celebrate the sacrament, in short, to participate with faith in the salvation God provided in Christ. The priesthood of Christ and the priesthood of Christians belong together.

The reality of the Christian community rather than the notion of religious individualism determined Luther's conception of ministry. For the existing community is the visible historical sign that God works in the world; it is the place where Christians share the "royal priesthood" with Christ (I Pet. 2:9). Thus Luther called the priesthood a "holy order" for all Christians, instituted by God, together with marriage and civil authority.[33]

Luther's doctrine of the common priesthood of all believers, developed particularly in his treatises of 1520, is one of the most revolutionary doctrines in the history of Christianity. Every Christian is priest in the sense of servant (I Cor. 4:1). Luther argued that the special class of priesthood in Christianity was produced only by the influence of pagan culture mixed with Jewish cultic ideas.[34] There is only a functional difference between those Christians who hold the office of the word and those who serve each other in mutual consolation. The consecration of priests is therefore not a sacrament or holy order (*ordo*), but a liturgical function of the congregation, a rite (*ritus*), through which Christians are called into the public office of the ministry.[35] One can be called into the office of the ministry directly, as God called prophets and apostles, or indirectly, through men. No one should arbitrarily ordain himself to be a preacher, for to do so is disobedience to God, who wills "that nothing be done as a result of one's own choice or decision, but everything as a consequence of a command [*Befehl*] or a call [*Beruf*]. That is especially true of preaching. . . ."[36] Accordingly, the ministry is but one vocation among others—a conclusion which had far-reaching consequences for Luther's ethical pronouncements.[37]

[33] Cf. *Confession Concerning Christ's Supper*, 1528. *LW* 37, 364.

[34] Cf. *Concerning the Ministry*, 1523. *LW* 40, 35.

[35] Cf. *The Babylonian Captivity of the Church*, 1520. *LW* 36, 106-117.

[36] Cf. *Psalm 82*, 1530. *LW* 13, 65.

[37] Cf. Carl C. Rasmussen (trans.), Gustaf Wingren, *Luther on Vocation* (Philadelphia: Fortress Press, 1957).

Luther's understanding of ministry, like his conception of the church, rested on his fundamental discovery of the word of God. The word begets faith and faith begets the church, which, in turn, proclaims the word. Thus Luther rejected the hierarchical interpretation of the church in medieval theology as well as the personalistic conception of the priesthood which, in spite of Luther's rejection, was to recur in subsequent neo-Lutheran periods of Protestantism.[38] He stressed the personal character of faith—the commitment to what Christ did for men—an emphasis which produced serious misunderstandings among Roman Catholics and Protestants alike. While the former often regarded Luther's conception of faith as "religious spiritualism," the latter reduced it to subjective experience. Thus both groups failed to comprehend the aspect of fellowship and communion in his ecclesiology.[39]

To sum up: (1) Luther's appreciation of the biblical world of ideas, as well as of Augustinian and late medieval strands of theology, drove him to an understanding of church and ministry in terms of the people of God whose faith is constantly nourished by the word of God. Those who belong to the people of God are called to live in communion with each other, a communion marked by the preaching of the word, the administration of the sacraments, and the "mutual consolation of the brethren." (2) Neither the universal church nor the local congregation is ever perfect as long as they exist in history; instead, they are always in a state of becoming (*Kirche im Werden*), that is, they are incomplete and even sinful until the end of time. Only then will God determine who really belongs to the body of Christ. There is no guarantee on earth that a particular church or congregation is the true church if the judgment is made in terms of ecclesiastical government, confessional orthodoxy, or moral propriety. The chief task of the church is to

---

[38] Cf. Walther von Loewenich, *Luther und der Neuprotestantismus* (Witten, 1963).

[39] This Introduction can only sketch Luther's basic concept of church and ministry. For a summary of problems of interpretation, cf. Althaus, *op. cit.*, pp. 287-344. For a Roman Catholic judgment, still popular, on Luther's "spiritualism," cf. Ronald Walls (trans.), Joseph Lortz, *The Reformation in Germany* (2 vols.; New York: Herder and Herder, 1968), I, 261: Luther exhibited "an irresistible allurement to the subjective caprice of all antinomians"! The on-going debate regarding Luther's concept of ministry is treated in Brian A. Gerrish, "Priesthood and Ministry in the Theology of Luther," *Church History,* XXXIV (1965), 404-422. On the critical issues in Luther's ecclesiology as a whole, cf. Pauck, *op. cit.*, pp. 37-59.

continue God's mission in faithfulness to his word rather than to proclaim or defend its establishment as the only guarantee of truth. (3) Finally, Luther viewed church and ministry in the perspective of concrete historical situations such as the trials of prophets and apostles in biblical times, the social and political problems of the citizen in the sixteenth-century Holy Roman Empire, and the consequences of ecclesiastical abuse. That is why his views at times contain ambiguities reflecting the dialectic between theological reflection and historical change. He sometimes appears to stand on fixed dogmatic principles—particularly in his opposition to left-wing radicals (*Schwärmer*) in his own camp, or to right-wing conservatives defending the papacy. Nevertheless, his childlike faith, as well as his theological sagacity which saw the real points at issue—combined with his inherent Saxon humor—provided subsequent generations of Christians with significant clues regarding a proper understanding of the church and its ministry. "What is Luther?" he asked in 1522, when his name began to be associated with political insurrection. "I ask that men make no reference to my name. . . . I neither am nor want to be anyone's master. I hold, together with the universal church, the one universal teaching of Christ, who is our only master" [Matt. 23:8].[40]

E.W.G.

[40] Cf. *A Sincere Admonition by Martin Luther to All Christians to Guard Against Insurrection and Rebellion,* 1522. *LW* 45, 70-71.

INTRODUCTION TO VOLUME 39

Luther's writings in this volume, selected from many others which stem from the same period (1520-1523), were written during the most dramatic years of Luther's career as a reformer. This period is highlighted by the "long hot summer" of 1520, when he made his most significant proposals for ecclesiastical renewal; by the heresy trial, initiated by Rome, leading to Luther's condemnation in the papal bull *Decet Romanum* on January 3, 1521; by the Edict of Worms, which declared him an enemy of the empire in the same year; by his voluntary exile at the Wartburg for several months after the edict; by his dramatic return to Wittenberg on March 6, 1522, to begin his successful battle against radical reformers; and by the realization of his constructive ideas through the establishment of new "Lutheran" ecclesiastical structures in Saxony and elsewhere.[1] Luther's fast rise to national and international prominence during these years exposed him to many pressures from many quarters: "Romanist" theologians continued the Leipzig Debate of 1519 by means of literary feuds with the Wittenberg professor; radicals in Luther's own camp attempted to involve him in programs ranging from the realization of "puritan" ideals to the establishment of military alliances against the emperor, such as the uprising of the German knights and the rebellion of the peasants; friends asked for pastoral advice; and political enemies, through German diets, called for the enforcement of the Edict of Worms. Luther reacted to all these pressures with an incisive mind and a fast hand, mainly with the publication of sermons, pamphlets, and polemical treatises. For example, in the six months following the Leipzig Debate, he published sixteen treatises in addition to the lengthy *Lectures on Galatians*,[2] without relinquishing his daily routine of lecturing and preaching. The material flowed from his pen. "I have a fast hand and a rapid memory," Luther explained. "When I write, it just

[1] For historical details, cf. the Introductions to *LW* 31 and 32, and E. G. Schwiebert, *Luther and His Times* (St. Louis: Concordia Publishing House, 1950), pp. 331-570.

[2] Cf. *LW* 27.

and *Dr. Luther's Retraction of His Error, Forced upon Him by the Most Highly Learned Priest of God, Sir Jerome Emser, Vicar in Meissen.* These works reveal his basic stance in theological controversy: an analytical mind pursuing the opponent's trend of argument, a mastery and knowledge of Scripture and tradition, and a fine Saxon sense of humor. The most important of these four treatises is probably the *Answer to the Hyperchristian, Hyperspiritual, and Hyperlearned Book by Goat Emser in Leipzig,* where Luther reiterates his argument for the common priesthood of all believers, which had already been stated programmatically in his address to the German nobility. At the same time, the treatise discloses Luther's basic principles of evangelical exegesis from which his concepts of church and ministry emerged. While both Emser and Thomas Murner (a Franciscan monk and author of satirical pamphlets) branded Luther a destroyer of civil and ecclesiastical order, Luther used the literary feud to advance the basic features of his concept of the priesthood, simultaneously exposing the weak argumentation of his two opponents.

Luther's polemical treatise *Against the Spiritual Estate of the Pope and the Bishops, Falsely So Called* contains his categorical rejection of the doctrine of "holy orders" as represented by Archbishop Albrecht of Mainz, Luther's old enemy dating from the indulgence controversy of 1517.[8] Now Luther threatened him with the power of a reformer who had shaken the foundations of the medieval ecclesiastical establishment. Writing his own "bull" against the Roman heresy, he laid bare the many weaknesses and immoralities of the spiritual estate such as celibacy, political tyranny, and financial greed. At the same time he portrayed the true "face" of the Christian priest in contrast to the "masks" of sixteenth-century ecclesiastical princes.

The final treatise in this volume is Luther's argument for congregational authority in *That a Christian Assembly or Congregation Has the Right and Power to Judge All Teaching and to Call, Appoint, and Dismiss Teachers, Established and Proven by Scripture.* The concept of the church as the communion of saints—centering in the idea of mutual consolation and common priesthood—is here applied to a concrete situation in the Saxon town of Leisnig:

[8] Cf. *LW* 31, xv-xvi.

since all Christians are equal through baptism, they have the right to exercise the office of the keys.[9] Drawing on the experience of early Christianity as reflected especially in the pastoral epistles of the New Testament, Luther charged the congregation with the exclusive responsibility to call and to ordain ministers.

Even though Luther's writings in this volume reflect his dramatic involvement in radically different situations—the plight of the man in the pew, the arrogance of conservative theological scholarship, the clash with the spiritual estate, and the reorganization of congregational life—they disclose, at the same time, the formation of his ecclesiological principles in the rhythm of his theology as a whole: his constant reflection on the word of God in the light of concrete problems of Christian existence. He was able to bring the questions arising in the context of fast historical change to the level of genuine theological reflection, which resulted in practical proposals for ecclesiastical reform. It is significant to note, in reading the ecclesiological treatises of the young Luther, that he developed his new concepts of church and ministry with due regard for existing ecclesiastical practice—although some of his writings exhibit the impatience, and even disgust, of a theologian who never received a proper hearing before his ecclesiastical superiors. This obstinacy on the part of ecclesiastical authorities determined to defend their human tradition as God's law convinced Luther that personal faith and institutional tradition could become irreconcilable. These writings are evidence that Luther knew the tyranny of tradition and the freedom of faith. "I too was once in error," he confessed to his worst enemy, Archbishop Albrecht of Mainz, "but the Father of all mercy did not look at my vice, blasphemy, and my very sinful, evil life; instead, out of the infinite richness of his grace, he permitted me to know his Son, Jesus Christ, and to teach [him] to others, until we were certain of his truth."[10]

E.W.G.

[9] Cf. *The Keys*, 1530. *LW* 40, 321-377.
[10] Cf. below, p. 248.

LUTHER'S WORKS

VOLUME 39

A SERMON ON THE BAN

1520

Translated by

Eric W. and Ruth C. Gritsch

INTRODUCTION

Luther's *Sermon on the Ban* was motivated by his pastoral concern for proper ecclesiastical practice. In a Lenten sermon preached in Wittenberg on March 17, 1518, he had already attacked the misuse of the ban. "So far has this childish veneration and holiness gone," he complained about the use of ecclesiastical power, "that they have started this game of excommunication, and the letters are flying about like bats, all because of a trifling thing."[1] According to Luther, the ban, like the letters of indulgence, was no longer used for the edification of troubled Christian consciences. Instead, it had become a means to enforce the fiscal policies of the church. Many a Christian community had been "banned" because it had not paid ecclesiastical dues in time or was unable to raise the money.[2]

In another sermon preached May 16, 1518, in the Town Church of Wittenberg, Luther used the text for Exaudi Sunday (John 15: 26–16:4) to offer his own understanding of the ban. Published in August, 1518, with the title *Sermon on the Virtue of Excommunication,*[3] it caused much consternation among the ecclesiastical authorities because Luther had incited people to defy the ban in the name of a righteous cause. Later, in a letter to his friend Wenceslaus Link in Nürnberg, he complained that he had wanted a public debate on the matter but that it had been put off by his bishop because "it stirred up some officials."[4]

Since a public debate on the ban was not possible, Luther continued to warn the Wittenbergers about the misuse of the ban. The *Sermon on the Ban,* probably preached in December, 1519, but not published before 1520,[5] repeated much that Luther had already said a few months earlier. It is intimately linked with his discussion of *The Blessed Sacrament of the Holy and True Body*

[1] Cf. *LW* 51, 42.

[2] Cf. Boehmer, *Road to Reformation,* pp. 223-225.

[3] *Sermo de virtute excommunicationis. WA* 1, 638-643.

[4] The letter was written July 10, 1518. Cf. *WA,* Br 1, 185-186; Smith (ed.), *Luther's Correspondence,* I, 98.

[5] The exact date is not known. For a discussion of the date, cf. *St. L.* 19, 885.

of Christ, and the Brotherhoods,[6] which dealt with the question of what it means to take part in the fellowship (*communicare*). Here he discusses what it means "to put under the ban" (*excommunicare*).

The first edition of the *Sermon on the Ban* appeared from the press of John Grünenberg in Wittenberg, followed by other editions in Leipzig, Augsburg, and Basel between 1520 and 1523. The following translation is based on the German Grünenberg text, reprinted in *WA* 6, 63-75, under the title, *Ein Sermon von dem Bann.* There is another English translation by J. J. Schindel, available in *PE* 2, 33-54.

[6] Cf. *LW* 35, 45-73.

A SERMON ON THE BAN

Jesus

1. Since we have already heard[1] that the sacrament of the holy body of Christ is a sign of the community of all saints, we must now learn what the ban is which is exercised through the power of the spiritual estate in Christendom. For its principal, real function and power is to deprive a sinful Christian of the holy sacrament and to forbid it to him. That is why the one cannot be understood without the other as long as they stand in opposition to each other. The Latin word *communio* means "fellowship," and this is what scholars call the holy sacrament. Its opposite is the word *excommunicatio,* which means "exclusion" from this fellowship, and this is what scholars call the ban.

2. Fellowship is of two kinds, just as there are two things, namely, sign and significance, in the sacrament, as I said in the sermon.[2] The first kind of fellowship is inward, spiritual, and invisible, for it is in the heart. It means that through faith, hope, and love a man is incorporated into the fellowship of Christ and all the saints—as signified and given in the sacrament. This is the work and power of the sacrament. No man, be he bishop or pope, nor any creature or even angel may either grant or take away such fellowship. Only God himself, through his Holy Spirit, must pour it into the heart of the man who believes in the sacrament, as was said in the sermon.[3] Here, too, no ban is able to reach or to exist, except the unbelief or sin of man himself. Consequently, he excommunicates himself and separates himself from the grace, life, and blessedness of the community. St. Paul proves this in Romans 8 [:35, 38]: "Who shall separate us from the love of God?" Can fear and distress do it? Or hunger and poverty? Or danger, persecution,

[1] Cf. *The Blessed Sacrament of the Holy and True Body of Christ, and the Brotherhoods,* 1519. *LW* 35, 45-73.

[2] Cf. *LW* 35, 49.

[3] Cf. *LW* 35, 58.

may never become anything, but a deprivation of the outward sacrament or of association with people. Just as, if I were put in prison, I would certainly be deprived of outward association with good friends, but I would not be deprived of their favor and friendship. In the same way, he who is put under the ban is forced to live without the common sacrament and association with men; nevertheless he is not abandoned on that account by their love, intercession, and good works.

7. It is certainly true that wherever the ban is rightly and deservedly imposed it is a sign, a warning, and a punishment. In this way he who is put under the ban should acknowledge that he himself has delivered his soul up to the devil through his own transgression and sin, and that he has deprived himself of the fellowship of all the saints with Christ. For his mother, the holy church, wants to show her dear son this unbearable damage of sin, by way of the punishment of the ban, and thereby wants to bring him back from the devil to God again. It is just the same as when a natural physical mother threatens and punishes her son when he does evil. She does not deliver him to the hangman or to the wolves, nor does she make a knave of him, but rather she restrains him and shows him by way of this same punishment how he could end up with the hangman. And so she keeps him in his father's home. In the same way, when a spiritual authority puts someone under the ban it should keep this in mind: "Look, you have done this and that whereby you have delivered your soul up to the devil, earned God's wrath, deprived yourself of the fellowship of all Christians, and fallen under the inward, spiritual ban before God, and you neither want to stop it nor to return. Well then, I therefore put you too under the outward ban before men. In order to shame you I am depriving you of the sacrament and the fellowship of people until you come to your senses and bring back your poor soul."

8. Every bishop, provost, or official[7] who has a different opinion about the ban should beware of putting himself under the ban eternally so that neither God nor any creature may save him

[7] The "officials" were officers at the episcopal court, usually judges. Cf. Luther's attack against them in *To the Christian Nobility of the German Nation,* 1520. *LW* 44, 160.

from it. To no one is the ban more harmful and dangerous than to those who impose it—even though it is imposed rightly and solely because of transgression—because they never give this a thought, are completely without fear, and do not consider how they themselves are perhaps worthy of a hundred bans before God, just as the Gospel of Matthew 18 [:23-30] says of the servant who owed ten thousand talents to his lord and still would not have patience with his own servant regarding a hundred pennies. What then is to become of the poor and miserable slave drivers who so often created such a state of affairs with their banning for the sake of money, so that Turks and pagans almost have an easier life than Christians? It is quite evident that many of them are under the ban before God, deprived of the fruits of the sacrament and of inward, spiritual fellowship. Day and night they do nothing but summon others to appear, harass them, and put them under the ban. They deprive people of the external sacrament who are inwardly a thousand times higher before God and who live in the spiritual fellowship of the sacrament. Oh, you miserable business! Oh, you terrible food of such abominable manipulation! I do not know yet whether these officials[8] were wolves before, or whether they want to become wolves, but their deeds are certainly wolflike!

9. Consequently, it is true that the ban as such destroys, condemns, and makes no one worse. Rather, it seeks and finds a ruined and condemned soul to bring it back, for it is the nature and character of all punishment to correct sin. The ban is a pure and motherly punishment. That is why it makes no one either worse or more sinful. Instead, when it is justly imposed, it is instituted only to restore the inward spiritual fellowship, and when it is unjustly imposed it is to be corrected. St. Paul proves this when he says in II Corinthians 13 [:10], "I should deal with you according to the power God has given me not for destroying but for improving." He also said, in I Corinthians 5 [:5], when he punished the man who married his stepmother, "I, together with you, deliver this man to Satan for the destruction of his body so that his soul may be preserved on the Last Day." Thus he also said above that we should not regard him who is under the ban as an enemy, but

[8] Luther calls them *publicusse,* an ironic deviation from the Latin *publicus.*

should punish him as a brother, that he may be ashamed but not condemned.[9] Indeed, Christ himself, according to his humanity, did not have the power to exclude a soul and to deliver it to the devil, as he says in John 6 [:37, 39]: "I will not reject whatever comes to me, and this is the will of my Father who sent me, that I not destroy or lose anything he gives me." Again, "The Son of man came not to destroy men's souls but to save them" [Luke 9:56]. If, therefore, Christ himself and all the apostles have no other power than to help souls, and have left no other power to the church, how dare the blind tyrants boast that they have the power to curse, to condemn, and to destroy? It is even denied them by their own canon law, according to *Lib. VI.* [*V.*] *De Sen. Exc. Cum Medicinalis:*[10] "Since the ban is a medicine rather than a poison, it only punishes for the sake of improvement and does not annihilate for the sake of destruction, insofar as he who is subjected to it does not despise it; therefore, every spiritual judge should diligently attempt to prove himself one who seeks to do nothing with the ban but to improve and to cure."

10. It is evident from this text that, when it is not despised, the ban is wholesome and harmless and not fatal to the soul as some dumb and timid consciences, frightened by blasphemous misuse on the part of a few others, imagine—although in apostolic times it had the power to deliver a body to the devil and to kill it.[11] This might perhaps still occur if the judges would use the ban not with blasphemous power but with humble love and faith for the improvement of their neighbor. It further follows that the ban brings greater danger and terror to those who impose it without being very careful to seek only the improvement and cure of him who is banned, according to the text [of canon law]. For the ban cannot be anything but a kind motherly scourge, aimed at temporal possessions and the body, so that no one is cast into hell but rather is saved from it and forced from damnation into his salvation. That is why we should not only endure it patiently, but

---

[9] II, Thess. 3:15. Cf. above, p. 9.

[10] Cf. *Decretalium D. Bonifacii Papae VIII,* lib. v, tit. XI, *De Sententia Excommunicationis,* C. I. *CIC* 2, 1093. Luther's translation, which is offered here, differs slightly from the text of this critical edition of *CIC.*

[11] This is Luther's interpretation of I Cor. 5:5. Cf. also Acts 5:5.

should also receive it with joy and all honor. But [the ban] will bring terrible harm to the tyrants who seek nothing but their own power, respect, and profit in it. For they pervert the ban and its work and turn a medicine into poison, only seeking a way to become terrifying to frightened people. They never think of improvement, and they will have to pay a heavy price for this. Woe to them!

11. They have coined for themselves the proverb, "Our ban ought to be feared, be it just or unjust." They freely comfort themselves with such a saying, boasting and puffing themselves up like adders, and they almost dare to defy heaven with it and threaten the entire world. They have propagated this bugaboo far and wide, imagining that there is much more to these words than there really is. That is why we want to point up their true nature[12] and prick this bladder with its three peas which makes such a frightful clatter.[13] Granted that it is true that one should fear the ban and not despise it, be it just or unjust, why do you apply this only to the ban, which is a motherly scourge, and not to all the other great punishments and adversities? How have you magnified the ban by basing it on fear? For we ought also be afraid when we are sick, poor, slandered, and despised, or when we are deprived of or refused possessions, profit, and justice or indeed if Turks and enemies plague and trouble us. In all these and other adversities, whether they occur justly or unjustly, we ought to be afraid, suffer, and surrender, and accept all things as though we deserved them, as the Lord teaches in Luke 6 [:30], "Of him who takes away your goods, do not ask them again."

Why are you not also afraid, dear tyrant, when you suffer injustice, when your profit is denied, when your goods are stolen, and when justice is denied you? Why do you not think to yourself that you ought to endure it with fear, be it just or unjust? Do you think others are commanded to endure your power with fear, be it just or unjust, and that you are freed from the same commandment so that you need not endure tyranny or injustice with fear?

[12] *Ausstreychen* is difficult to translate. We have used the conjectural reading *herausstreichen*. Cf. *BG* 3, 302, n. 8.

[13] A reference to a medieval children's toy consisting of a dried pork bladder filled with air and dried peas. Cf. *BG* 3, 302, n. 9.

You certainly will find that you, too, are a man and are under the same commandment with which you threaten others and with which you puff yourself up in your own folly.

12. Now look at this perversity! Spiritual authorities come along with the ban, saying that it should be feared and endured, be it just or unjust. But if they themselves are subjected to tyranny and injustice, they refuse to endure it to the extent of even a single penny. Rather, without any fear at all, they want to add up their own account and demand what is theirs. Thus they exempt themselves from God's commandment when they should be the prime example to others in obeying it. If it is true that pope, bishop, and the entire spiritual estate may fearlessly resist injustice, injury, and contempt in their own interest, then it is also true that one may resist the ban and reject it just as vigorously as they seek their own interest. For there is no distinction in God's commandment—it applies to everyone in equal measure. But God forbid! As the gospel teaches us, both are to be endured with fear, be it the ban or whatever adversity may occur. Take heed, therefore, for when someone does you an injustice, takes your profit, and you do not endure it with fear, but instead want to frighten him with the ban,[14] especially when you do not seek his improvement but your own advantage or wanton will—then you are already worse than he is. For you want to pull yourself out of fear and push him into it, which you have no right to do; and he should heed the gospel you tear up! How will you face God? So when they say, "Our ban should be feared, be it just or unjust," we reply, "This is indeed true; but it is also true that your unjust ban is harmful to no one but to yourself alone, body and soul, and the just ban is more dangerous to you than it is to me. Therefore, you too should endure your injury with fear, be it just or unjust. And when you blast me with your ban, I shall blast you because of your suffering. It is just as if a criminal took my coat and said, 'You ought to endure it with fear and humility'; I would say, 'I will, not because of your theft, which does not hurt me, but because of Christ's commandment.' Thus I do not fear your ban for its own sake; it does

[14] Cf. the *Gravamina,* the grievances of the German nation against the curia, for examples of this type of misuse of the ban. *DRTA. JR* 2, 685.

not hurt me; rather it hurts you more. But I fear it because of Christ's commandment."

13. Although it is certainly true that the ban ought to be feared, be it just or unjust, the one who imposes the ban is always in greater danger than the one who is under the ban. The one who is under the ban faces no other danger than that of despising the ban and not bearing it, be it just or unjust. But the one who imposes the ban faces these dangers: (1) that he does not endure injustice with fear; (2) that he fearlessly avenges himself through the ban; and (3) that he does not seek with singleness of purpose only the improvement of his sinning neighbor, but instead is simply attacking someone who is injuring him. All this is against the gospel. So it happens that in our own day those who impose the ban with terrible perversity are multiplying their own problems.[15] They put other people under the ban outwardly and condemn themselves inwardly. Moreover, they have become so deluded that they boast that their outward ban is to be feared, and inwardly they are condemning themselves freely and fearlessly, and enjoying it like foolish and mad people. That is why I am sure that it was not the Holy Spirit who composed the arrogant saying, "Our ban ought to be feared, be it just or unjust." It is not fitting for a Christian, even less for one who belongs to the spiritual estate,[16] to do injustice to others. How much less fitting it is, then, for this same man to be obstinate and to boast that his injustice is to be feared! It is appropriate for me to say, "I ought to be afraid of your injustice;" you, on the other hand, should take care and be afraid if you do me an injustice and moreover add the threat that I should endure this with fear. Your injustice can harm me only temporally, but it can harm you eternally. We live in such evil and miserable times that furious tyrants unashamedly and publicly boast of their sin and eternal harm—something which would be horrible to hear even in the midst of Turks and pagans—so that in this world only they may defy and mock the misfortune

[15] Luther uses a German proverb which literally says, "They pick up the spoon, but smash the bowl" (*Den leffell auff heben und tzu treten die schussell*). It means that in correcting a small error they make a bigger one. Cf. Ernst Thiele, *Luthers Sprichwortersammlung* (Weimar, 1900), No. 276.

[16] I.e., a clergyman.

of those who suffer. They seek not the improvement but rather the fear and false terror of people.

In short, the higher estate, in all that it does, is always in greater danger than the lower estate; and where the lower estate has to fear once, the higher estate has to fear ten times over. Therefore, those who impose the ban have no reason to be obstinate and arrogant toward those who are under the ban; they should weep about themselves instead. For God's judgment will not fall on the lowly but rather on the mighty, as the wise man says [Wisd. of Sol. 6:8].

14. It would certainly be better if Christians would teach that we should love rather than fear the ban, just as we were taught by Christ to love and not to fear punishment, pain, or even death. But these prattlers only emphasize the fear of the ban, although they teach that all other punishment and adversity should be borne with joy. In this way they disclose their blind and blasphemous intention of ruling the people of Christ by force and at the same time of making the free Christian church a captive of fear. Therefore, let us understand what is to be recognized as the most significant aspect of the ban, namely, that one should bear it without fear or impatience for two reasons: first, the power of the ban is given by Christ to the holy mother, the Christian church, that is, to the congregation of all Christians. Therefore, we should honor and endure our dear mother the church and Christ in this matter. For we should certainly accept, love, and fear in a childlike way whatever Christ and the church do. Second, the fruit and work of the ban are useful and wholesome and never harmful to him who endures them and does not despise them. To use a simple parable: when a mother punishes her dear son, whether or not he deserved it, it is quite certain that she does not do it with evil intent. It is a motherly, harmless, and wholesome punishment if the son endures it. But if he becomes impatient, does not give in, or does not improve in the things for which he is punished, and instead revolts against his mother and despises her, then the real harm to him begins. For then he opposes God's commandment, "You shall honor your father and your mother," and transforms a small and harmless, indeed, even a meritorious punishment, into terrible guilt and sin, to his own eternal pain and punishment.

15. Thus it happens in our own time that some officials and their associates are murdered, beaten, imprisoned, or are no longer safe. No doubt this certainly would not occur, or at least would occur less often, if the common people would not have the false notion that the ban does them more harm than good. That is why they venture everything and do such nonsensical things in their desperation. Although such things are horrible, these tyrants still deserve whatever they get through God's providence because they hide from the people the goodness and usefulness of the ban and misuse it, without intending any improvement but only to strengthen their own power. For even though every man ought to endure the ban, they ought not to despise a poor sinful or innocent man either, as Christ says in Matthew 18 [:10], "See that you do not despise any one of these little ones who believes in me; for I tell you that in heaven their angels always behold the face of my Father who is in heaven." Why then should they be surprised when at times, through God's providence, they are beaten over the head because of the unjust, tyrannical ban, and when their commandment is despised because they act so arrogantly and ceaselessly against the commandment of God? True, there is wrong on both sides. But if the common people were taught about the wholesome and necessary power of the ban, and that it has been instituted and was used not for their harm but for their good, then they [the tyrants] would face less opposition and find much greater and readier obedience and, indeed, even love, favor, and honor among all the people.

16. That is why the common people should be taught in some way such as this: "My dear people, do not be troubled about those who use and hold the power of the ban, whether they are godly or evil, or whether they do you justice or injustice. The power of the ban may not do you any harm, but should always be helpful to the soul, provided you bear and endure it rightly. Their abuse of the ban does not impede its virtue. Or, if it cannot be endured, you should humbly extricate yourself from it, but not with calculation or revenge in word or deed. Do not keep your eyes on them in this matter, but on the dear mother, the church. What do you care whether she lays her scourge or punishment upon you through a godly or through a wicked man? It is and remains your

dearest mother's most wholesome scourge." Since the beginning of the world it has been true, and it remains true, that spiritual and temporal authority are more often given to the Pilates, Herods, Annases, and Caiaphases than to godly men such as Peter, Paul, and others. There are always more evil men than godly ones in the government as in all other estates. Moreover, it cannot be supposed or hoped that we shall ever inherit a purely pious government. Indeed, if a good regiment, government, or blessed use of power is to be had at all, it must come as pure grace, or through special prayer and merit. For God punishes evil subjects with evil rulers, as he says in Isaiah 3 [:4], "I will make boys their princes, and childish people shall rule over them," and, "I will take from them every mighty, brave, wise, and able man," etc. [Isa. 3:2]. Since to have incapable or evil rulers is God's punishment, and there are so many among us who deserve such punishment, we should not be surprised when the government behaves tyrannically toward us and misuses its power over us. Indeed, we should wonder and thank God when the government is not tyrannical and does us no injustice.

17. Because of the abundance of horrible sins, the world is now overburdened with young, imprudent, and inexperienced rulers, mostly in the spiritual estate. Therefore our age is extraordinarily perilous, and we must act very wisely and see to it that we hold government and power in the highest honor, just as Christ honored the power of Pilate, of Herod, of Annas, of Caiaphas, and even of secular princes. We must not let such grave misuse and childish governing of the prelates move us to despise authority. Otherwise, we despise not only the unworthy persons who rule but their power itself. Rather, we should joyfully bear everything it imposes, or humbly and respectfully refuse to bear it. For God neither likes nor tolerates blasphemous and wanton resistance to authority, as long as it does not drive us to act against God or against his commandment—although it [authority] itself may act as much against God as it wants to, or hurt us as much as it wants to. He himself intends to judge and to condemn those who are great and powerful tyrants, as well as to help those who are oppressed sufferers. That is why we should yield to his will and let the tyrants fall under his sword and judgment. On the other hand, we should let ourselves be

helped by him, as St. Paul says in Romans 12 [:19], "Oh, dearest brethren, do not avenge and protect yourselves, but leave it to the wrath of God; for it is written, 'Vengeance is mine alone, and I will repay everyone, says the Lord.' "

These same prelates should be humbly told—especially the preachers should rebuke them, but only in such a way that they show them with the word of God how they are acting against God, and what he expects of them. Furthermore, there should be diligent and serious intercession for them before God, just as Jeremiah wrote to the children of Israel in Babylon [Bar. 1:11; Jer. 29:7] that they should diligently pray for the king of Babylon, who had imprisoned them, destroyed them, strangled them, and done all kinds of evil things to them, as well as for his son and his kingdom.

We could do this easily if we saw that the ban and every unjust authority can do no harm to our soul if we endure them, and that they must always be useful unless they are despised. Moreover, they [the authorities] are a thousand times worse off than we. Thus they are more to be pitied than blasphemously despised. For this reason the law of Moses commands that no one should slander the authorities, whether they are good or evil, even though they might certainly give enough grounds for doing so. In short, then, we have to have evil and childish rulers. If the Turk does not do the job, then Christians have to do it. The world is much too evil to be worthy of good and godly lords. It must have princes who go to war, levy taxes, and shed blood; it must have spiritual tyrants who suck it dry and burden it with bulls, letters of indulgence,[17] and laws. These and other punishments are its deserved reward. To oppose them means to oppose God's punishment. As humbly as I conduct myself when God imposes a sickness upon me, so humbly should I also conduct myself toward the evil authority that the same God now imposes upon me.

18. When we are under a just and deserved ban we should pay more attention to the matter for which we were put under the ban, either doing it or not doing it [as the case may be]. For the ban is always imposed because of sin (which is much worse than the ban). But here too, as in all other things, we wrongly tend to consider only

[17] Cf. *To the Christian Nobility of the German Nation,* 1520. *LW* 44, 155.

how painful the scourge is and not why we are being punished. Where, today, do you find those who are so afraid to sin and to make God angry that they are afraid of the ban? So it comes about that we fear the wholesome punishment more than the horrible sins. But this, too, must be endured and allowed to happen because of our sensuality which does not see the spiritual harm of sin, but only feels the pain of punishment. However, the fear of the ban has become too great through the tyrannical coercions and threats of the spiritual judges who drive the common people into the fear of punishment more than into the fear of sin. But wherever the ban is unjust, we should surely beware of doing or not doing, saying or not saying, that for which we were put under the ban, unless we do it without sin or harm to our neighbor. Instead, we should prefer humbly to endure the ban and freely to die under it if it cannot be otherwise. Nor should we be in any way afraid when we do not receive the sacrament and are buried in unconsecrated ground. Why? Because truth and righteousness belong to the inward spiritual fellowship. He who discards them falls under the ban of God which is eternal. Thus they should not be abandoned for the sake of an outward fellowship which is immeasurably less important, or for the sake of the ban. Moreover, to receive the sacrament and to be buried in consecrated ground are much less important than to desert truth and righteousness because of them. So that no one may wonder about this, I will go even further and say that he who dies under a just ban is not condemned, unless he did not repent his sin and despised the ban. For repentance and sorrow make all things right, even though one were exhumed or thrown into the water.[18]

19. Therefore, the unjust ban is much more desirable than the just ban or the outward fellowship. It is a noble and great merit before God, and blessed is he who dies under the unjust ban. For God will eternally crown him who is put under the ban for the sake of truth. Here he should sing with Psalm 109 [:28], "They cursed me, but you have blessed me!" Only let us beware of despising authority, and humbly declare our innocence. If this does not help, then we are free and excused before God. For if it is our duty to

[18] Possibly a reference to John Wycliffe, whose body was exhumed, cremated, and the ashes cast into the Rhine in 1427, and to John Huss, whose ashes were thrown into the Rhine in 1415.

make friends with our adversary, according to the commandment of Christ in Matthew 5 [:25], how much more should we make friends with the power of the Christian church, be it exercised over us justly or unjustly, through worthy or unworthy authorities! Just as an innocent child is not really harmed by an unjust scourging from his mother, even though he is undeservedly punished and in fact becomes even dearer to and more accepted by his mother, so we will become much more dear to God if we endure the undeserved punishment of our spiritual mother, the church, through its evil government. For she remains the mother as long as Christ remains, and she does not change into a stepmother because of evil government. Nevertheless, prelates, bishops, and their officials should be temperate and should not use the ban hastily. To use the ban often is nothing but to institute many laws and many commandments. To institute many laws means to set many traps for poor souls. Therefore, hasty and excessive use of the ban creates much scandal and gives many reasons for sinning. These things make God angry, although the ban was instituted to appease him. And even though we owe obedience to it, they have a much greater duty to direct, to change, and to institute their commandment and power according to our ability, necessity, improvement, and salvation, as was said above by St. Paul,[19] [namely,] that the authority is not given to tear down but to build up [II Cor. 13:10].

20. The ban should not only be used against those who oppose faith, but also against those who sin in public, as was indicated above by St. Paul,[20] who calls for the ban against slanderers, usurers, fornicators, drunkards, etc. But in our own time one leaves such sinners alone, especially when they are big shots,[21] and to the disgrace of this noble power—one puts someone under the ban because of a financial debt sometimes so small that correspondence and costs amount to much more than the original debt. To cover this up they invented something new and say they put no one under ban because of debt, but because of disobedience when the summons was not heeded. But if there were no debt they certainly would forget about disobedience. It becomes clear that they allow many

[19] Cf. above, p. 11.

[20] Cf. above, p. 8.

[21] Literally, "big Johns" *(grosse hansen).*

other sins, including their own, to be left out of the ban. A poor man certainly must become disobedient many times when he is summoned from so many miles away, and at the cost of his work has to lose time and money to obey. It is sheer tyranny to summon a man to court such a distance across country. I praise the secular rulers[22] who do not tolerate such a ban and such malpractice in their lands and among their people. What are rulers and counselors for if in their city, community, and among their own subjects, they do not deal with and judge such temporal matters and debts? Spiritual authorities should deal with the word of God, with sins, and with the devil; they should lead souls to God, leave temporal goods alone, and judge the world, as Paul writes in I Corinthians 6 [:2-3]. Indeed, as things are now, it might almost be necessary to use the ban to drive people into church rather than out of it.

21. It does not matter whether someone is justly or unjustly under the ban—no one is to drive him out of the church until the Gospel has been read or the sermon preached.[23] For no one may ban someone or himself be banned from hearing the Gospel and the sermon. The word of God shall remain free, to be heard by everyone. Indeed, those who are under the just ban should hear it most so that thereby they might perhaps be moved to come to their senses and to improve themselves. Thus we read that it was ancient practice in the church to drive out those under the ban after the sermon. If an entire congregation should be under the ban, the sermon should be permitted to proceed as if there were no ban. In addition, he who is under the ban, even though he dare not stay for the real mass after the sermon and does not want to come to the sacrament either, should nevertheless not neglect to come to the sacrament spiritually; that is, he should heartily desire it and believe that he will partake of it spiritually, as was said in the sermon on the sacrament.[24]

Finis 1520

[22] In 1518 the Saxon princes George and Frederick took the position that spiritual jurisdiction should be limited to spiritual matters. Cf. G. Gess (ed.), *Akten und Briefe zur Kirchenpolitik Herzog Georgs von Sachsen* (2 vols.; Leipzig, 1905), I, 44.

[23] Early Christian public worship was divided into two parts: the service of the word, which included everyone who came (*missa catechumenorum*); and the eucharistic service, which excluded those under the ban, or those who were not yet baptized (*missa fidelium*).

[24] Cf. *LW* 35, 60-62.

A DISCUSSION ON HOW CONFESSION SHOULD BE MADE

1520

Translated by

Eric W. and Ruth C. Gritsch

INTRODUCTION

Luther's new understanding of penance, popularized in 1519 in a series of writings climaxing in the sermon on *The Sacrament of Penance,*[1] raised questions regarding the proper use of the confessional. Most people went to confession out of fear of eternal damnation. Medieval artists pictured God sitting on a rainbow, angry and merciless in his judgment of human sins. But Luther asserted that God is merciful in Christ and ready to forgive the sins of him who believes. "This sacrament does not depend on the priest, nor on your own actions, but entirely on your faith."[2] Not fear of God but loving trust should be the stance of the penitent who, through his baptism, has become a child of God.

Among those who urged Luther to apply his new understanding of penance to the practice of auricular confession was George Spalatin, since 1516 adviser and court chaplain to Elector Frederick of Saxony. A good friend of Luther, he offered his house on the Schlossberg at Lochau (now Annaberg) as a meeting place between Luther and Charles von Miltitz, papal chamberlain, after agreements had been reached between Rome and Wittenberg to hold a colloquy on the indulgence problem.[3] During the colloquy, which took place on January 4 and 5, 1519, Spalatin seems to have pressed Luther for personal advice on how confession should be made. On January 14, 1519, Luther told his good friend in a letter that he was busy drafting a statement on "the form of confession" (*forma confessionis*).[4] Ten days later, on January 24, 1519, he sent the Latin draft of the statement to Spalatin.[5]

Luther's statement on confession soon made its way from Spalatin to the printer Melchior Lotther in Leipzig. A German translation appeared, entitled *A Brief Instruction on How Con-*

[1] Cf. *LW* 35, 9-22.

[2] Cf. *LW* 35, 16.

[3] For the detailed story, cf. Schwiebert, *Luther and His Times,* pp. 370-379.

[4] Cf. *WA,* Br 1, 303.

[5] Cf. *WA,* Br 1, 311.

fession Should Be Made.[6] Luther heard of it through another friend, Canon Bernard Adelmann of Augsburg, who, unhappy with the copy he had read, contacted Luther and urged him to revise it. Luther agreed and demanded a copy of the original from Spalatin. "I fear," he wrote to Spalatin on January 18, 1520, "that it might be printed in its present form, as our Adelmann writes. He wants me to send him a revised and altered copy."[7]

A Discussion on How Confession Should Be Made represents the results of Luther's revision of Spalatin's copy. Luther completed the revision on March 25, 1520, and sent it to Spalatin. A short time later it was printed by John Grünenberg in Wittenberg. Upon Luther's request, Spalatin prepared a German translation, which appeared on May 8, 1520, with a dedication to Duke John of Saxony. A comparison of the translation of the Leipzig edition of 1519 with Spalatin's translation of the Wittenberg edition of 1520 warrants the thesis that Spalatin translated both. Moreover, he seems to have heeded Melchior Lotther's request to have the first version printed in Leipzig. Luther did not chide Spalatin for releasing his earlier personal advice on confession to the public. His main concern was to create a clearer statement on confession for public consumption.

Luther dedicated the first Latin edition of *A Discussion on How Confession Should Be Made* to his friend Alexius Chrosner, canon of Altenburg, asking him to publish it under his own name.[8] But the treatise appeared under Luther's name and without the letter of dedication to Chrosner because the printer seems to have forgotten to include the letter accompanying the manuscript.[9] The following translation is based on the first revised Latin edition, entitled *Confitendi Ratio,* printed in *WA* 6, 157-169, with the letter to Alexius Chrosner. Five other Latin editions and four of Spalatin's German translations appeared in 1520. C. M. Jacobs prepared an English translation in *PE* 1, 73-101.

---

[6] *Ein kurtz underweysung wie man beichten soll: auss Doctor Martinus Luther Augustiners wolmeinung getzogen, 1519. WA* 2, 59-65.

[7] Cf. *WA,* Br 1, 612-613.

[8] Cf. below, p. 27.

[9] Cf. the Introduction to the treatise in *WA* 6, 154.

A DISCUSSION ON HOW CONFESSION SHOULD BE MADE

Jesus

To the Most Honorable Dr. Alexius Chrosner of Coldiz, Canon at Altenburg, from His [Friend] in Christ.

Greetings! Dr. George Spalatin,[1] your colleague and our mutual friend, once exacted a letter from me in which I briefly delineated how confession should be made. For the complaint which came to me (among others) from all sides and disturbed me was that the method of confessing was extremely complicated and totally confused. Since I recognized that I was asked about something which was troublesome and intolerable to the ecclesiastical tyrants, I postponed it for some time, until I was forced to calm my friend somewhat by way of a personal and private letter. But when he shared this booklet or letter with a few others here and there—something he certainly was justified in doing without offending me—it began to be endangered and it seemed desirable to print it.

Well aware of how my friends watch every single syllable of mine, I was forced to recall the vagabond,[2] to review it once again —although hurriedly, because I was occupied with other matters— and, altering and adding a few things, to forestall its publication by others. I certainly am aware that this matter should have been left to far more learned people and that it should have been held back for nine years (as they say) and reflected upon. But the die was cast and we could not do otherwise than we did. I have begun to take for granted the spirit which knows nothing of slow endeavors. Thus I ask you to allow this to appear under your name, no matter how trifling or important a matter it may be; for you, who are so

[1] George Spalatin (1484-1545), court chaplain to Elector Frederick of Saxony.
[2] Cf. Luther's letter of January 18, 1520, to George Spalatin. *WA*, Br 1, 612-613.

like Spalatin in almost everything, should not appear to be dissimilar in this matter. Farewell and commend me to the Lord and excuse me.

Wittenberg, April 7, 1520[3]

A Discussion on How Confession Should Be Made

I

In our time almost every conscience has been seduced by human teachings into a false trust in its own righteousness and works, and learning about faith and trust in God has nearly ceased. That is why it is necessary, above all, that he who confesses should not put his trust in the confession he is about to make or has made. Rather, he should put his trust in the most merciful promise of God alone, with complete faith and with the certainty that he who promised the forgiveness of sins to the person about to confess them will most faithfully fulfil his promise. For we are to glory not in making confession but in him who promised forgiveness to those who confess. That is, [we glory] not in the merit and sufficiency of our confession (for such do not exist), but in the truth and certainty of his promise, just as Psalm 25 [:11] says, "For your name's sake, O Lord, you will pardon my sin." It does not say, "For my sake, or my merit, or my name," but, "For your name's sake," etc. Therefore, the work of confession is nothing but an occasion on which God is requested to fulfil his promise—or rather, whereby we are trained to believe that we shall undoubtedly obtain the promise. Accordingly, [we say,] "Not to us, O Lord, but to your name give glory" [Ps. 115:1], and, "Rejoice, not because we have blessed you, but because you have blessed us, as you say through Ezekiel [20:44]." Thus it will happen that he who glories will glory in the Lord; he will not praise himself, but glorify the grace of God. Thus it will come to pass that confession and splendor are the work of God (Psalm 111 [:3]).

[3] This is the date which was supplied by the printer in the first edition in which this dedication appeared. Circumstantial evidence presented in *St. L.* 21, 37, n. 2; 249, n. 5; and *WA* 6, 154, suggests that Luther wrote this dedication around March 21. Cf. also *St. L.* 19, 37.

II

It must be demonstrated from Scripture that God has promised forgiveness (for the glory of his grace and mercy). First, Psalm 32 [:5]: "I said, 'I will confess my transgressions to the Lord' and you forgave the guilt of my sin." Then, II Samuel 12 [:13], from which this psalm has been taken: as soon as King David said, "I have sinned against the Lord," Nathan immediately responded, "The Lord has put away your sin; you shall not die." And Jeremiah 18 [:8], "If that nation turns from its evil, I will repent of the evil that I intended to do to it." Again, I John 1 [:9], "If we confess our sins, he is faithful and just, and will forgive our sins and cleanse us from all iniquity." And this is the true definition of the righteous man in Proverbs 18 [:17]: "The righteous man is his own first accuser"; therefore, he is righteous because he accuses himself. From this it follows, "His friend (Christ) comes and examines him," that is, he will search for him and will not let him perish; he will deliver him even from the depth of hell. Thus Joshua 7 [:19] calls the confession of sin the glory of God, saying to Achan, "My son, give glory to God and confess; and tell me what you have done." And St. Jerome comments on it, "The confession of sin is the praise of God."[4] No wonder! For he who confesses his sins certainly speaks the truth. However, God is the truth; therefore he [who confesses] simultaneously confesses God. Thus Manasseh, king of Judah, says in the last chapter of II Chronicles, in his most beautiful prayer (well suited for anyone about to make confession), "But you, O Lord, according to your goodness, have promised repentance and forgiveness of sins," etc.[5] Indeed, "you have promised according to your goodness" because our confession is nothing unless the promise of God stands firm; it is by his divine goodness alone that he promises forgiveness which cannot be obtained by any righteousness

[4] Jerome (*ca.* 345-420), translator of the Vulgate and renowned church father. The commentary on Josh. 7:19 is found in *MPL* 28, 520. The exact quotation could not be located.

[5] A reference to the apocryphal book The Prayer of Manasseh (vs. 7), which was added to the last chapter of the canonical II Chronicles in the Vulgate text. Luther added a translation of this prayer to *A Discussion on How Confession Should Be Made*. Cf. below, pp. 46-47.

unless he has given the promise. Thus faith in this promise is the first and supreme necessity for whoever is about to make confession, lest he boldly presume that it is his own diligence, his own recollection, and his own powers which move God to the forgiveness of sins—when God himself has anticipated him already and is fully prepared to forgive; so it is really he who through the goodness of his sweetest promise draws out and calls forth the acceptance of forgiveness and the offering of confession.

III

Before someone confesses to the priest, the "vicar," he should certainly first confess to God himself, the "prince." Indeed, he should treat this matter seriously because, just as there is nothing hidden from the divine eye, so there is nothing that deceives it. That is why he should ponder, without any pretense, his intention to lead a better life and his hatred of sin. For almost nothing deceives most people who are about to make confession more than the kind of subtle and profound pretense whereby they often pretend, even to themselves, a violent hatred of sin and an intention to lead a better life. This is sufficiently proven by the miserable result that after confession they soon return to their natural way of life and, as if relieved of the great burden of confession, once again live without care, being as negligent as they are unmindful of their intention. This fact alone can sufficiently expose their most miserable fiction. That is why a man should be completely free here to state unhesitatingly to himself and within himself what he would feel and what he would do if there were no punishment, no God, no commandment, etc., and if he were to whisper these things into the ear of a certain secret friend to whom he could reveal everything about himself without being ashamed in any way. Indeed, just as he would want to speak most freely with himself about his vices, so should he speak before God who loves us much more than we love ourselves.

For if there is anyone who does not find himself seriously affected by good intention, I am not sure it is safe for him to make confession. I do know that it would be better for him to abstain from confession. Nor should he in this case care in any way about the commandment of the church, regardless of whether it excommunicates him or does less than that. It is better not to listen to the church than to come before God at one's own peril, with a false heart. For in the latter case one sins against God, whereas in the former case one sins only against the church—if indeed one sins at all by not listening to the church. The church certainly has no right to command anything endangering the soul; such a matter is always excepted from the commandments of the church. For whatever the church itself commands it commands for God and for the salvation of the soul, assuming that a man is capable of receiving its commandment and fit to fulfil it. If this assumption is false the commandment does not hold either, since the church cannot decree anything contrary to God's commandments, which bind the conscience.

It is certainly to be feared that many people come [to confession] because they fear the ecclesiastical commandment, although in their hearts they still like their former sinful life.

IV

However, if a man is afraid to stay away [from confession] because he is seized by anxiety, yet feels (if he were to speak the truth) the lack of intention to lead a better life, then he should seize the one thing left and listen to the advice of the prophet who says, "Pour out your hearts before him" [Ps. 62:8]. He should fall on his knees and plainly confess to God all the evil of his heart, and pray and wish for good intention. Indeed, who is so proud as to think that he does not need such advice, since there is no one whose intention is as good as it should be? Thus he should freely ask God for what he feels he does not find in himself, until the idea of a better life seriously and truly begins to please him and his own [life] begins to displease him. For the teachings which have been handed down and inculcated in us about how good intention is to be created should not be understood in the sense that man himself should create and work it out for himself (for such an understanding would mean death and perdition, just as it says, "O man of God, there is death in the pot!" [II Kings 4:40]—although, alas, a great many people are being tormented in this affliction because they have evidently been taught to strive after the impossible). Rather, he should in his sheer despair while pouring his heart out before God say, "O Lord God, I do not have what I should have, and I cannot do it. Grant what you command and command what you will." For this is the way St. Augustine prays in confession.[6]

V

But I want what has been said about intention to be understood with caution. For good intention should be of two kinds. The first [intention] concerns such obvious mortal sins as adultery, murder, fornication, theft, robbery, usury, slander, etc. The intention to avoid these properly belongs to sacramental confession, and it also applies before God as soon as [these sins] have been committed, according to the saying in Ecclesiasticus [21:1], "My son, have you sinned? Do so no more so that you do not add more"; and again, "Do not delay to turn to the Lord" [Ecclus. 5:7]. The second [intention] concerns all the sins called "venial"—of which more below. It is utterly useless to strive to create good intention. For if a man understands himself correctly, he will find this to be impossible, at least if he wants to live in the flesh, since this life (as Augustine says)[7] cannot be lived without such things as laughter, words, thoughts, sight, sound, taste, superfluous and thoughtless touch, etc. Sometimes they are of such a nature that it is uncertain whether they are sins or temptations leading to merits. And yet, in this regard, it is amazing how a man making a confession is oppressed and burdened by the very wordy manner in which he should confess. For his intention must be certain about those things which are certain and which can be avoided in ordinary life, like the obvious mortal sins already mentioned.

VI

Whether the secret sins of the heart—that is, those known only to God and to the man who commits them—belong to sacramental confession, is beyond my understanding. I would very much like to

[6] Augustine (354-430), bishop of Hippo, whose writings Luther esteemed. Cf. *Confessions,* 10, 29. *MPL* 32, 796; *PNF* 1, 153.

[7] Cf., for example, *Confessions,* 10, 33. *MPL* 32, 799-800; *PNF* 1, 156-157.

deny it because it can in no way be proven, either by reason or by Scripture. I have often suspected that it was all an invention either of avaricious or inquisitive prelates, or certainly of tyrannical ones, who used this method to make the people of Christ fear them. This means (in my opinion) to lay a hand on God's judgment and to violate God's court, especially if people are forced into it.

Here is where this whole sea of laws and impossible questions about "cases of sins,"[8] etc., comes up, since it is impossible for a man to know when he was mortally proud, or lustful, or envious in his heart. And how should the priest, who alone is in a position to judge mortal sins, know? How should he who does not fully know his own heart know a strange one? Thus it happens that many people confess many sins not knowing whether or not they are sins. They are driven to it by this statement of Gregory, "Pious minds should admit guilt even where there is none."[9] For (so monstrous is the arrogance of popes and priests and so very haughty is the presumption of the Pharisees) they want a matter which should be brought before God to be brought before them also. Meanwhile, they do not see that if this has to be brought before man, all of life would consist of nothing but confessing; and even the confession itself would have to be confessed in another confession by the man afraid of guilt where there is no guilt, since even good works are not without guilt and Job is afraid of all his works [Job 9:28].

VII

Therefore let someone else explain it. I am content with the fact that not all sins of the heart have to be confessed. But if some are to be confessed, I assert that it should be only those which a man himself clearly knows to have established themselves in his heart against the divine commandments; that is, not simple thoughts about a virgin or a woman, nor, on the other hand, a woman's thoughts about a young man; nor affections themselves or the ardor of mutual lust, or the inclinations toward the opposite sex, however

[8] A reference to the medieval science of "casuistry," which used general ethical principles to judge individual cases, determining the exact moral value of a person's thoughts and deeds and the degree of his guilt.

[9] Possibly Pope Gregory I (590-604). The passage could not be found in his works.

filthy; nor, I would add, any passions of this sort. For such thoughts are frequently passions—aroused by the flesh, by the world, or by the devil—which the soul is forced to bear against its will, sometimes for a long time, occasionally indeed for a whole day or a week, just as the apostle Paul confesses about his "thorn in the flesh" [II Cor. 12:7].

That is why the intention to avoid all these things is impossible, vain, and deceitful. Moreover, the inclinations and mutual attraction of the sexes do not stop as long as there is an opportunity; the devil never rests, and our whole nature is sin. But those who want to be without sin and who believe man to be sound are the ones who erect these crosses for us, so that we do not cease confessing (even to the priest) whatever titillates us moderately or minimally. Therefore, if these secret sins of the heart are to be confessed at all, confession should be made only about those which involve full consent to the deed. But that happens either rarely or not at all in those people who want to live a pious life, although they are constantly vexed by such affections and passions.

VIII

The class of certain hyperaudacious theologians who are virtually born to shake the whole world with false terrors after the true fear of God has been extinguished in the hearts of men belongs here. It seems quite possible that Christ spoke about them when he mentioned the terrors from heaven [Luke 21:11]. These are the ones who dared to distinguish between mortal and venial sins for us. Accordingly, when men hear that a certain sin is venial they feel safe and completely discard the fear of God (as though he counted a venial sin for nothing). Again, when they hear that the consent of the heart is a mortal sin, or if someone has not listened to the commandments of the church, or unknowingly has committed some trifling offense, then Christ no longer has any place in their heart because of the confusion created by the roaring sea and the stormy waves of a very troubled conscience.

In opposition to such [theologians] it ought to be known that a man must despair of ever being able to confess all his mortal sins, and that the doctrine propagated in the church from decretals[10]—according to which every Christian must make confession of all his sins once a year (so the words read)—either is a diabolical and murderous doctrine or is in dire need of a loose interpretation.

I say that one should not confess all sins, be they mortal or venial. Indeed, a man should know that after he has made every effort he still has only confessed a minor part of his sins. How does this come about? Because Scripture says, Psalm 19 [:12], "Cleanse me from hidden faults, O Lord!" God alone knows these hidden faults. And again, "Create in me a clean heart, O God" [Ps. 51:10]. Even this holy prophet confesses that his heart is unclean. And the entire holy church prays, "your will be done," thus confessing that it does not do the will of God and is a sinner itself.

Furthermore, we are so far from being able to know our sins, not to mention confessing them, that even our good works are damnable and mortal if God were to judge them severely and not acknowledge them with forgiving mercy. If, therefore, all mortal sins are to be confessed, it should be done with a brief word, such as saying once, "All that I am, whatever I say, do, and speak, is mortal and damnable." This accords with Psalm 143 [:2], "Enter not into judgment with your servant; for no man living is righteous before you," and also with Romans 7 [:14, 18, 19], "But I am carnal, sold under sin. I find nothing good in my flesh but the evil I do not want is what I do," etc.

The most mortal of all mortal sins, however, is not to believe one is guilty of damnable and mortal sin before God. This is the madness for which these theologians strive with their rule about the offer of good works. Moreover, they most perniciously attract the consciences of men by teaching that venial and mortal sins must be distinguished—and this must be done according to their practice. Thus we read in Augustine,[11] Cyprian,[12] and other church fathers that not mortal sins but "criminal" sins—that is, those of which men can be accused and convicted—should be bound and loosed.

[10] Cf., for example, *Decretalium D. Gregorii Papae IX,* lib. v, tit. XXXVIII, *De Poenitentiis et Remissionibus,* C. XII. *CIC* 2, 887-888.

[11] The passage could not be found in Augustine's works.

[12] Cyprian, bishop of Carthage (248-258). The passage could not be located in his works.

That is why the decretal[13] should understand "all sins" in terms of all those offenses of which a man is accused, either by others or by his own conscience. By conscience I do not mean a conscience cauterized by the traditions of men [I Tim. 4:2] and fashioned in the worst form; but rather a right conscience, instructed by divine commandments and knowing that much more is to be left to divine goodness alone than is to be committed to one's own efforts.

But what if the devil reproaches a man with his unconfessed sins at the point of death, as we read in many examples?[14] I answer: Let these sins go along with those about which it is said, "Who can discern errors" [Ps. 19:12], and with others of which it is written, "Enter not into judgment with your servant," etc. [Ps. 143:2]. If some contrary examples have been presented, they have been produced by either diabolical illusion or incorrect understanding. It is sufficient that you wanted to confess everything, if you had known and had been able to. God wants his mercy to be glorified. But how? Through our righteousness? No, through our sins and our afflictions. Scripture should be preferred to all other examples.

IX

But to come to the matter itself: The man about to make confession (who is celebrated far and wide) should do away completely with the confusion of distinctions such as these: what [he has done] through fear dragging him down to evil or through love arousing him to evil; what [he has sinned] against the three theological virtues of faith, hope, and love, and against the four cardinal virtues; what [he has sinned] through the five senses, through the seven mortal sins, against the seven sacraments, against the seven gifts of the Holy Spirit, against the eight Beatitudes, against the nine alien sins, against the twelve articles of faith;[15] what silent sins, or sins crying to heaven [he has committed], or whatever else there is through which or against which sins occur. For this most

[13] Cf. above, p. 35, n. 10.

[14] A reference to stories used in sermons to illustrate ecclesiastical doctrines. Cf. *LW* 44, 57, n. 29.

[15] The Apostles' Creed.

hateful and tedious catalogue of distinctions is utterly useless, indeed, altogether harmful. Some have added to these evils the most troublesome business of circumstances. All this produced two results: (1) He who is about to make confession is kept so busy with these trifles that he is totally unable to care about that which is most important, namely, the desire of good intention. He is forced to put such a burden upon his memory, to fill his heart with so much business of how he should correctly express his cares and anxieties, that while he looks for forgotten sins or a way to make confession, he may in the meantime completely lose the pangs of conscience and the whole usefulness of the salutary confession. As a result, after having been absolved, he rejoices more about his final liberation from this tormenting misery of how he should make confession than about his absolution. For he sought not so much for absolution, but rather for an end to his agonizing torment of how to make confession. Thus everything was turned upside down everywhere while we were sleeping securely. (2) Such people are most tedious to the confessor; they pilfer his time and stand in the way of others.

That is why one should briefly examine God's commandments themselves, which undoubtedly contain all sins if understood correctly.[16] But not all of them [commandments] should be included; the last two are to be completely excluded from confession. For the confession must be brief and above all a confession of those sins which hurt immediately and, as they say, "move to confession." The sacrament of confession is instituted to appease rather than perturb the conscience.

For example, regarding the commandment, "Thou shalt not commit adultery," one should quickly say in what manner he has succumbed to lust, be it by deed, word, or consent, as though he were describing himself completely, including all his limbs and senses, in this commandment. Why then, should one uselessly bring in the five senses, mortal sins, and that ocean of distinctions? Likewise, regarding the commandment, "You shall not kill," one should quickly say by what kind of anger he had sinned, whether by hate,

[16] A reference to the Ten Commandments, which Luther regarded as a complete guide for Christian living.

slander, cursing, or by the deed itself. And so on with the rest, as I have tried hard to show in my *Preceptorium*[17] and notes on the Decalogue.[18]

It should not be at all disturbing that in the decretals on penitence[19] and in the fourth book of the *Sentences*[20] this matter is treated differently. They are all filled with human inventions. No wonder, since they have taken all their materials out of a certain apocryphal and unlearned book entitled *On True and False Penitence*,[21] which is ascribed to St. Augustine under this lying title and which is everywhere revered.

X

In making confession, one should be very careful to distinguish sharply between sins committed against the divine commandments and sins committed against the statutes of men. I say this because today the madness is prevalent which views with the greatest concern sins committed against papal decretals, and sins committed against God with little or indeed no concern at all.

Let me give you some examples:

You will find priests and monks who tremble as though confronted by a terrible monster if they stammer or if they repeat a syllable in the canon of the mass,[22] even though this may be due to a defect of the tongue or to some kind of accident and no sin

[17] *The Ten Commandments, Preached to the People of Wittenberg (Decem Praecepta wittebergesi, predicata Populo),* 1518. *WA* 1, 398-521.

[18] *The Ten Commandments, with a Brief Exposition of Their Fulfilment and Violation (Die zehen gepot gottes. Mit einer kurtzen ausslegung jrer erfullung und ubertretung),* 1518. *WA* 1, 250-256. Cf. also *Instruction for a Brief Confession of Sins, According to the Decalogue (Instructio pro confessione peccatorum abbrevianda, secundum Decalog),* 1518. *WA* 1, 258-265.

[19] *De pe,* an abbreviation for *on penitence,* a section of canon law. Cf. *Decretalium D. Gregorii Papae IX,* lib. v, tit. XXXVIII, *De Poenitentiis et Remissionibus,* C. I-XVI. *CIC* 2, 884-889.

[20] Book IV of Peter Lombard's (*ca.* 1100-1160) *Four Books of Sentences (Sententiarum Libri Quatuor),* the standard theological textbook of the Middle Ages, deals with the seven sacraments and with the last things. Cf. *MPL* 192, 839-962.

[21] *De Vera et Falsa Penitentia.* This popular medieval penitential work was not written by Augustine, but by an unknown author or authors. Luther totally rejected Augustine's authorship. Cf. *WA* 8, 158.

[22] That part of the liturgy in which the transubstantiation of the elements takes place.

is committed. Again, there is not one [of them] who does not confess he has been distracted or has failed to read his preparatory lessons, or some other such very old-womanish trifle. There was one who, while already celebrating at the altar, summoned a priest three times to confess that something had come to his mind. Finally, I have seen many of them take these endless pranks of the devil so seriously that they almost went insane. But that they nourished hate or secret envy in their hearts, cursed before or after mass, lied with ease and engaged in slander—this did not move them at all. Where does such perversity arise? From the traditions of "men who reject the truth" (as the Apostle says [Titus 1:14]), and because we have neglected to offer God a confession of real sins. He has given us up to our own base minds [Rom. 1:28]. Consequently, we delude ourselves with fictitious sins and deprive ourselves of the benefit of the sacrament through the very effort with which we seem to seek it most. It is this sort of people who make the neglect of canonical hours[23] an almost unforgivable sin, while, in the meantime, they easily forgive fornications which are against the commandment of God, or the neglect of good will toward one's neighbor. You will find some who have such a preference for St. Severin's[24] fancy or example that they think they cannot keep the canonical hours either before or after the appointed time without sinning, even if they were prevented from keeping them at the appointed time by the most just cause—such as the necessity to serve their neighbor in his needs, which has six hundred times more merit than their extremely cold and perhaps damnable prayers. In their thoughtless mumbling of the words of the canonical hours they reach a point when they no longer see that God's commandment, in service to one's neighbor, should be preferable to the commandment of men. This sort of people includes those who think it a crime to speak or to call a boy [acolyte] during the canon of the mass, even in cases of the greatest need and danger. Finally, they make natural fasting one thing and ecclesiastical fasting another; and if someone has unexpectedly swallowed a few drops of liquid, or has taken a bit

[23] The fixed hours of daily prayers observed in monasteries and later incorporated into the clerical prayer discipline outlined in the breviary. Daily reading from the breviary was required of all the clergy.

[24] St. Severin (d. 482), an Italian monk known for his ascetic severity.

of medicine, they keep him away from the sacrament completely and declare it a sin, even the greatest of sins. I wonder where such people get the authority to establish these laws and to confuse the consciences with sins they themselves invented. Other similar cases may be judged according to these examples. Indeed, one layman confessed that he liked to taste sweets, another that he listened to pleasantries, smelled perfumes, and touched soft things.

Let us move on to greater things! The common people are persuaded that it is heretical to eat butter or eggs on fast days. So atrociously do the laws of men rage in the church of God! And we freely delight in the people's superstition—indeed, in our tyranny—without in any way caring that God's commandments are considered a joke everywhere, as long as people fear and turn pale at our laws. No one calls an adulterer a heretic; fornication is a light sin; even schisms and discords, inspired, preserved, and increased by the authority and in the name of the church, are merits; but to eat meat on Friday is the greatest of all heresies. This is what we teach and permit to be taught to the people of Christ.

I am disgusted, nauseated, ashamed, and filled with pity because of this endless chaos of superstitions which this miserable ignorance of true theology has inflicted upon this most salutary sacrament of confession—[an ignorance] which has exercised its tyranny ever since human laws have been established.

XI

I advise, as John Gerson[25] advised several times, that a man should at times go to the altar or to the sacrament with a scruple of conscience, that is, without confessing, when he has been drinking too much, or talking, or sleeping, or has done anything else, or has not prayed a single one of the canonical hours. Do you want to know why such advice is given? Listen: it is given so that man learns to trust God's mercy more than his own confession or effort. For not enough can be done against this accursed trust in our own works. Therefore, when any occasion either of temptation or of

[25] John Gerson (1363-1429), a professor at the University of Paris and a cardinal. Luther liked to refer to him because he asserted the authority of the general council over the pope. The passage could not be found in Gerson's works.

death assails a man, and the secret sins begin to appear which could never be seen or confessed, then he should have already prepared the practice of trusting in God's mercy offered to the unworthy, according to the saying, "His heart is prepared to trust in the Lord" [Ps. 28:7]. How else should a man hope, in the face of such a mass of sins which suddenly break in at that time, if he has not learned in this life, while he still had time, to hope in the Lord with regard to even the smallest or imagined sin? If you say, "What if this means despising the sacrament and tempting God?" I answer: It is not tempting God if it is done for the glory of God; that is, if you do it not because you despise God's sacrament or tempt him—since you are prepared to confess everything—but rather so that you may accustom a troubled conscience to trust in God and not to tremble at the sound of every falling leaf. You should not doubt that everything that brings about trust in God is most pleasing to God. For this is his total glory that we trust his mercy with all our heart. However, I do not want this to happen every time; rather, I say, only at times, and then only to arouse trust in God and to destroy trust in our own confession. A person can hardly celebrate [mass] without sinning if he goes there with greater certainty because he has confessed rather than because God is merciful. This is indeed nothing but sheer ungodliness. To sum up, "Blessed are those who trust in the Lord" [Ps. 2:11]. When you hear "in the Lord" you certainly know that whoever trusts in whatever is not the Lord himself is without blessing. That is the sort of man these artists of confession produce. For what has the art of correct confession done but to destroy the art and practice of trusting, so that we have learned to confess much, but to trust not at all?

XII

Many people are troubled about "reserved cases."[26] Since I know that the laws of men should be subject to equity[27] and should

[26] Reserved cases were sins for which absolution could be granted only by a higher ecclesiastical authority than the confessor. Thus they were "reserved" for later absolution.

[27] *Epiiciae,* from the Greek *epieikeia.*

be applied with mildness rather than with rigor, I follow the custom and advice of those who hold that no case of secret sins should be reserved. That is why all those should be absolved whose sins are hidden, whether they are sins of the flesh, or of every kind of lust, abortion, and the like. For it should not be presumed that any pope wanted to devise so many snares and pitfalls to endanger souls with regard to secret sins. But wherever there has been a public crime, or a clear reserved case, it should certainly be brought before the appropriate authority, be it equitable or inequitable. In that case the confessor may moderate the power of the keys[28] to such an extent that he does not let the man who confesses go without absolution for at least those sins which he knows are not reserved. Although I have doubts at this time and have not yet found the place for a proper discussion of the question of whether any case dealing with the remission of guilt[29] can be reserved or is ever reserved, there is no doubt that the penalty can be reserved. However, others should be the judge of this. But in dealing with the remission of penalty, neither the confessor nor the man who confesses should be excessively scrupulous; I am thinking of the penalty of excommunication, or any other censure of the church—what they call their "thunder and lightning." For since excommunication is merely penalty and not guilt and can be imposed on an innocent man or remain imposed on a man who has regained his senses, and since it is sometimes necessary to postpone satisfaction several times because of a long journey or poverty, he who confesses should nevertheless be absolved from all his sins if he so desires, and should be referred to the [appropriate] authority to be freed from the bond of excommunication and to make satisfaction. Thus, absolved in the court of God and from the guilt of conscience and from sins, he should be sent to the court of the church to be absolved from the penalty. This is what is meant when

[28] The power to bind and to loose sin (Matt. 16:19; John 20:23).

[29] Scholastic theologians distinguished between "guilt" and "penalty" and classified sins as either venial or mortal. If, for example, a mortal sin was absolved, the sinner was freed of "guilt" and eternal punishment in hell, but he still had to render satisfaction in terms of a temporal penalty. Consequently, a sinner would always receive a penalty. If the sin was absolved on earth he had to render temporal satisfaction as a penalty; if the sin was not absolved he would suffer an eternal penalty, sometimes in purgatory. On Luther's controversy with the church on this point, cf. the *Ninety-five Theses. LW* 31, 20, 26.

it is said that the desire [to render] satisfaction[30] is sufficient for the sinner who is to be absolved.

Conclusion[31]

One should also consider the subject of vows, which is almost the most important question in this matter. It is much more confused than the reservation of cases and exercises its "Babylon" [Rev. 14:8] with great tyranny. If one wishes to speak freely here, "the land is not able to bear all his words," as the impious Amaziah says about Amos [Amos 7:10].

If pontiffs and preachers wanted to dissuade and deter the people from their proneness to make vows, their first and best advice would be to show them that visiting the Holy Land, Rome, Compostella,[32] or other holy places, as well as fasting, praying, and doing self-chosen works are nothing when compared with the works demanded by God and the vows we have taken in baptism.[33] Everyone can keep these vows in his home in dealing with his neighbors, his wife, his children, his servants, and his masters, and thus gain incomparably greater merit than he could find in self-chosen works or vows not commanded by God. The stupid opinion of the common people and the pomp of bulls brought it about that these vows of pilgrimages, fasting, prayer, and all kinds of other works were far more observed than the works of the commandments of God, which we never have enough strength to do. In my own judgment, there should be no vows at all for Christians, except those which we have taken in baptism—as appears to have been the practice in former times; and I wish that everyone understood what is required in obedience to God's commandments. For the vows of baptism seem to have been cheapened in every way because of too much custom, pomp, dispensation, and redemption of these vows. I say let us put all our strength into this task, and we

[30] *Votum satisfactionis,* that is, the serious desire to render satisfaction suffices for salvation whenever the actual reception of the sacrament is impossible. *NCE* 11, 81.

[31] *Ultimo* ("last"). The Jena Edition of Luther's works (1556) entitled this section "Concerning Vows."

[32] A famous place of pilgrimages in Spain, where, according to Spanish tradition, St. James was martyred in A.D. 44. Cf. Acts 12:2.

[33] Cf. *The Holy and Blessed Sacrament of Baptism,* 1519. *LW* 35, 40-42.

shall find that we have vowed more in baptism than we shall ever be able to fulfil.

Some vows, oaths as it were, are made to men, others to God. Those made to men are valid as much and as long as the man to whom they are made desires. Therefore, as Gerson correctly thinks, one should know that oaths or vows usually taken at universities, or made to secular lords,[34] are not to be regarded so highly that we should judge every violation of them to be a violation of a vow or an act of perjury. Rather, it is more equitable not to regard vows of this kind as violated unless it is done out of contempt or obstinate malice. It is different with those vows made to God.

Regarding vows made to God, I can see dispensations granted by pontiffs. But I shall never be persuaded that the one to whom such dispensation is granted is safe. For such a vow is of divine law, and neither an intermediate nor a supreme pontiff has any more power in this matter than any Christian brother, although I know that some decretals and glosses on decretals venture to assert many things I do not believe.

This, however, I would like to believe: a vow of chastity given before puberty neither holds nor binds, because he who made the vow was ignorant of what he vowed, since he had not yet felt the stimulus of the flesh. Consequently, it is my pious opinion that such a vow is regarded as foolish and voided by God, and that, if we are concerned about the care of souls, a general edict of the church should prohibit the fathers of monasteries from receiving a young man before his twentieth, or at least before his eighteenth year, or a girl before her fifteenth or sixteenth year.

Moreover, it is exceedingly thoughtless, in the matter of changing and relaxing vows, to impose "a better work" (as they call it). For there is certainly no difference in works before God, who does not judge according to the magnitude or quantity of works but rather according to the good will of him who does the work, as it is written, "The Lord knows what is the mind of the Spirit" [Rom. 8:27]; and he frequently prefers the manual labor of a poor craftsman to the fasting and prayers of a priest, as was illustrated

[34] The feudal oath of allegiance. The passage could not be found in Gerson's works.

by St. Anthony[35] and a certain tanner of Alexandria.[36] Who then dares to presume that he wants to change a vow into some "better work"? But this subject should have been discussed in another place, for here we undertook to treat only the rite of confession relating to God's commandments, for the sake of quieting and consoling troubled consciences.

I shall add only one more thing. Many people set dangerous traps for married couples, especially in the case of incest, as, for example, when a man has defiled the sister of his wife, or his mother-in-law, or someone else related to him with any degree of consanguinity (which can happen and, indeed, does happen!). They then deprive him of his right to demand marital duty; and yet they allow him—indeed, they force him—not to leave the bed of his wife. I ask you, what kind of monstrosity is that? What kind of new medicine against sin? What sort of satisfaction for sin? Is it not apparent that these tyrants freely impose their rule upon the infirmity of others while indulging too much in their own? Give me a legislator, no matter how penitent and chaste, who would permit such a law to be made for himself! They put dry wood on the fire and say, "Don't burn"; they put a man into the lap of a naked woman and forbid him to touch her or to know her; and they do this on their own authority, without a commandment from God. What madness! My advice is that a confessor should beware of such tyrannical decrees or laws and confidently sentence such a sinner either to some other penance or desist totally from punishing him, relinquishing to him the rights of marriage which were given him not by man but by God. No angel in heaven, not to mention a man on earth, has the power to inflict such a penance (that is, the most glorious opportunity for continuous sinning). Therefore one should in no way heed those who want such things done; and whoever makes confession should be liberated with confidence from this scruple and danger. But who can recount all the tyrannies with which the troubled consciences of confessing and

[35] St. Anthony (d. 356) took up the life of a hermit, *ca.* 270. The story is repeated by Melanchthon in *Apology of the Augsburg Confession*, Art. XXVII, 38. Cf. Tappert (ed.), *The Book of Concord*, pp. 275-276.

[36] The story is recorded in the *Lives of the Fathers (Vitae Patrum)*, III, 130. Cf. *MPL* 73, 785.

penitent Christians are burdened—the deadly constitutions and customs with which they are daily harassed by silly manikins who bind and place on the shoulders of men very heavy and unbearable burdens which they themselves do not want to touch even with one finger? Thus this most salutary sacrament of penance has become nothing but sheer tyranny imposed by the magnates; finally, it has become a disease and a means to increase sins—so that it signifies one thing but works another thing for troubled sinners. This is the way in which the godless priestlings, uneducated in the law of God, administer the church of God, which they have filled with their own laws and dreams.

The Prayer of Manasseh, King of Judah Among the Captives in Babylon[37]

O Lord Almighty,
  God of our fathers,
of Abraham and Isaac and Jacob
  and of their righteous posterity;
you who have made heaven and earth
  with all their ornament;
who have shackled the sea by your word of command,
  who have confined the deep
  and sealed it with your terrible and glorious name;
at whom all things shudder
  and tremble before your power,
for your glorious splendor cannot be borne,
  and the wrath of your threat to sinners is irresistible;
yet immeasurable and unsearchable is your promised mercy,
  for you are the Lord Most High,
of great compassion, long-suffering, and very merciful,
  and repent over the evils of men.
You, O Lord, according to your great goodness
  have promised repentance and forgiveness.
Therefore you, O Lord, God of the righteous,
  have not appointed repentance for the righteous,

[37] Cf. p. 29, n. 5. This translation is based on the R.S.V.

for Abraham and Isaac and Jacob, who did not sin against you,
but you have appointed repentance for me, who am a sinner.
For the sins I have committed are more in number than the sand of the sea;
my transgressions are multiplied!
I am weighted down with many an iron fetter,
so that I am rejected because of my sins,
and I have no relief:
for I have provoked your wrath
and have done what is evil in your sight,
setting up abominations and multiplying offenses.
And now I bend the knee for your goodness.
I have sinned, O Lord, I have sinned,
and I know my transgressions.
I earnestly beseech you,
forgive me, O Lord, forgive me!
Do not destroy me with my transgressions, or lay up evil for me;
For, unworthy as I am, you will save me in your great mercy,
and I will praise you continually all the days of my life.
For all the host of heaven sings your praise,
and yours is the glory for ever. Amen.

ON THE PAPACY IN ROME AGAINST THE MOST CELEBRATED ROMANIST IN LEIPZIG

1520

Translated by

Eric W. and Ruth C. Gritsch

INTRODUCTION

When Luther debated with John Eck in Leipzig, July, 1519, the chief emphasis was on Thesis 13 of the debate, concerning the authority of the pope and the jurisdiction of the church of Rome.[1] While Eck asserted that papal authority was instituted by Christ and derived from God, Luther contended that the papacy was a human institution subject to the vicissitudes of history. Eck rested his case on papal decretals and conciliar decisions; Luther argued on the basis of historical research, culminating in the thesis that for eleven hundred years there was no papal authority in the church. Although Luther did not win the support of the major universities such as Paris, Louvain, Cologne, and Erfurt, many scholars did agree with him. In fact, the debate appeared far from being settled by the spring of 1520.

Early in May, 1520, the Franciscan monk Augustine Alveld[2] published a Latin treatise against Luther, entitled *Concerning the Apostolic See* (*Super apostolica sede*). Commissioned by the bishop of Merseburg, Adolph von Anhalt, and encouraged by the papal chamberlain, Charles von Miltitz, Alveld announced in the subtitle his intention to prove "on the basis of the holy canon of the Bible" that the apostolic see was "a divine institution" (*iure divino*), a thesis "which all scholars would have to acknowledge." He dedicated the treatise to Bishop Adolph von Anhalt and signed it "priest of the regular observance [of the Franciscan Order] of the Saxon province, under the holy cross, public lecturer of the canon of the Bible in the convent of Leipzig."[3] He even asked to be relieved of all liturgical duties during Lent to devote himself completely to the task of refuting Luther.

Luther regarded the treatise as irrelevant and not worth answering. "At last brother Augustine Alveld has come out with his stuff," he wrote to George Spalatin on May 5, 1520. "Truly, he

[1] Cf. *LW* 31, 318.

[2] So called because he was a native of Alfeld. His name appears as "Alvelt," "Alveldianus," "Alveldius," and "Alveldensis." Cf. *WA* 6, 277, n. 1. On his life and writings, cf. *RGG* 1, 301.

[3] Cf. the lengthy Latin subtitle in *WA* 6, 277.

is too stupid for me to lose time answering him. . . . Others will answer him, and I will give it as an exercise to my *famulus*[4] to make verses and orations against this stolid ox."[5]

A brief glance at Alveld's treatise confirms Luther's judgment: referring to Luther as a "wolf among the sheep," "heretic," and "madman," Alveld wanted to pierce Luther with "seven swords."[6] The first he called "correct reasoning" (*recta ratio*), arguing that the church must have a single administrative head because every human community must have one. The second he called "canonical Scripture" (*canonica scriptura*), using Matt. 5:17-18 and I Cor. 10:6 for his assumption that the apostolic see is prefigured as a divine institution in the Old Testament and fulfilled in the New Testament through Christ's mandate to Peter (Matt. 16:18). The third he called "true knowledge" (*vera scientia*), that is, the teachings of the church fathers who testify to the Petrine foundation of the apostolic see. Their testimony is further confirmed by the fourth sword, the "sacred piety" (*pietas sacra*) of individual popes who, in the name of God, refuted error and blasphemy. The fifth sword was "sane intellect" (*sanus intellectus*), by which accusations against the sacred piety of the popes were refuted, such as the charge that popes were immoral men. The sixth sword, "simple and chaste knowledge" *(simplex et pudica scientia),* proved that worldly environment was responsible for papal immorality rather than the popes themselves. Finally, "pure and uncorrupted knowledge" (*pura et integra scientia*), embodied in Alveld himself, must come to the conclusion that Rome has to be the center of Christendom.

Luther simply jotted down a few counterarguments for his *famulus* John Lonicer, who published his reply on May 12, 1520, under the title *Against the Romanist Friar Augustine Alveld, Franciscan from Leipzig, Public Lecturer of the Canon of the Bible and Torturer of the Same.*[7] Printed by John Grünenberg in Wittenberg,

[4] A student who waited on a professor in return for tutoring. Luther's *famulus* was John Lonicer, a young Augustinian, who studied in Wittenberg until December, 1521.

[5] *WA*, Br 2, 98; Smith (ed.), *Luther's Correspondence,* I, 317.

[6] A detailed summary of Alveld's Latin treatise is given in *WA* 6, 277-279.

[7] *Contra Romanistam fratrem Augustinu Aluelden, Franciscanu Lipsicu Canonis Biblici publicu lictore & tortore eiusdem.*

it was a satirical commentary on Alveld's work, homing in on its stylistic and logical weaknesses. Lonicer concluded with the statement that Luther had better things to do than to argue against such an ass. Henceforth Alveld was known in Wittenberg as the "ass of Leipzig."

John Bernhardi, a young scholar and a friend of Luther at Wittenberg University, had already written a more detailed refutation of Alveld's treatise, entitled *Confutation of the Inept and Impious Booklet of Friar Augustine Alveld.* It was printed by Melchior Lotther in Leipzig and was for some time wrongly regarded as a work by Melanchthon.[8]

Alveld's superiors in Leipzig were not happy with the results of his scholarship and encouraged him to withdraw from the ensuing controversy. But Alveld wanted to continue in the role of defender of the apostolic see. He was prepared to publish a German treatise on the same subject and asked Charles von Miltitz to secure permission from Rome for its publication.[9] By the middle of May, 1520, the treatise was published under the title *A Very Fruitful and Useful Booklet About the Papal See and About St. Peter; Also About Those who Are the True Sheep of Christ whom Christ Our Lord Has Commanded to Be Under Peter's Protection and Rule, Made by Friar Augustine Alveld, of the Franciscan Order in Leipzig.*[10] It was written for simple laymen and was published by Melchior Lotther, who was easily impressed with pseudoscientific arguments. Using essentially the same arguments he had advanced in the Latin treatise, Alveld used moderate language and simple words to convey the thesis that it is foolish to argue against the authority of Rome and its jurisdiction over the entire church.

Luther was infuriated when he saw the treatise. In less than two weeks (May 17-30), he wrote his reply, *On the Papacy in Rome, Against the Most Celebrated Romanist in Leipzig,* which Melchior Lotther printed in Wittenberg on June 26, 1520. "If he [Alveld] had not put his apelike book into German to poison poor

[8] *Confutatio Inepti et impii Libelli F. August. Alveld.*

[9] In a letter dated May 8, 1520; quoted in WA 6, 280.

[10] *Eyn gar fruchtbar und nutzbarlich buchleyn von dem Babstlichen stul: unnd von sant Peter: und von den, die warhafftige scheflein Christi sein, die Christus unser herr Petro befolen hat in sein hute und regirung, gemacht durch bruder Augustinum Alueldt sant Francisci ordens tzu Leiptzk.*

laymen, he would have been much too insignificant for me to bother with," he declared at the end of the treatise.[11] Without even mentioning Alveld's name, he used the controversy as an opportunity to teach laymen the meaning of Christianity.[12] Thus originated Luther's first major treatise on the nature of the church, one of the most significant milestones in the formation of his new theology.

Luther's treatise did not end the controversy. Peter Mosellanus, noted humanist and rector of Leipzig University, asked Luther not to defame the city together with Alveld. Though Luther told him that the city deserved it, in the end he limited his attack to Alveld.[13] Alveld himself wrote another inept pamphlet in response to John Lonicer's defense of Luther,[14] in spite of the fact that Leipzig University had asked him to make a public statement "that it had nothing in common with his writings"[15] since he had so obviously disregarded the canons of scholarship. Alveld had no ear for them, and wrote a reply to Luther's treatise in the form of a sermon in December, 1520.[16] Another friar, John Fritzehans, had already retorted to John Bernhardi's earlier defense of Luther in the form of a public letter of exhortation (*Epistola exhortaria*) to Alveld.[17] Luther remained silent, obviously unconcerned about the continuing "prattling" of the Leipzig friars.

The following translation is based on the first German edition of Luther's treatise, as printed in *WA* 6, 285-324, entitled *Von dem Bapstum zu Rome: widder den hochberumpten Romanisten zu Leiptzck*. We have occasionally consulted the English translation of Augustus Steimle in *PE* 1, 327-394. A revision by Theodore G. Tappert of the Steimle translation is available in *SW* 1, 197-249.

---

[11] Cf. below, p. 103.

[12] Cf. below, p. 57.

[13] Cf. Luther's letter to Mosellanus, written in June, 1520. *WA*, Br 2, 133-134.

[14] Cf. the lengthy Latin title of Alveld's tract in *WA* 6, 283.

[15] Cf. *WA* 6, 283.

[16] Cf. the lengthy German title in *WA* 6, 284.

[17] Cf. the lengthy Latin title in *WA* 6, 283.

ON THE PAPACY IN ROME AGAINST THE MOST CELEBRATED ROMANIST IN LEIPZIG

Preface

After years of abundant rain and much new growth, something new has appeared on the field. Previously many people struck out at me with slander and glorious lies, without much success. Now, the very latest to distinguish themselves are the brave heroes in the marketplace of Leipzig. They not only want to be noticed, they also want to fight everyone. They are so well armed that I have never seen the likes of it before. They have put the helmet on their feet, the sword on their head, the shield and breastplate hang on their back, they hold their spears by the blade, and this whole armor, worn in this new knightly fashion, becomes them very well.[1] They want to prove that they have not wasted their time on dream books (as I have accused them), never learning anything; in fact, they want to win a prize as people who were conceived, born, nursed, cradled, fondled, educated, and matured in Holy Scripture. It would only be fair if anyone who could, would be afraid of them, so that their effort and good intention might not be in vain. If Leipzig can produce such giants, it must indeed have rich soil.

But just so you understand what I mean, listen to this: Sylvester,[2]

[1] Cf. Augustine, *Confessions,* 3, 7. *MPL* 32, 689; *PNF* 1, 64.

[2] Sylvester Prierias (*ca.* 1456-1523), a Dominican monk and official theological adviser to Pope Leo X. He published three books against Luther prior to 1520. Luther responded with several tracts. Cf. *LW* 41, 286, n. 56.

Cajetan,[3] Eck,[4] Emser,[5] and now also Cologne and Louvain[6] truly proved their knightly prowess against me. They have received the honor and glory they deserve. They have so defended the cause of the pope and of indulgences against me that they wished they had done better. In the end, some of them thought it best to attack me as the Pharisees attacked Christ [Matt. 22:35]. They put up somebody, thinking, "If he wins, we have all won; but if he loses, he alone is defeated." And this hyperlearned and cautious blockhead[7] thinks I will not notice. Well then, I shall pretend not to understand their game at all, so that not everything goes wrong for them. I ask them in return not to notice that when I hit the pack I was aiming at the mule. And if they refuse to grant me this request, I shall stipulate that whenever I say anything against the new Roman heretics and slanderers of Scripture, it does not pertain just to the poor immature scribe in the cloister of the barefoot friars[8] at Leipzig, but also to the magnanimous flag-bearers who are not allowed to reveal themselves even though they would like to win a victory under someone else's name.

I ask every devout Christian to understand that my words, though they are perhaps mocking and cutting, come from a heart which must break with great sorrow and turn seriousness into mockery, in view of the fact that this blasphemer publicly speaks and writes in Leipzig, where there are indeed devout people who would save Scripture and the word of God at the cost of their body and soul. This blasphemer values and treats the holy words of God no better than if they had been invented by some fool or

[3] Thomas of Gaëtano, called Cajetan (1469-1534), vicar-general of the Dominican Order, was the papal legate at the Diet of Augsburg in 1518. On his encounter with Luther, cf. *Proceedings at Augsburg*, 1518. *LW* 31, 253-292.

[4] John Eck (1486-1543) wrote and debated against Luther at Leipzig in 1519. Cf. *The Leipzig Debate*, 1519. *LW* 31, 307-325.

[5] Jerome Emser (1478-1527), a humanist who became an adviser to Duke George of Saxony, Catholic ruler of Saxony and an enemy of Luther. Cf. *To the Goat in Leipzig*, 1521, below, pp. 105-115.

[6] The theological faculties of the universities of Cologne and Louvain condemned certain aspects of Luther's teachings in August and November, 1519. Cf. the printed condemnations and Luther's response in *WA* 6, 174-195.

[7] *Neydhard*, or *Neidhammel* in modern German, meaning literally, "envious ram." Luther used this designation to indicate that Emser wanted to "ram through" his arguments against him instead of engaging in rational scholarly debate.

[8] A term for Franciscan monks.

jester to use as stories during Shrovetide. Therefore, since my Lord Christ and his holy word, which he dearly purchased with his precious blood, are considered a mockery and foolish talk, I have to drop my own seriousness and see whether I, too, have learned to play the fool and to mock. You, my Lord Jesus Christ, know how my heart feels about these arch-blasphemers—that is what I am relying on. Let justice be done in your name, Amen. They will indeed [have to] let you be Lord. Amen.

I notice that these poor people seek no more than to make a name for themselves at my expense. They cling to me like dirt to a wheel. They would rather have a disgraceful uproar than stay at home. The evil spirit uses the schemes of such people only to prevent me from doing better things. But I welcome this as an opportunity to teach laymen something about Christendom[9] and to combat these alluring masters. That is why I also intend to devote myself more to the matter itself than to answering their idle talk and to mentioning their names. Consequently, they will be unable to gain what they seek or to become arrogant, as though they were worthy of arguing with me about Scripture.

The Argument and the Matter in Question

We are arguing about a matter which, taken by itself, is unnecessary, for one would certainly remain a Christian without investigating it. But our loafers, who trample on all the main articles of the Christian faith itself, must take up this matter and plague other people, so as not to live on earth in vain. This, then, is the matter in question: *Whether the papacy in Rome, possessing the actual power over all of Christendom,* as they say, *is derived from divine or from human order;*[10] and, if so, whether it would be a Christian statement to say that all other Christians in the whole world are heretics and schismatics—even though they adhere to

[9] *Christenheit.* Throughout the treatise Luther distinguished between "Christendom," "church" *(Kirche),* and "community" or "congregation" *(Gemeyne)* and "assembly" *(Vorsamlung).* We maintain this careful distinction in our translation.

[10] This had been the chief issue at the Leipzig Debate between Luther and Eck. "Order" *(ordnung)* implies "origin" as well as "ordinance" or "law."

the same baptism, sacrament, gospel, and all articles of faith in harmony with us—if they do not have their priests and bishops confirmed by Rome or, as is the case now, buy them with money and let themselves be aped and mocked like the Germans. The Muscovites,[11] the white Russians, the Greeks, the Bohemians, and many other great nations in the world are some examples—all of them believe like us, baptize like us, preach like us, live like us, and also honor the pope without spending money for the confirmation of their bishops and priests. Moreover, they do not let themselves be plagued and shamed with indulgences, bulls, seals, parchments, and whatever more there is in the Roman stock, as do the drunken and obese Germans. They too are prepared to hear the gospel from the pope, or from the pope's ambassadors; and yet, nothing happens to them. Now the question is whether all of them (for of such alone and of no others do I speak and write) should be branded heretics by us Christians, or whether we are not the real heretics and schismatics when we brand such Christians heretics and schismatics for the sake of money alone. For when the pope does not send the gospel or the proclamation of it to those who would like to have it and receive it, it is as clear as day that he only seeks useless power and money through the confirmation of bishops and priests. They do not agree to this and are therefore branded heretics and schismatics.

I have held and still hold that they are neither heretics nor schismatics; perhaps they are better Christians than we are—although not all of them are, just as not all of us are good Christians. The fine, barefoot booklet from Leipzig attacks this [judgment] too, after others have done so; it marches along in wooden shoes, indeed on stilts, and thinks that among all the others it alone does not step into the dirt. It might even like to dance if someone would buy it a flute. I must have a try at it.

---

[11] The Russian Orthodox Church. The metropolitan patriarch of Moscow opposed union with Rome, which Rome proposed in 1439. The metropolitan patriarch of Kiev, second to Moscow, favored union. Eventually a "Russian rite" developed within the Roman Catholic communion. Cf. *NCE* 12, 749-755. For the history of Russian Orthodoxy, especially Kiev Christianity, cf. George P. Fedotov, *Kievan Christianity* ("The Russian Religious Mind," Vol. I [Cambridge, Mass.: Harvard University Press, 1946]).

First of all, I say that no one should be so foolish as to believe it is the serious opinion of the pope or of all his Romanists and flatterers that his powerful authority is derived from divine order. This is clearly shown by the fact that everything derived from divine order is disobeyed in Rome down to the last iota. Indeed, it is mocked as foolishness if anyone thinks of it at all. This is as clear as day. Moreover, they allow the gospel and the Christian faith to collapse everywhere in the world, and do not intend to lose a hair over it. In addition, all evil examples of spiritual and worldly knavery flow out of Rome, as from a sea of malice, into all the world. In Rome they just laugh about it, and whoever is sad about it is [considered] a "simple Christian,"[12] that is, a fool. If they were seriously concerned about the order of God, they would have to do many thousand more necessary things, especially those things they now laugh at and mock. Since St. James says, "Whoever keeps the whole law[13] but fails in one point has become guilty of all of it" [Jas. 2:10], who wants to be so foolish as to believe that they seek God's order in one point when they mock all the others? It is impossible for anyone to take one point of God's order to heart and not be at least affected by all the others. But there are many, many people who take papal power very seriously, yet not one of them dares to say a word in order that even one [part] of this other much greater and more necessary order should not be so blasphemously mocked and despised in Rome.

Furthermore, if all of Germany were to fall on its knees and pray to the pope and the Romans to keep this same power but to confirm our bishops and priests free of charge, as the Gospel says, "You received without pay, give without pay" [Matt. 10:8]; and to provide all our churches with good preachers, since they are abundantly rich and have so much that they might as well give [rather than take] money; and if they were strongly reminded that this is their duty according to divine order, then you may be sure that all of them would discover even stronger [arguments] than

[12] *Bon Christian,* an Italian term used by papal courtiers to describe the uneducated, common man, especially in Germany. Luther probably became acquainted with it during his stay in Rome in 1510. Cf. Heinrich Boehmer, *Luthers Romfahrt* (Leipzig, 1914), p. 143.

[13] *Ordnung.*

ever before that it is not divine order to make such a great effort without being paid. They would soon find a little gloss to help them wriggle out of it, just as they now discover them to push their way in. No begging would ever drive them to do these things. Since money is at stake, whatever they consider to be divine order must be divine order.

Within the memory of men, the bishopric of Mainz has bought eight episcopal capes[14] from Rome, each of which cost about thirty thousand gulden. I am not even mentioning the innumerable other bishoprics, prelacies, and benefices. Thus one blows the noses of us German fools and says afterward that it is divine order to have no bishop without Roman power. I am surprised that Germany, which indeed is half, if not more, under spiritual rule,[15] still has a penny left for these unspeakable, innumerable, and unbearable Roman thieves, knaves, and robbers.

It is said that the Antichrist shall find the treasures of the earth. I think the Romanists have found them, to the point of hurting us in life and limb. If the German princes and the nobles do not do something about it soon, and with decisive courage, Germany will be desolated or forced to devour itself. This would really please the Romanists, who regard us as nothing but beasts and who have coined a proverb about us in Rome, saying, "One should lure the gold from the German fools in any way possible." The pope does not prevent this blasphemous knavery. They all wink at it; indeed, they consider this chief knave higher than the holy gospel of God. They claim it to be divine order—as though we were fools unto death—that the pope has his hand in every dirty concoction and does with everyone as he pleases, as though he were a god on earth, although he should serve everyone freely (if he wanted to be, or were, the greatest). But before they do that they would

[14] A reference to the pallium, a woolen shoulder cape with the insignia of the archbishop's office on it. Since there had always been an archbishop in Mainz, the conferring of pallia, a source of papal revenue, involved considerable financial arrangements. Cardinal Albrecht of Mainz (1490-1545) held two archbishoprics and one bishopric at the same time. Cf. *LW* 31, 21. For the history of Mainz as an ecclesiastical center, cf. *RGG* 4, 613-614.

[15] *Geystlich*, that is, in possession of the church. "Spiritual fees" *(spiritualia)* were collected by the church from the clergy and laity, such as tithes, annates, and the cost of pallia. Besides these, there were "temporal fees" *(temporalia)*, that is, income from endowments of land and the like.

rather drop this power and call it no more a divine order than any other order.

If you say, "Why do they fight you so hard on this matter?" I answer, I have attacked them on a few higher matters pertaining to faith and the word of God. This they could not knock down. Moreover, they saw that Rome does not care about such good things at all, so they dropped them too and attacked me on the matter of indulgences and papal power. Thus they hoped to win the prize here for they knew very well that where money is concerned the principal school of knaves in Rome would be on their side and would not remain silent. But Dr. Luther is a bit arrogant and does not care much about the Romanists' grunting and squealing, and this almost breaks their heart. My Lord Christ does not care about that, and neither does Dr. Luther; we think that the gospel must and should go on. Then let a layman ask these Romanists, and let them answer, why they desolate and mock all divine order, and why they rage so fiercely because of this [papal power] without being able to show why it is useful, good, or necessary. For since the time it became established, nothing but sheer corruption has arisen from it for Christendom, and no one can show anything good or useful coming from it. I shall speak more on this if this Romanist shows up again, and, God willing, I shall expose the holy see of Rome as it deserves.

I have said this, not because I have thus provided sufficient arguments to dispute papal power, but rather to show up the perverted opinion of those who fight gnats but let elephants go, who see the speck in their neighbor's eye but do not notice the log in their own [Matt. 7:3; 23:24]. For with any unnecessary matters they kill others if they can, or brand them as heretics and freely slander them if they cannot. This delicate pious Romanist in Leipzig is one of them. Let us now have a look at him.

I find three strong arguments with which the fruitful and noble booklet[16] *of the Romanist in Leipzig attacks me.*

The first, and by far the strongest, is that he brands me a heretic, a senseless, blind fool, a madman, a snake, a poisoned worm, and many other things—not only once, but on almost every page of

[16] An allusion to Alveld's title of the German tract. Cf. the Introduction, above, p. 53.

the entire booklet.[17] These invectives, insults, and slanders count as nothing in other books. But if a book is produced in the cloister of the barefoot friars in Leipzig by a Romanist of the high and holy observance of St. Francis,[18] such words are not only an example of moderation, but also a strong reason to defend the power of the pope, indulgences, Scripture, faith, and Christendom. Moreover, it is unnecessary to prove any of them with Scripture or reason. It suffices that they are simply put down by a Romanist and holy observant of St. Francis. Since this Romanist also writes that the Jews used these reasons[19] to overcome Christ himself on the cross, I too must surrender and confess that, as far as so much slander, cursing, reviling, and blaspheming are concerned, the Romanist certainly has overcome Dr. Luther. I must really let him win on this score.[20]

The second argument, to put it briefly, is natural reason and goes like this:

A. Every community on earth, if it is not to disintegrate, must have a physical head under Christ the true head.

B. Since all of Christendom is a single community on earth, it must have a single head who is the pope.[21] For the sake of clarity, I have designated this argument with the letters A and B. I also want to indicate that this Romanist knows the alphabet all the way down to B.

[17] Alveld's Latin tract abounds in such language. Cf. the Introduction, above, p. 52.

[18] The Minor Brethren of the Regular Observants *Fratres minores regularis Observantiae)* split from the Franciscan Order in 1368 in Italy to follow the strict rule of St. Francis as confirmed by Pope Honorius III in 1223. Alveld used this designation in the title of his Latin tract. Cf. the Introduction, above, p. 51.

[19] "Don't you see how the gates of hell, namely, these most cruel Jews, these filthy satellites and cohorts of demons, prevailed against Christ, since they seized him, bound him, dragged him, beat him, spit upon him, robed him, mocked him, whipped him, and even crowned him, not with a crown made of yellow gold—so that his innocent face might shine after the manner of a king—but with a wreath of thorns, so that the divine face became red from the spilling of this most precious blood, and then condemned and crucified him?" Cf. Alveld's Latin tract, *WA* 6, 290, n. 3.

[20] Cf. the comment of John Lonicer in his tract against Alveld: "When Luther was admonished to respond to this monstrosity, he said, 'What shall I do? Look here! You respond that a certain Alveld certainly has won a victory against me, as long as he confused and mixed rudeness, ignorance, fear, blasphemy, monstrosity, and extravagance into a single mass so that I trust I cannot be dragged down by this kind of dignity.' " *WA* 6, 290, n. 4.

[21] Cf. the Introduction, p. 52.

My answer to this argument is: Since the matter in question is whether the power of the pope exists because of divine order, is it not a bit ridiculous to refer to reason drawn from experience in temporal things and compare it with divine law, especially since this poor, presumptuous man promises to argue against me with divine law?[22] For whatever worldly order and reason disclose is very far below divine law. Indeed, Scripture forbids one to follow reason. Deuteronomy 12 [:8]: "You shall not do what is right in your own eyes." Reason always resists God's laws, according to Genesis 6 [:5], "All of the human heart and mind always desire the greatest evil." Therefore, the attempt to guard or to base God's order upon reason, unless previously it has been grounded in and illumined by faith, is the same as if I wanted to illumine the sun with a dark lantern or use a reed as the foundation for a rock. For Isaiah 7 [:9] puts reason under faith, saying, "If you will not believe you shall have neither understanding nor reason."[23] He does not say, "If you have no reason, you shall have no faith." That is why this scribe should have left his perverted reason at home, or first grounded it in passages of Scripture, so as not to claim, in such a ridiculous and perverted manner, to prove faith and divine law with mere reasoning. For if this reasoning concludes that a physical community must have a physical lord or disintegrate, it should conclude further that, just as a physical community cannot continue to exist without women, so Christendom must also be given a physical, common woman so as not to perish. Indeed, she would have to be a real whore. And again, a physical community does not exist without a common, physical city, a house and a country; thus Christendom must be given a common city, a house and a country. Where is it to be found? In Rome, to be sure, they are always eager to acquire one, for they have made almost the entire world their own. Again, Christendom must have common, physical property—servants, maids, cattle, fodder, and the like—for no community can continue to exist without such things. You can see how gracefully this reasoning walks on its stilts.

A teacher[24] should first have considered such clumsy things

[22] Alveld expressed this intent on the reverse side of the title page of his Latin tract.

[23] This is Luther's free translation of the Vulgate text.

[24] *Lesemeyster,* literally, "master of reading."

and proven divine work or order with Scripture rather than with temporal analogies and worldly reasoning. For it is written that divine commandments are justified in and by themselves [Ps. 19:9], not by other external help. Again, the wise man says about God's wisdom, "Wisdom has overcome the proud with its own power" [Prov. 11:2].[25] It is quite disgraceful that we should want to defend the word of God with our reason; for we should use God's word to defend ourselves against all enemies, as St. Paul teaches [Eph. 6:17]. In a fight would not he who wanted to protect his breastplate and sword with his bare hand and head be a great fool? The same applies when we want to protect God's law, which is our armor, with our reason.

From this I hope it becomes clear that this blabbermouth's rotten argument is defeated and found to be without foundation, along with everything he has built on it. But to make him understand his own mummery fully, we will see that, even if I were to admit that reason could exist solidly without Scripture, neither of these points, either the first A or the second B, holds true.

First, A says that every community on earth must have a single, physical head under Christ. This is simply not true. How many principalities, castles, cities, and families can be found where two brothers or lords rule with equal power? Even the Roman Empire and many other empires in the world for a long time governed themselves very well without a single head! How do the Swiss govern themselves in our own time? Again, there is no single overlord in worldly regiment since we are all one human race and have come from one father, Adam. The kingdom of France has its king; Hungary, Poland, Denmark each have their own. But they all are still one people of the worldly estate within Christendom, even though they do not have a single head; nor does this cause these kingdoms to disintegrate. Even if no government were without its one ruler, what would prevent a community from electing for itself many overlords with equal power, rather than a single one? That is why it is a bad pretense to measure anything in God's order on the basis of such a worldly and inconstant analogy, for it does not even hold true in the human order. If, once again, I were to admit

[25] A very free translation of the Vulgate text.

that this dreamer's dream is true, that no community could exist without a single, physical head, why would it have to follow that it has to be so in Christendom? I see very well that the poor dreamer thinks, according to his own understanding, that the Christian community is equal to any other worldly community. Thus he publicly discloses that he has never learned what "Christendom" or "Christian community" means. I would never have believed that such crude, fat, and stubborn error and ignorance could ever exist in any man, much less in a Leipzig saint. *That is why I first have to explain* to this crude mind and to others who have been seduced by him *what Christendom and head of Christendom mean.* But I have to speak bluntly and use the same words they have employed in their own wild reasoning.

Scripture speaks about Christendom very simply and in only one way; they have brought two more ways into general usage.

The first way, according to Scripture, is that Christendom means an assembly of all the people on earth who believe in Christ, as we pray in the Creed, "I believe in the Holy Spirit, the communion of saints." This community or assembly means all those who live in true faith, hope, and love. Thus the essence, life, and nature of Christendom is not a physical assembly, but an assembly of hearts in one faith, as St. Paul says in Ephesians 4 [:5], "One baptism, one faith, one Lord." Accordingly, regardless of whether a thousand miles separates them physically, they are still called one assembly in spirit, as long as each one preaches, believes, hopes, loves, and lives like the other. So we sing about the Holy Spirit, "You have brought many tongues together into the unity of faith."[26] This is what spiritual unity really means, on the basis of which men are called a "communion of saints." This unity alone is sufficient to create Christendom, and without it, no unity—be it that of city, time, persons, work, or whatever else it may be—can create Christendom.

In this connection we have to listen to Christ's word before Pilate, when he answered the question concerning his kingdom, "My kingdom is not of this world" [John 18:36]. This is indeed a clear saying which distinguishes Christendom from all worldly com-

[26] Luther's rendering of the hymn *Veni Sancte Spiritus* from the eleventh century. Cf. *LW* 53, 265-267.

munities as being nonphysical. But this blind Romanist makes it a physical community just like any other community. He [Christ] says even more clearly in Luke 17 [:20-21], "The kingdom of God is not coming with signs to be observed; nor will anyone say, 'Lo, here it is!' 'There!' for behold, the kingdom of God is within you." I am surprised that these Romanists regard such a clear and strong saying of Christ as nothing but a carnival mask. Everyone can clearly understand from it that the kingdom of God (for this is what he calls his Christendom) is not in Rome, is not bound to Rome, and is neither here nor there. Rather, it is where there is inward faith, whether the man be in Rome, or wherever he may be. Therefore, it is a stinking lie[27] and opposes Christ as though he were a liar to say that Christendom is in Rome, or is bound to Rome, much less that its head and power are there because of divine order.

In addition, he [Christ] prophesied the deception now ruling under the name of the Roman church in Matthew 24 [:24-26], saying, "Many false Christs and prophets will arise in my name, say that they are Christ, and seduce many with signs and wonders, so as to lead astray even the elect. Lo, I have told you beforehand, so if they say, 'Lo, he is in the wilderness,' do not go out; if they say, 'Lo, he is in the inner rooms,' do not believe it." Would it not be a horrible error for these preachers of dreams to count the unity of the Christian community—separated by Christ himself from all physical and external places and locations and given a spiritual place—as a physical community, which is of necessity bound to a place and a location? How is it possible, and what mind may grasp it, that spiritual unity and physical unity are one and the same thing? There are many Christians who are in the physical assembly and unity but through their sins they exclude themselves from the inward spiritual unity.

Therefore, he who says that an external assembly or unity creates Christendom speaks his mind arbitrarily. And whoever uses Scripture to support this brings divine truth down to the level of his lies and makes God a false witness, which is what this miserable Romanist does when he brings everything that is written about

[27] Proverbial German, *Es ist erlogen und erstuncken.*

Christendom to the level of the external pomp of Roman power. But he cannot deny that the majority of this mob, particularly in Rome itself, is not in the spiritual unity, that is, in true Christendom, because of their unbelief and evil life.[28] For if the fact that one is in the external Roman unity created true Christians, there would not be a sinner among them. They would need neither faith nor the grace of God to become Christians. Instead, this external unity would be enough.

From this it follows, and must follow, that, just as being under the Roman unity does not create Christians, so also being outside this unity does not make either heretics or non-Christians. I would like to hear someone dissolve this [logic]! For whatever is necessary to being a true Christian must make one. If it does not make a true Christian then it must not be necessary, just as I am not made a true Christian by being in Wittenberg or in Leipzig. Now if it is clear that the external unity of the Roman assembly does not make Christians, then being outside of it certainly does not make heretics or schismatics either. That is why it cannot be true to say that being under the Roman community is divine order. For whoever obeys one part of divine order obeys all of it; one part may not be obeyed without the others [Jas. 2:10]. Thus it must be an open, blasphemous lie against the Holy Spirit to say that the external unity of Roman power is the fulfilment of one divine order; for there are many people in it who neither respect nor fulfil any part of the divine order. That is why being either here or there does not make heretics; rather, not having true faith makes heretics. It is clear then that being in the Roman assembly does not mean to be in faith, and being outside it does not mean to be in unbelief. Otherwise, all those who are in it would be believers and saved, since no one article of faith is believed without all the other articles.

Therefore, all those who make the Christian unity or community physical and external, equal to other communities, are true Jews. For they, too, wait for their messiah to establish an external kingdom at a particular external place, namely, Jerusalem. Thus they drop the only faith that makes Christ's kingdom spiritual and internal.

[28] Cf. Alveld's argument in the Introduction, above, p. 52.

Again, if every physical community derives its name from its head, just as we say, "This city is electoral, that one is ducal, this one is Franconian," then all of Christendom should by rights be called "Roman" or "Petrine," or "papal." Why then is it called "Christendom" and why are we called "Christians?" Because of our head—even though we are still on earth. This indicates that all of Christendom has no other head than Christ, even on earth, because it has no other name than the one derived from Christ. That is why St. Luke writes in Acts [11:26] that the disciples were first called "Antiochians," but this was soon changed and they were called "Christians."[29]

It follows further that, although man consists of two natures, body and soul, he is not counted as a member of Christendom according to his body, but according to his soul, indeed, according to his faith. Otherwise, it might be said that a man is a more noble Christian than a woman, since the physical nature of man is better than that of woman; or that a man is a greater Christian than a child, a healthy man a stronger Christian than a sick one, a lord, a lady, a rich man, or a mighty man a better Christian than a servant, a maid, a poor man, or a slave. St. Paul contradicts this in Galatians 5 [:6; 3:28], "In Christ there is neither Jew nor Greek, there is neither slave nor free, there is neither male nor female." Rather, as far as the physical person is concerned, everyone is equal. But whoever believes, hopes, and loves more is a better Christian. Thus it is plain that Christendom is a spiritual community which is to be numbered with the worldly community just as little as minds with bodies and faith with temporal goods.

It is certainly true that just as the body is a figure[30] or image of the soul, so is the physical community a model of the Christian spiritual community which has a spiritual head just as the physical community has a physical head. But who could be so senseless as to say that the soul must have a physical head? This would be like my saying that a living animal must have a painted head on its

[29] Luther's rendering of "In Antioch the disciples were for the first time called Christians."

[30] *Figur,* from the Latin *figura.* On Luther's and Alveld's use of the term, cf. below, p. 77, n. 42.

body. If this scribbler[31] ("book writer," I should say) had understood what Christianity is, he would undoubtedly have been ashamed of thinking of such a book. Is it any wonder that not light but only black darkness emerges from such a dark and confused mind? St. Paul says in Colossians 3 [:3] that our life is not on earth but is hidden with Christ in God. For if Christendom were a physical assembly, one could tell by looking at every single body whether or not it is a Christian, a Turk, or a Jew, just as I can tell by looking at someone's body whether it is a man, a woman, or a child, black or white. Again, with regard to a worldly assembly, I can tell whether a person has assembled together with others at Leipzig or at Wittenberg, or wherever. But I cannot tell at all whether or not he believes. Therefore, whoever does not want to err should remember clearly that Christianity is a spiritual assembly of souls in one faith, and that no one is regarded as a Christian because of his body. Thus he should know that the natural, real, true, and essential Christendom exists in the Spirit and not in any external thing, no matter what it may be called. For any non-Christian can have all these other things, but they will never make him a Christian; true faith alone makes Christians. Thus we are called "believers in Christ," and on the day of Pentecost we sing, "Now let us pray to the Holy Ghost above all for true faith."[32]

This is the way Holy Scripture speaks of the holy church and of Christendom. It cannot speak about it in any other way.

Beyond that, there is a *second way* of speaking about Christendom. According to this, Christendom is called an assembly in a house, or in a parish, a bishopric, an archbishopric, or a papacy. To this assembly belong external forms such as singing, reading, and the vestments of the mass. Here, above all, bishops, priests, and members of religious orders are called the "spiritual estate"—not because of faith, which they might not have, but because they are blessed with external anointing, wear crowns and special vestments, say special prayers, do special works, hold mass, stand in the choir, and seem to perform all such external worship. Although

[31] *Buchstaber*, a pun on *Buchstabe*, meaning "letter."

[32] Luther's rendering of the popular German hymn *Nun bitten wir den Heiligen Geist*, dating from the middle of the thirteenth century. Cf. *LW* 53, 263-264.

the little words "spiritual" or "church" are violated here when they are applied to such externals, since they refer only to the faith which makes true priests and Christians in the soul, this manner of speech has spread everywhere—to the not unimportant seduction and error of many souls who think such external glitter is the spiritual and true estate of Christendom or of the church.

There is not a single letter in Holy Scripture saying that such a church, where it is by itself, is instituted by God. And I here defy all those people and their followers who have made or want to protect this blasphemous, damned, heretical booklet, even if all the universities were on their side. If they can show me that a single letter of Scripture speaks of it, I will recant all my words. I know that they will not do me that favor. Canon and human laws do call such externals "church" or "Christendom." But that is not the point right now. Therefore, for the sake of better understanding and brevity, we shall call the two churches by two distinct names. The first, which is natural, basic, essential, and true, we shall call "spiritual, internal Christendom." The second, which is man-made and external, we shall call "physical, external Christendom." Not that we want to separate them from each other; rather, it is just as if I were talking about a man and called him "spiritual" according to his soul, and "physical" according to his body, or as the Apostle is accustomed to speak of an "internal" and "external" man [Rom. 7:22-23]. So, too, the Christian assembly is a community united in one faith according to the soul, although, according to the body, it cannot be assembled in one place since every group of people is assembled in its own place.

This Christendom is ruled by canon law and by prelates within Christendom. Included in it are all popes, cardinals, bishops, prelates, priests, monks, nuns, and all those who are regarded as Christians according to externals, no matter whether they are true and real Christians or not. For, although such a community does not make a true Christian—all the estates mentioned may continue to exist without faith—it never really exists without some people who are also true Christians, just as the body does not keep the soul alive, but the soul does exist in the body as well as without the body. But those who are in the second community without faith and outside the first community, are dead before God; they are hypocrites and are merely like images of true Christendom. Israel has therefore been a figure of the spiritual people assembled in faith.

According to the *third way* of speaking, it is not Christendom that is called the church, but rather the houses that are built for worship. The little word "spiritual" is then further applied to temporal goods—not those which are truly spiritual through faith but those which belong to the second, physical Christendom. They are called its "spiritual" or "ecclesiastical" goods.[33] On the other hand, the goods of laymen are called "worldly," even though the laymen who belong to the first and spiritual Christendom are much better and are truly spiritual. This is the way almost all works and government in Christendom are now heading. The term "spiritual goods" has even been applied to worldly goods, so that today no one understands anything else by it, to the point that one respects neither the spiritual nor the physical church any longer. They fight and quarrel over temporal goods like pagans, saying that they do it for the sake of the church and spiritual goods. Canon law and human law brought about this perverted use of language and things, to the unspeakable ruin of Christendom.

Now let us consider the head of Christendom.

From all this it follows that the first Christendom, which alone is the true church, may not and cannot have an earthly head. It may be ruled by no one on earth, neither bishop nor pope. Here only Christ in heaven is the head and he rules alone.

This is proven, first of all, in this way. How can a man rule something he neither knows nor recognizes? But who can know who truly believes or does not believe? Indeed, if papal power were to extend this far it could take faith away from Christian people and could guide, multiply, and change it as it pleases, just as Christ can.

Second, it is proven by the manner and nature of the head. For it is the nature of every head that is joined to a body to infuse all life, mind, and activity into its members. This can also be proven in worldly heads. For the prince of a land infuses his subjects with everything he wants and has on his mind, thus making all his

[33] Cf. above, p. 60, n. 15.

subjects receive the same mind and will and do what he wills. This is then truly called work that is instilled in the subjects by their prince, because without him they would not have done it. But no one is able to instill either into another man or into his own soul the faith, mind, will, and activity of Christ except Christ alone. Neither pope nor bishop can cause faith and whatever else a Christian member should have to spring up in a human heart. What a Christian must have is the mind, sense, and will that Christ in heaven has, as the Apostle says in I Corinthians 3 [2:16]. Furthermore, it can happen that a Christian member has the faith neither pope nor bishops have. How could he [i.e., the pope or bishop] then be the head of such a Christian? Since he is unable to give himself the life of the spiritual church, how is he to instill it in someone else? Indeed, who has ever seen a live animal with a dead head? The head must instill life. That is why it is clear that on earth there is no head of spiritual Christendom other than Christ alone. Even if a man were the head here, Christendom would have to fall as often as a pope died, for the body cannot live when its head is dead.

It follows further that Christ cannot have a vicar in this church. That is why neither pope nor bishop can ever be, or be allowed to become, Christ's vicar or regent in this church. This is proven in this way: if he is obedient to his lord, a regent works, pursues, and instills in the lord's subjects precisely the same work the lord himself instills; we see this take place in the worldly regiment, where the lord, the regent, and the subjects are of one will and opinion. But the pope is unable to instill or produce the work of Christ his Lord (that is, faith, hope, and love, and all grace with virtue) in a single Christian man. He could not do it even if he were holier than St. Peter.

And even if such an analogy and proof could not hold up, although they are grounded in Scripture, there are the strong and immovable words of St. Paul in Ephesians 4 [:15-16], where he attributes only one head to Christendom, saying, "We are to grow up in every way (that is, to be not external but solid, true Christians) into him who is the head, into Christ, from whom the whole body, joined and knit together by every joint supplying it when each part is working properly, grows bodily and builds itself up in love." Here the Apostle clearly says that the improvement and growth of Christendom, which is a body of Christ, comes from Christ alone, who is its head. Where then could another head be found on earth to whom such a nature could be attributed, especially since these heads quite frequently have nothing, neither love nor faith, themselves? Moreover, he said these words to himself, to St. Peter, and to everyone else. If another head were necessary he would have been disloyal to remain silent about it.

I certainly know some people who, in regard to this and similar sayings, dare to say that Paul was silent and therefore did not deny that St. Peter is a head, too; rather, he was giving milk to the babes in Christ [I Cor. 3:1-2]. Look out there! They want to make it necessary for salvation to have Peter as the head, and they are so arrogant that they dare to say Paul was silent regarding these things that are necessary for salvation. Thus these senseless bucks must first slander Paul and God's word before they allow their error to be defeated. They call preaching Christ milk and preaching St. Peter solid food, just as though Peter were something higher, greater, and more difficult to understand than Christ himself. This is called interpreting Scripture and defeating Dr. Luther. This is the way to run out of the rain and fall into the trough. How would these blabbermouths fare if we were to have a debate with the Bohemians[34] and the heretics? Indeed, no better than if we all became laughingstocks and gave them reason to think that all of us are senseless and out of our minds. Through our folly they would only hold on to their faith even more.

But if you ask, "If the prelates are neither heads nor regents over this spiritual church, what are they then?" let laymen give you the answer. They say, "St. Peter is one of the 'twelve messengers,'[35] and other apostles are also members of the twelve. Why is the pope ashamed to be a messenger, if Peter is no more than that?" But, you laymen, beware of having the hyperlearned Romanists burn you as heretics, since you want to make the pope a messenger and letter-carrier. Nevertheless, you certainly have good reason to

[34] The Hussites, who became schismatics after the martyrdom of John Huss during the Council of Constance in 1415.

[35] *Zwelff bottenn,* an old German word for apostles, meaning "one of the twelve messengers."

do so, for "apostle" in Greek means "messenger" in German, and this is what the entire gospel calls them.

If they are all messengers of the one Lord Christ, who will be so foolish as to say that such a great Lord, who has such a great cause for the entire world, has only one messenger, and that this same messenger should then produce other messengers of his own? In that case St. Peter should not be called "one of the twelve messengers" but rather "the only messenger," and none of the others would be "one of the twelve messengers." Instead they would be "one of the eleven messengers" of St. Peter. What is the custom at the courts of the nobility? Is it not true that one lord has many messengers? Indeed, how often are many messengers sent with one message to one place, as there are now priests, bishops, archbishops, and the pope ruling over one city, not to mention some tyrants who rule in between? Christ sent all the apostles into the whole world with equal, full authority and with his word and message, as St. Paul says [II Cor. 5:20], "We are ambassadors for Christ," and in I Corinthians 3 [:5], "What then is Peter? What is Paul? Servants through whom you believed." This message means tending sheep, ruling, being bishop, and the like. But when the pope subjects all of God's messengers to himself, it is the same as if one of a prince's messengers stopped all the others and sent them wherever he pleased while he himself ran nowhere. Would this please the prince, if he found out?

If you should say, "Well, one messenger may indeed be above the others," I say, "One may be better and more skilled than the other, just as St. Paul was, when compared with Peter, but since they all deliver the same message, none of them, for the sake of the office, can be above the others." Why then is St. Peter not one of the twelve messengers but lord over the eleven messengers and a special one? What is the advantage of one over the others, since they all have one and the same message and vocation from the one Lord?

Therefore, since according to divine order all bishops are equal and occupy the place of the apostles, I can certainly confess that according to human order one is above the other in the external church. For here the pope instills what he has in his mind, for example, his canon law and human work, so that Christendom is ruled with external pomp. But, as was said, this does not make Christians.[36] Moreover, those who are not under these same laws and this pomp, or under human order, are not heretics. Many countries have many customs. All this is confirmed by the article, "I believe in the Holy Spirit, one holy Christian church, the communion of saints." No one says, "I believe in the Holy Spirit, one holy Roman church, the communion of Romans." So it is clear that the holy church is not bound to Rome; rather, it extends to the end of the earth, assembled in one faith, a spiritual and not a physical assembly. For what is believed is neither physical nor visible. All of us see the external Roman church. That is why it cannot be the true church, which is believed and which is a community or assembly of the saints in faith. But no one can see who is holy or who believes.

Not Rome or this or that place, but baptism, the sacrament,[37] and the gospel are the signs by which the existence of the church in the world can be noticed externally. Wherever there is baptism and the gospel no one should doubt the presence of saints—even if they were only children in the cradle. But Rome or papal power are not signs of Christendom, for this kind of power does not make a Christian, as baptism and the gospel do. That is why it does not belong to true Christendom either and is a human order.

I therefore advise this Romanist to go to school for one more year to learn what Christendom and head of Christendom really mean, before he drives the poor heretics away with such high, deep, wide, and long writings. It hurts my heart to have to permit such mad saints so arrogantly, so freely, and so unashamedly to tear up and slander Holy Scripture and to dare to deal with Scripture at all when they are not even fit to tend pigs. Until now I was of the opinion that whenever something is to be proven by Scripture, Scripture itself should serve the point in question. But now I learn that it suffices to throw many passages together helterskelter whether they fit or not. If this is the way to do it, I certainly

[36] Cf. above, p. 70.

[37] The Lord's Supper.

shall prove, with Scripture, that Rastrum beer[38] is better than Malmsey wine.[39]

He uses the same method when he writes in Latin and in German that Christ is head of the Turks, of the heathen, of Christians, of heretics, of robbers, of whores and knaves.[40] It would not be surprising if all the stones and wood in the monastery were to stare this unfortunate wretch to death and scream at him because of his horrible blasphemy. What shall I say? Has Christ become a keeper of whores, the head of all murderers, heretics, and rogues? Woe to you, you unfortunate wretch for holding up your Lord to slander in this way before the whole world! This poor man wants to write about the head of Christendom, and in his great insanity thinks that head and lord are one and the same thing. Christ certainly is a lord of all things, of those who are godly and those who are evil, of angels and of devils, of virgins and of whores. But he is the head only of the godly, faithful Christians assembled in the Spirit. For a head must be joined to the body, as I have proven with St. Paul, Ephesians 4 [:15-16],[41] and the members must derive from the head and have their activity and life from it. That is why Christ cannot be the head of some evil community, although it is certainly subject to him as to a lord; just as his kingdom, Christendom, is not a physical community or kingdom, yet everything is subject to him, both spiritual and physical, hellish and heavenly.

---

[38] *Rastrum* is a Latin term meaning a scraping instrument, such as a toothed hoe or a rake. Leipzig students judged this beer to be extraordinarily bad. An old Erfurt tract on various drinks at the time of the Reformation contains the remark, "Leipzig students call the beer *Rastrum,* a metaphor taken from the farmers because, just as they turn and soften all the hard surface of the field with hoes, mattocks, and rakes, so does the Leipzig beer injure, attack, and corrupt, like a hoe, all the intestines with its acidity." Cf. *WA* 6, 301, n. 1.

[39] *Malmesier,* from *Monemvasia,* a Greek town producing this strong, sweet wine later known as Madeira.

[40] In the German tract Alveld wrote, "It is not enough to have Christ as a shepherd or head. If it were enough, all the pagans, all the Jews, all those who err, and all heretics would be true Christians. . . . Christ is a lord, a guardian, a shepherd, and a head of the whole world, whether one likes it or not." Cf. *WA* 6, 301, n. 3. In the Latin tract he wrote, "No community [*civilitas*] or assembly [*pluralitas*] of mortals can be rightly administered without the unity under one head, under the head Christ Jesus." He supports this statement with several examples, saying, "No brothel, no band of thieves, plunderers, and robbers, nor any unit of soldiers can be governed, or held together, or long endure, without a governor, a prince or lord, or one head." Cf. *WA* 6, 278.

[41] Cf. above, p. 72.

So we have seen that this blasphemous scribe has vilified and slandered me in the first argument. But in the second argument he has vilified Christ much more than me. For although he thinks highly of his own holy prayer and fasting in comparison with that of a poor sinner like me, still he did not make me a keeper of whores and an arch-knave as he did Christ.

Now comes the *third argument,* in which the high majesty of God has to suffer and the Holy Spirit has to become a liar and heretic so that only the Romanists can remain true.

The third argument is taken from Scripture, just as the second was taken from reason and the first from unreason, so that everything is truly put in order. It goes like this: "The Old Testament was a figure[42] of the New Testament. Since the former had a physical high priest, the New Testament must also have one. How else could the figure be fulfilled, since Christ himself has said [Matt. 5:18], 'Not an iota, not a jot, will pass from the law until all is accomplished'?" This is his argument.[43]

I have never encountered a more foolish, a sillier, or a blinder book than this one. Someone else has already published the same argument against me.[44] It was so crude and so foolish that I had to hold it in contempt. But since they have not yet sharpened their wits, I shall have to talk crudely to such crude heads. I can certainly see that the ass does not know how to use the lyre; I have to offer him thistles.

First, it is evident that the figure and the fulfilment of the figure correspond to each other as a physical thing [corresponds] to a spiritual one, or an external thing to an internal one. Everything seen with physical eyes in the figure must in its fulfilment be seen by faith alone. Otherwise it is not fulfilment. I must prove this with an illustration: the Jewish people physically came out of

[42] *Figur,* used by Alveld and Luther in the sense of "prefiguration" or "foreshadowing" of true reality. This basically Platonic idea paved the way for a biblical theology which regarded the Old Testament as "promise" and the New Testament as "fulfilment."

[43] Cf. the Introduction, above, p. 52.

[44] Jerome Emser, in his tracts *Concerning the Leipzig Debate (De disputatione Lipsicensi)* and *Formal Declaration of the Capricorn Regarding the Lutheran Game (A Uenatione Luterania Aegocerotis assertio).* Cf. *WA* 6, 302, n. 3; on the controversy between Luther and Emser, cf. below, pp. 107-110.

the physical land of Egypt through many miracles, as is written in Exodus. This figure does not mean that we, too, should physically go out of Egypt. Rather, our souls should leave the sins and spiritual power of the devil through true faith. Thus the physical assembly of the Jewish people means the spiritual, internal assembly of the Christian people in faith. Accordingly, whereas they drank water from a physical rock [I Cor. 10:3-4] and ate physical bread from heaven, so do we drink and eat with the heart's mouth from the spiritual rock, the Lord Christ, if we believe in him. Again, Moses set a serpent on a pole and whoever looked at it was restored to health [Num. 21:6-9]; this [figure] signifies Christ on the cross, and whoever believes in him shall be saved. And so on throughout the Old Testament: whatever references it makes to physical, visible things mean in the New Testament spiritual and invisible things which cannot be seen but which are possessed in faith alone. This is also the way St. Augustine understood figures; for he said concerning John 3 [:14], "The difference between a figure and its fulfilment is such that the figure granted temporal goods and life, whereas its fulfilment grants spiritual and eternal life."[45] Now the external pomp of Roman power can grant neither temporal nor eternal life. That is why it is not only no fulfilment of the figure; it is less than the figure of Aaron, which was of divine order. For if the papacy were to grant temporal or eternal life, all the popes would be saved and alive. But whoever has Christ and the spiritual church is truly saved and possesses the fulfilment of the figure, although only in faith. As long as the pope's external glory and unity can be seen with eyes, and we all see it, it is impossible for him to be the fulfilment of any figure. For the fulfilment of figures must be believed and not seen.

Just look at these fine experts! They make the Old Testament high priest a figure for the pope—yet the latter lives in more physical glory than did the former. Thus something physical is to fulfil a physical figure. This means nothing else than that the figure and its fulfilment are identical. But if the figure is to hold up, then the new high priest has to be spiritual, and his ornamentation and finery must be spiritual. The prophets saw this too when

[45] Augustine, *On the Gospel of John*, 12, 3, 2. *MPL* 35, 1490; *PNF* 7, 81. Luther translated freely from the original.

they said about us in Psalm 132 [:9], "Let thy priests be clothed with faith or righteousness, and let thy saints be ornamented with joy"; it is as if they were to say, "Our priests are figures, they are clothed externally in silk and purple, but your priests will be clothed internally with grace." Therefore, this miserable Romanist falls down with his figure, and his jumbling together of so much Scripture is in vain. The pope is an external priest, and they think of him in terms of external power and splendor. That is why Aaron may not, and cannot, have been his figure. We must have someone else.

Second—so that they may understand how far away they are from the truth—even if they had been wise enough to grant a spiritual fulfilment of the figure, it still would not hold up unless they had a clear passage of Scripture to bring together figure and spiritual fulfilment. Otherwise, everyone could do with it whatever he pleased. For example, John 3 [:14] teaches me that the serpent which Moses hung on a pole means Christ. If this were not the case, my reason would invent rather strange and wild things on the basis of this same figure. Again, I have to learn from St. Paul in Romans 5 [:14-15], rather than from myself, that Adam was a figure for Christ. Again, Paul, rather than reason, says in I Corinthians 10 [:4] that the rock in the desert means Christ. Therefore, no one but the Holy Spirit himself, who instituted the figure and created its fulfilment, can interpret the figure, so that word and work, figure and fulfilment, and the interpretation of both are God's own and not man's. Consequently, our faith is founded on divine, not human, works and words. What else leads the Jews astray but the fact that they interpreted the figures according to their own reason, without Scripture? What else led many heretics astray but their interpretation of figures without Scripture? Even if the pope were something spiritual, it is not valid to make Aaron his figure, unless there were a text which clearly states, "Look here! Aaron has been a figure for the pope." Otherwise, who could prevent me from holding the opinion, for example, that the bishop of Prague is prefigured in Aaron? St. Augustine has said figures are invalid in a dispute unless accompanied by Scripture.[46]

[46] Cf. Augustine, *On the Unity of the Church (De unitate ecclesiae)*, 5, 8, *MPL* 43, 396-397.

This poor blabbermouth, then, lacks both: he has neither a spiritual, internal high priest, nor a passage from Scripture. He stumbles blindly out of his own dream and takes as a premise that Aaron was a figure of St. Peter—which would take the greatest power to establish and to prove. He prattles with many words that the law must be fulfilled and not one iota omitted.

My dear Romanist, whoever doubted that the old law and its figures must be fulfilled in the new? Your expertness is certainly not needed to establish that. You should prove your great mastery here and show that this same fulfilment comes through Peter or through the pope. But when there is a real need to speak you are silent as a stick, and you prattle when there is no need to speak. Did you not learn your logic any better than that? You try the major clauses no one debates, take for granted the minor clauses everyone debates, and draw any conclusion you please.

Listen to me: I will give you a better lesson in logic. I agree with you in saying, "Everything prefigured in the old high priest must be fulfilled in the new," as St. Paul says in I Corinthians 10 [:6]. Thus far we agree. Now you go on to say, "St. Peter or the pope is prefigured in Aaron." Here I say no. What do you want to do now? Be very scholarly, get help from all the Romanists together, and add one letter or iota from Scripture to it—and I will call you a hero. On what foundation did you build? On your own dream! But you boast you want to attack me with Scripture. It would not have been necessary to play the fool with me, for I would have had to defeat a fool in any case.

Listen to me further: I say that Aaron was a figure of Christ and not of the pope. I do not say this on my own, as you do. Rather, I shall truly prove both, so that not you, nor all the world, nor all the devils will overthrow it. First, Christ is a spiritual, internal priest. He is seated in heaven and intercedes for us as a priest; he teaches us internally, in the heart, and does what a priest is supposed to do between God and us, as St. Paul says in Romans 3 [:25], and in all of Hebrews. Therefore, the figure of Aaron is physical and external, whereas the fulfilment is spiritual and internal, and the two correspond to each other. Second, [to show] that I do not bring these two together in my own mind, I quote the passage in Psalm 110 [:4], "God has sworn and will not change his mind, 'You are a priest for ever according to the order of Melchizedek.'" Why do you not cite such a passage about St. Peter or about the pope? For I think you will not deny that this passage is said about Christ, since St. Paul cites it in Hebrews 5 [:6] and in many other places, and the Lord Christ applies it to himself in Matthew 22 [:44].

Thus we see how excellently the Romanists deal with Scripture, making whatever they want out of it, as if it were a wax nose to be pulled to and fro. We have confirmed, with passages in the New Testament, that Christ is the high priest. In addition, in Hebrews 9 [:6-12] Paul compares Aaron and Christ even more clearly, saying, "The priests went every day into the outer tabernacle, performing their ritual duties; but into the second only the high priest went once a year, and not without taking blood which he offered for his own and the people's sins. The Holy Spirit indicates thereby that the way into the true, holy tabernacle is not opened as long as the outer tabernacle is still standing—an image or figure necessary at the time. But Christ has come as a high priest of future spiritual goods. And he entered once and for all into a greater and much wider tabernacle (not made by hand, that is, not a temporal building), without the blood of goats or oxen but with his own blood. Thus he secured eternal redemption." What do you say to this, you hyperlearned Romanist? Paul says that Christ is symbolized through the high priest, whereas you say it is St. Peter. Paul says that Christ did not enter a temporal building, whereas you say he is in a temporal building in Rome. Paul says that he entered once and for all and secured eternal redemption. He makes the figure completely spiritual and heavenly, whereas you make it earthly and physical. What do you want to do now? Let me give you this advice: take your fist, strike him in the mouth, and say he lied, that he is a heretic and a poisoner, as you have done to me. Then you will be like your father Zedekiah who also struck Micaiah in the mouth [I Kings 22:24]. Do you see now, you miserable blasphemer, where your mad mind and your advice got you? Where now are the big shots[47] who suppressed my sermon

[47] *Grosse hansen,* one of Luther's favorite expressions.

on the two kinds [in the eucharist]?[48] It served them right, because they wanted neither to hear nor to endure the gospel. Now they shall hear instead the lies and blasphemies of the evil spirit, as Christ tells the Jews in John 5 [:43], "I have come in my Father's name, and you have not received me; if another comes in his own name, him you will receive."

But if you should say that besides Christ, St. Peter was also prefigured in Aaron, I say, if you won't give up, that you might as well say that the Turks are prefigured in Aaron. Who can prevent it, since you enjoy useless prattling? But you have promised to fight with texts. Then do so, and leave your dream at home! Furthermore, if one fights for the sake of faith, one should not fight with uncertain texts but with those referring to the point in question, in a sure, simple, and clear way. Otherwise, the evil spirit tosses us to and fro so that in the end we do not know where we are—as happened to many people regarding the little words "Peter" and *petra,* Matthew 16 [:18].[49] It would have been less of a lie and blasphemy if you had said that Aaron was the figure of Christ, and, in addition, also of Peter. But then you scream with all your might, saying that Aaron was not Christ's but Peter's figure. You strike St. Paul in the face with arrogant words and, to make your foolishness complete, you say that Moses was a figure of Christ. You argue this not only without Scripture, reason, or proof—just as though you were more than God, so that everything you spit out is to be regarded as gospel—but also against all of Scripture, which makes Moses a figure of the law, as St. Paul does in II Corinthians 3 [:7-11]. It is unnecessary to speak about this any further now. Perhaps you would strike him in the mouth again, arrogant and malicious as you are. You have sucked such poison from Emser

[48] Cf. *The Blessed Sacrament of the Holy and True Body of Christ, and the Brotherhoods,* 1519. *LW* 35, 45-73. This tract, arguing for communion in both kinds, was branded "Bohemian" (Hussite) by Duke George of Saxony and prohibited by the bishop of Meissen on January 20, 1520. In the ensuing controversy, Luther defended his position in the tract *An Explanation of Certain Articles by Dr. Martin Luther, Regarding His Sermon on the Blessed Sacrament (Vorclerung Doctoris Martini Luther etlicher Artickell yn seynem Sermon von dem heyligen sacrament),* 1520. Cf. *WA* 6, 76-83. Leipzig theologians, among them Alveld, bitterly opposed Luther. The "big shots," of course, are Duke George of Saxony and the bishop of Meissen.

[49] Cf. below, pp. 86-89.

and from his heretical and blasphemous booklet![50] I shall give it the answer it deserves, God willing, when Knight Eck arrives with his particular manure.[51] You cannot pull it off this way, dear Romanists! If I cannot prevent it by force, at least you shall not bring any Scripture to support you. Praise God, I am not yet ready to bite the dust.

I think it is clear that the third argument of this Romanist is heretical and blasphemous, since he flatly contradicts God the Holy Spirit, calls him a liar, and completely destroys St. Paul. For since Christ is symbolized by Aaron, St. Peter cannot be symbolized by him. For what Scripture attributes to Christ should not be attributed to anyone else, so that Scripture always retains a sure, simple, and unequivocal meaning upon which our faith may build without wavering. I will grant that Peter is one of the twelve jewels Aaron carried on his chest [Exod. 28:17-21]. This might symbolize that the twelve apostles, surely elected in Christ and recognized from eternity, are the greatest and dearest portion of Christendom. But in no way do I allow him to become Aaron. Again, I grant that St. Peter is one of the twelve lions standing beside Solomon's throne [I Kings 10:19-20]. But for me, Christ alone must remain the one King Solomon. I grant that the twelve apostles are the twelve fountains in the desert Elim [Exod. 15:27], but in such a manner that the bright cloud and the pillar of fire are nothing but Christ himself. Just as little power as one of the twelve apostles had over any of the others, so little power does St. Peter have over the other apostles, or does the pope, by divine order, have over other bishops and pastors.

One more thing, dear Romanists, and then I shall finish. I beg from you a gracious and correct answer [to this question]: If Aaron was a figure of the pope in his physical authority, vestments, and city, why was he not also a figure in all the other physical things? If one physical thing counts, why not all the others?

It is written that the high priest shall not marry a widow or one who is divorced, but only a virgin [Lev. 21:14]. Why then is not

[50] Cf. above, p. 77, n. 44.

[51] *Juchenn*, probably from *Jauche*. A reference to John Eck's tract *On the Primacy of Peter (De primatu Petri)*, which he announced as a great work before it appeared in 1520. Cf. Schwiebert, *Luther and His Times*, pp. 422-423.

the pope also given a virgin in marriage, so that the figure is fulfilled? Indeed, why does the pope prohibit marriage to the entire priesthood? This not only contradicts the figure but God, law, reason, and nature as well, and he has neither authority, power, nor right to do that. Moreover, the church has never commanded this, and could not command it. He arbitrarily and without any need or reason crowds Christendom with whores, sinners, and miserable consciences—as St. Paul says of him in I Timothy 4 [:1-3], "In the last days some will depart from the faith and cling to the teachings of demons with deceit and false, invented words. Their consciences are seared, who prohibit marriage and command abstinence from foods God created," etc. Did not St. Paul here strike at the Roman spiritual laws in which the priesthood is forbidden marriage and all Christians are commanded not to eat butter, eggs, milk, or meat on certain days—although God himself left it completely up to all Christians to eat or to marry as they please? Where are you now, you Romanist of the observance, with your noisy prattling that not a single letter of the figure is to be omitted and everything must be fulfilled? Indeed, where is the pope, the successor of St. Peter, who, together with St. Paul and all apostles, had a wife?[52]

Furthermore, the old [i.e., Old Testament] high priest was not allowed to cut his hair [Lev. 21:5]. Why does the pope allow himself and all other priests to have a tonsure? Where is the figure fulfilled to the very letter here?

Again, the old high priest was not allowed to own any part of the land of Israel, but instead lived just from the contributions of the people of Israel. Why then does the Roman see so furiously desire the whole world? Why did it steal and rob country, city, indeed, principalities and kingdoms, and now dares to produce, ordain, dismiss, and change as it pleases all kings and princes, as if it were the Antichrist? Where is the figure fulfilled here?

Again, the old high priest was a subject ruled by kings. Why then does the pope allow his feet to be kissed, and why does he want to be king of all kings—something even Christ himself did not do? Where is the figure fulfilled here?

[52] Luther could be mistaken here, since Paul probably was not married. Cf. I Cor. 9:5.

Again, the high priest was circumcised, and—to come to an end—if fulfilling the figure means that things in the New Testament should be as physical as in the old, why do we not become Jews again and obey the whole law of Moses? If we have to obey one part of it, why not all of it? And if not all, why one part? Indeed, if the New Testament is to be considered higher in temporal splendor than the Old Testament, would it not be reasonable to suppose that there should be more than one high priest in the New Testament, so that it should be more glorious and more magnificent than the Old Testament, which had only one? If reason were to judge here and to follow its own rules, what do you think it would do?

Again, at the time of the old high priest, there were many holy men who were not subject to him, as for example Job and his family. Indeed, he was not alone. There were also the king of Babylon, the queen of Sheba, the widow of Zarephath, the prince Naaman of Syria, and many others in the Orient who, together with their families, were all praised in Scripture. Why is the figure not valid in every letter here? And why does the pope not allow anyone to be a Christian unless he be subject to him and purchase seals and letters from him at any price his Romanists please? Or do the Romanists have the power to interpret the figures however and how often they please, without any Scripture at all? Do you not see yet, dear Romanist, how completely envy and hate have blinded you and your kind? Would it not have been better for you to have stayed in your monastery and to have prayed your vigils until you had been called or driven into this matter? You do not know what "figure" means or signifies. But you boast of being a "public expert on Scripture."[53] An expert indeed—but in corrupting it, in blaspheming God, and in slandering all truth. Come again some other time, dear Romanist, and I shall deck you out with lilies and present you as a New Year's gift to those who have sent you![54]

[53] Alveld had announced himself as such on the title page of his Latin tract. He also had himself released from the usual obligatory chapel duties in the monastery during the Lenten period of 1520. Cf. the Introduction, above, p. 51.

[54] Shakespeare used this same phrase in a similar satirical vein in *Merry Wives of Windsor,* III, 5. Cf. *PE* 1, 373, n. 1.

I, too, want to say one thing not contained in Scripture. In all the estates God has instituted, there are always some who become holy and are saved. There is no estate on earth without living saints, according to Christ's statement in Luke 17 [:34], "There will be two men in one bed; one will be taken and the other left," etc. If the papal estate were of God, it would be impossible for a pope to be condemned; for there is always only one person in that estate, and whoever became pope would therefore be certain of his salvation—which is contrary to all Scripture.

Now let us see how these pious people deal with Christ's holy words in this matter.

Christ says to St. Peter in Matthew 16 [:18-19], "You are Peter and on this *petra* (that is, on this rock) I will build my church. I will give you the keys of the kingdom of heaven, and whatever you bind on earth shall be bound in heaven, and whatever you loose on earth shall be loosed in heaven."

On the basis of these words they have attributed the keys to St. Peter alone. But the same St. Matthew, in Matthew 18 [:18], has barred such an erroneous interpretation, for Christ says to all of them in general, "Truly, I say to you, whatever you bind on earth shall be bound in heaven, and whatever you loose on earth shall be loosed in heaven." Here it is clear that Christ is interpreting himself, explaining chapter 16 [:18] in this chapter 18 [:18], that the keys are given to St. Peter in place of the entire community, and not to his person alone. Thus also John, in the last chapter [John 20:22-23]: "He breathed on them, and said to them, 'Receive the Holy Spirit. If you forgive the sins of any, they are forgiven; but if you retain the sins of any, they are retained.'" Many people have tried to reconcile the sole authority of St. Peter with these two passages which are opposed by only the one [Matt. 16:18-19]. But the gospel is only too clear. Up to now they have had to concede that nothing particular is given to St. Peter as a person in the first passage. Many of the ancient holy fathers also understood it this way. This is also proven by Christ's words when he asked not only Peter, but all of them together, before he gave St. Peter the keys, "But who do you say that I am?" Peter replied for them all, saying, "You are the Christ, the son of the living God" [Matt. 16:15-16]. That is why the words of Christ in chapter 16 are to be understood according to the words in chapter 18 and in the last chapter of John; the one passage is not to be considered stronger than the other two. Instead, the one is to be properly explained through the other two. Two [passages] are stronger proof than one, and it is only proper that the one should follow or give way to the two, and not vice versa.

Therefore, it is as clear as day here that all the apostles are equal in all power to Peter; aside from the words, this is also proved by their actions. For St. Peter never selected, made, confirmed, sent, or ruled over an apostle—although this would necessarily have been the case had he been their superior on the basis of divine order. Otherwise, they would all have been heretics. Furthermore, all the apostles together could not make St. Matthias and St. Paul apostles; rather, these two had to be made apostles by heaven, as is written in Acts 1 [:23-26] and 13 [:2]. How then could St. Peter alone be lord over them all? No one has cracked this little nut yet, and I trust that against their will they will be gracious enough to me to let it remain uncracked for a while longer. Just as this Romanist boasts that the Roman see maintained its power in spite of frequent attacks on it,[55] I, in turn, boast that the Roman see has many times desired and been madly pursuing such power, and still does, but it has never been able to attain it and, God willing, never will attain it. It is real Shrovetide boasting to say that something has always been retained which has never been possessed. Why does not this dear Romanist boast that the city of Leipzig, where he does not possess a single house, has never been taken away from him? It would certainly be the same boasting. Thus the prattling goes on; whatever he hears he has to repeat.[56] That is why I say that although the Roman tyrants have fought against the gospel and

[55] In the Latin tract Alveld wrote, "Indeed, the insanity of the Jews, the fury of tyrants, the folly of schismatics, and the mournful pride and atrocious presumption of heretics frequently strove to destroy and even more often undermined this apostolic see; but always in vain and without effect." The German version reads, "This assembly [*samlung*] has existed more than 1486 years under the see of Peter, which Christ erected. No one was able to destroy the assembly of sheep under this see, although it was tried more than twenty-three times." Cf. *WA* 6, 310, n. 1.

[56] *Was nur ynsz maul fellet, das musz erausz,* a proverbial expression which literally means "whatever falls into the mouth must come out again." Cf. Thiele, *Luthers Sprichwörtersammlung*, No. 8.

tried to transform the general power into a power of their own, the word which Christ spoke has remained in force, "The powers of hell shall not prevail against it" [Matt. 16:18]. If it [Roman power] had been of divine order, God would not have abandoned it; it would have been fulfilled sometime. For he says that neither an iota nor a letter will pass away; it must be fulfilled [Matt. 5:18]. But not a single letter of Roman power has been fulfilled throughout all of Christendom. Moreover, it does not help to say it is not the fault of the Romans but of the heretics that there is no fulfilment. Heretics here, heretics there! The gates of hell (not to mention heretics) can neither prevent nor hinder what is divine order and promise. He [God] is so strong that he can and will fulfil it in spite of the heretics. But since he has never done so and allows it to remain unfulfilled, regardless of the great seriousness, diligence, effort, labor, cunning, and trickery employed by the Romans, it is, I trust, conclusively demonstrated that, whatever the pope's power over other bishops and priests, it is of human and not of divine order. The kingdom of Christ has always existed throughout the entire world, as it is written in Psalm 2 [:8] and Psalm 19 [:4]. But not even for one hour has it ever been completely under the pope, despite those who say otherwise.

Even though all this is quite true, we shall nevertheless go on and destroy their useless fairy tales, saying: Even if it were invalid to have the two passages in Matthew [18:18] and John [20:22-23], which make the power of the keys a common possession, interpret the one passage in Matthew [16:18], which reads as though the keys were given to Peter alone, it does not advance the matter. For it is doubtful that the one passage should follow the other two, or vice versa. Moreover, I defy them with two passages as strongly as they [defy me] with one. But we have assurance in this doubt, and it is up to us whether or not we want to have the pope as a head. For no one is a heretic where something hangs in the balance of doubt, no matter whether he holds this opinion or that one, as they all say themselves. And so once again their argument has broken down and they cannot come up with anything but an uncertain doubt like this one. That is why they must either drop all three of these passages as useless for the confirmation of their cause, since they are doubtful, or cite other passages clearly showing us that the two should follow the one. This they have to grant me. I dare them to try it.

But I shall cite passages to prove that the one passage is to follow the other two. For thus says the law and Christ quotes it, that each case should be established through the mouth of two or three witnesses [Matt. 18:16], and, "No one shall die on the evidence of one witness alone [Deut. 17:6]. Since I have two witnesses against one, my case must take precedence, and the one passage must follow the other two, namely, that Peter received the keys not as Peter, but in place of the community, as Matthew 18 [:18] and John 20 [:22-23] clearly say—and not as Peter alone, as Matthew 16 [:18-19] seems to say.

Furthermore, I am very surprised at their great arrogance when they want to make a power to rule out of the power of the keys. This goes together like summer and winter, because the power to rule is far greater than the power of the keys. The power of the keys extends only to the sacrament of penance, to loosing and binding sins, as is clearly written in Matthew 18 [:18] and in the last chapter of John [20:22-23]. But the power to rule also extends to those who are pious and do not have anything needing to be bound or loosed. It extends to preaching, admonishing, consoling, celebrating the mass, offering the sacraments, and the like. That is why none of the three passages fits the power of the pope over all of Christendom, unless one made him just a confessor, a penitentiary, an anathematizer, so that he ruled only those people who are evil and are sinners—but this they do not want to do.

Moreover, if these words are to confirm papal power over all Christians, I would very much like to know who could absolve the pope when he sins. If these words make everyone subject to the pope, as they say, then he himself certainly has to remain in a state of sin. It would not even help if he were to give his power to someone else to exercise over him. For this would make him a heretic acting against divine order.

Of course, some people have invented the fiction that in the pope person and office are two different things,[57] as though the

[57] Alveld wrote in his Latin tract, "The office is something different from the person functioning in the office." The German version reads, "There is a difference between the office and the person in the office. Even though the person dies, the office does not perish." Cf. *WA* 6, 312, n. 1.

person could subject himself and the office could not. This glitters for a moment, but then it becomes like the usual glittering merchandise. For with great noise and pomp they themselves have in their laws forbidden any lower bishop to confirm a pope, although this [confirmation] is not the institution of the office but the induction of the person into the office. If the person is not subject to anyone in this case, he certainly is not subject to anyone in absolving either. But they have a fraudulent spirit in all their affairs, glosses, and interpretations, so that they say now this and now that. While they try to subjugate God's words, they lose the correct understanding of them, so that they do not know where they are and go completely astray; and yet they want to rule the whole world.

Therefore, every Christian should hold the view that neither St. Peter nor the apostles have in these passages been given power to rule or be on top. What then is in these passages? I shall tell you.

The words of Christ are nothing but gracious promises to the whole community, given to all of Christendom, as was said,[58] so that the poor sinful consciences are consoled when they are "loosed" or absolved by a man. Thus the words apply only to the sinful, stubborn, and troubled consciences which, if they but believe, will be strengthened thereby. Now if these comforting words of Christ, given for the benefit of all poor consciences in the whole community, are used to strengthen and to justify papal power, I will tell you what it reminds me of. It reminds me of a rich and mild prince who opens up his rich treasure and gives all the poor and needy the freedom to get what they need. If there were a scoundrel among these needy people who used this freedom only for himself and did not admit anyone else [to the treasure] unless one let oneself be captured in accordance to his will, and if he rushed in and interpreted the words of the prince to mean that he alone had this freedom—can you imagine what the mild prince would think of this scoundrel? If you cannot imagine it, then hear what St. Matthew, Matthew 24 [:48-51], says of this servant: "But if that wicked servant says in his heart, 'Hah! My lord is long delayed,'

[58] Cf. above, p. 86.

and begins to beat his fellow servants, and eats and drinks with the drunken, the master of that servant will come one day when he does not expect him and at an hour when he does not know, and will give him what he deserves and put him with the hypocrites; and there will be weeping and gnashing of teeth."

Now look, just as this servant interprets his master's opinion so also do the Romanists interpret the word of God; and yet this is the very best interpretation they can achieve. For whenever they go really insane, they act as though this same servant had not only sold his master's kindness for his own profit, but as though he had exchanged the goods, giving chaff and stubble for wheat, copper for gold, lead for silver, and poison for wine. Therefore, it is still a favor that they grant the keys to the pope so that we may at least buy them with money and everything else we have. But all evil takes over when they preach their laws, their power, their ban, their indulgences, and the like, instead of the gospel. This is what the Lord calls the beating of the fellow servants by the evil servant when he should be feeding them instead.

I shall offer a crude illustration so that everyone can distinguish correctly between the true and the false interpretation of these words of Christ: the Old Testament high priest had, by divine order, a particular garment to use for his office [Exod. 28:2-43]. When King Herod elevated himself over the people of Israel, he took the same garment for himself and, although he himself did not need it, he usurped the power to use it; and the people had to buy their God-given right from him. This is also true today. The keys are given to the whole community, as was proven above.[59] But now the Romanists come along and, although they themselves never need them, nor exercise the office, they still usurp the use of the keys; thus we have to buy with money what is our own, given by Christ. As if this were not enough, they apply the words of Christ used about the keys neither to the keys nor to their use but to their own usurped might and power over the keys. Consequently, the power of the keys, freely given by Christ, is now imprisoned in the power of the Romanists, and both powers are to be understood

[59] Cf. above, pp. 86-89.

by the one word of Christ. This is as though Herod had said that Moses spoke of his own power when he spoke of the garment of the high priest.

Thus a tyrant, for example, could seize a last testament and interpret the words by which the property was allotted to the heir as though the power over this testament were given to him and [he could decide] whether he would let the heir have it for nothing or sell it to him instead. It is exactly the same when the power of the keys and the authority of the pope are understood as synonymous even though they are two things. Not only are they different, but the authority [of the pope] is greater than the power of the keys; yet they make of it one and the same thing.

I have many times refuted[60] their statement that the physical authority of the pope is instituted by the words of Christ, "On this rock I will build my church" [Matt. 16:18], "the rock" being understood to mean St. Peter and his authority. Now I will say only this: First, they have to prove that the rock means authority. They do not do this, and cannot do it. Thus they prattle their own ideas, and their drivel is supposed to mean divine order. Second, the rock can mean neither St. Peter nor his authority, because of Christ's subsequent word, "And the gates of hell shall not prevail against it." Now it is clear as day that no one is edified in the church, or prevails against the gates of hell, by being under the external authority of the pope. For the majority of those who strongly believe in the authority of the pope and rely upon it are possessed with all the power of hell and are filled with sin and malice. Furthermore, some popes have themselves been heretics, have instituted heretical laws, and have nevertheless remained in authority. That is why the rock cannot mean an authority which is unable to prevail against the gates of hell; it can only mean Christ alone and the faith against which no power can do anything.

The fact that this authority continues to exist even though some fight against it[61] does not mean it prevails against the gates of hell. For the Greek church, too, has continued to exist, as well as

[60] Cf. especially *Luther's Resolution About Thesis XIII Concerning the Power of the Pope (Resolutio Lutheriana super propositione sua tercia decima de potestate papae)*, 1519. *WA* 2, 185-240.

[61] Cf. above, p. 87, n. 55.

all the other Christians in the world; so have the Muscovites and Bohemians. Indeed, even the kingdom of Persia has continued to exist more than two thousand years, and the Turks almost a thousand years now, although they have been fought in many ways. And to tell you even more—which should certainly surprise a hyper-learned Romanist like you—the world, in its evil, has prevailed from the very beginning and continues to exist until the Last Day and eternally, even though God himself, with all holy angels and men, continually preaches, writes, and works against it. If you wish, dear Romanist, then defy God and all the angels, and the continued existence of the world, against all their words and deeds.

Should not you, you miserable and blind Romanist, first learn what "to prevail against the gates of hell" means before writing something? If every "prevailing" means as much as prevailing against the gates of hell, then the kingdom of the devil prevails with a greater following than the kingdom of God. But "to prevail against the gates of hell" does not mean to continue existing physically in the external community, power, authority, or assembly, as you prattle regarding the Roman community and unity. Instead it means to be built, in strong and true faith, upon Christ the rock, so that no power of the devil can suppress this rock, even though it has a greater following and uses innumerable quarrels and cunning and power against it. Now a majority of the Roman community, and even some of the popes themselves, have intentionally and without a struggle left the faith and live under the tyranny of the devil, as is evident. Moreover, the papacy has frequently been subjected to the gates of hell. And to speak bluntly, this same Roman authority—ever since it dared to rise above all of Christendom—not only missed its purpose, but also caused almost all the schisms, heresy, disunity, sects, unbelief, and misery existing in Christendom; and it has never freed itself from the gates of hell.

If there were no other passage proving that the Roman authority is of human and not divine order this passage alone would certainly be sufficient, when Christ says that the gates of hell shall not prevail against his building on the rock [Matt. 16:18]. The gates of hell have frequently contained the papacy; the pope has not been godly, and his office more than once has existed without faith, grace, or good works. God would never have permitted this to happen if, in Christ's words, the rock meant this same papacy. For then his promise would not be true, and he would not fulfil his own words. That is why the rock and Christ's building upon it must be something quite different from the papacy and its external church.

Accordingly, I say furthermore that frequently the Roman bishop has been deposed or appointed by other bishops. Now if his authority came by God's order and promise, then God would not have permitted this. For it would be against his word and promise, and if God were ever found inconstant in a single word, faith, truth, Scripture, and God himself would perish. Since, then, God's words are constant, they have to prove to me that the pope has not once been subject either to the devil or to men. Here I would like to hear what my dear Romanists can say in contradiction. I hope that they are struck with their own sword, like Goliath [I Sam. 17:51]. For I can prove that the papacy was not only subject to the devil, but also to bishops, and indeed to worldly power, namely, to emperors. Where did the rock prevail here against the gates of hell? I shall leave them the free choice: either the papacy is defeated in these words, or God is a liar. Let us see which they will choose.

Furthermore, it is not enough to extricate yourself with words, saying that even though the papacy has been subject to the devil from time to time, devout Christians have certainly always continued to exist under it. I reply that Christians continue to exist even under the Turks, and in all the world as well, as they have previously existed under Nero[62] and other tyrants. What good does that do? The papacy and the pope himself must never be subject to the devil if Christ's word is to be said about them, namely, that it is a rock against the gates of hell. See, this is the way our Romanists cite Scripture, according to their insane masks. Whatever means faith must mean authority to them; whatever means spiritual building must mean external pomp to them. They do not want to be heretics, they want to make heretics of everyone else. These are Romanists!

They, on their part, cite still one more passage, namely, the

[62] Nero, Roman emperor (54-69) who persecuted Christians.

Lord saying to Peter three times, "Tend my sheep" [John 21:15-17]. Here they are really true experts, saying that since Christ says to Peter in particular, "Tend my sheep," he gave him authority above all others.

We shall see here to what trouble, effort, and labor they are put to maintain this. First, we must know what they mean by "tending." "Tending" in Romanist language means to burden Christendom with many human, injurious laws; to sell for the highest price the vestments of bishops; to tear annates[63] from every benefice; to annex all religious foundations, to make servants of all bishops by means of horrible oaths; to sell indulgences, to tax the whole world with letters, bulls, seals, and wax; to prohibit the preaching of the gospel; to garrison the entire world with knaves from Rome; to make themselves the arbiters of all quarrels; to increase quarrels and disputes—in short, not to let anyone come freely to the truth or have peace.

But if they say that by "tending" they mean authority in itself, not this abuse of authority, it is not true. This I can prove by the fact that whenever, with due respect to authority, one only grumbles a little against such abuse, they rave and threaten with thunder and lightning; they scream that it is heresy and spoken against authority and that one wants to tear apart the seamless robe of Christ. They want to burn heretics, revolutionaries, schismatics, and the whole world. Thus it becomes clear that they mean nothing else by "tending" than this "wolfing" and extortion! Meanwhile, we prefer to think that tending does not mean wolfing; let us see what it really is.

They have a keen, high, and subtle speech (as they imagine) when they say that person and office are not one and the same thing, and that the office still continues to exist and is good, even if the person is evil.[64] From this they draw the conclusion, and it must follow, that Christ's little word, "Tend my sheep," means an office and external power which an evil man may, of course, hold.

[63] Annates *(annatae, annalia)* were originally the various revenues a bishop received from the vacant benefices in his diocese. Since 1317 they had been incorporated into the network of papal and curial revenues. Various German diets complained about them. Luther attacked them in *To the Christian Nobility of the German Nation,* 1520. *LW* 44, 143-146.

[64] Cf. above, pp. 89-90.

The office makes no one holy. Well, we welcome this, and we want to pose a question to the Romanists.

He who keeps and fulfils Christ's words is certainly obedient and godly, and will be saved because his [Christ's] words are Spirit and life [John 6:63]. Since tending therefore means to sit at the head and to have an office, even though one is a knave, it follows that he who sits at the head and is pope is tending. He who tends is obedient to Christ; he who is obedient in one thing is obedient in all things and is holy. Thus it must be true that he who is pope and sits at the head is obedient to Christ and is holy, be he a knave, a scoundrel, or whatever he pleases. Thank you, dear Romanists! Now I really begin to see why the pope is called "most holy." This is the way Christ's words are to be interpreted, making knaves and scoundrels into holy and obedient servants of Christ—just as you have made Christ into an arch-knave and a keeper of whores above.[65]

Furthermore, if tending means to sit at the head, then in turn being tended must mean to be subject. Likewise, just as tending means to rule externally, so being tended means to be ruled and, as they say, to live in the Roman unity. Thus it must certainly also be true that all those who are in the Roman unity, whether they are evil or good, must be real saints because they are obedient to Christ and let themselves be tended. For no one can be obedient to Christ in one thing unless he be obedient in all things, as St. James says [Jas. 2:10]. Is this not a fine church under Roman power, in which there are no sinners, only saints? What then will become of the poor indulgences if no one needs them any longer in the Roman unity? What will become of father confessors? How is the world to be taxed if penance disappears? Indeed, what will become of the keys if they are no longer needed? But if there are still sinners around, it means that they are not tended and are disobedient to Christ. What do you want to say now, dear Romanists? Let us hear your pipes! Do you not see that "tending" must mean something different from having authority, and that "being tended" must be something different from being externally subject to Roman power? Do you not see how foolishly the saying of Christ, "Tend my sheep,"

[65] Cf. above, p. 76.

is applied to Roman authority to substantiate external unity or assembly?

Christ also says in John 14 [:23-24], "Whoever loves me keeps my words, whoever does not love me does not keep my words." Prick up your ears, dear Romanists! You, of course, boast that Christ's word "Tend my sheep" is a commandment and word of Christ. We ask you, where are those who keep it? You say that even knaves and scoundrels keep it. Christ says that no one keeps it unless he loves and is godly. Come to some understanding with Christ so that we may know whether you or he are to be charged with lying! Therefore, the pope who neither loves nor is godly does not tend or keep Christ's word. Consequently, he is no pope either; he has neither power nor anything which is contained in the little word "tending," whatever it may be. For Christ stands fast here, saying, "He who does not love me does not keep my word." Accordingly, he does not tend either, that is, he is no pope as they interpret it. Thus it happens that precisely those passages cited in support of the papacy are against it. This serves the people right who treat the word of God according to their own insane minds, as if it were fool's talk. They want to make what they please out of it.

However, if you said, "If someone who is subject to worldly authority can be obedient even though this authority is not godly, why should not someone be obedient to the authority of the pope? That is why 'tending' and 'being tended' need not necessarily include obedience," I answer: Scripture does not call worldly authority "tending." Moreover, in the New Testament no one is told by a clear word of God to rule in a worldly way, although no power rises without his [God's] own hidden order. That is why St. Peter calls such authorities human orders [I Pet. 2:13], because they rule without the word of God, but not without God's providence. Accordingly, they need not be godly. But since there is a word of God here, namely, "Tend my sheep," neither the shepherd nor the sheep can do justice to this word unless they are obedient to God and are godly. Therefore, I let bishop, pope, and priest be what they please; if they do not love Christ and are not godly, they have nothing to do with the word "tending." Moreover, they are something different from the shepherds and "tenders" who are referred to in this word. Accordingly, it is not proper to apply these words of Christ to external power which itself may be either obedient or disobedient. Tending can only mean to be obedient.

Christ intended this too. For when he said to Peter three times, "Tend my sheep," he had previously asked him three times whether he really loved him; and Peter answered three times that he loved him. So it is clear that where there is no love there is no tending. For this reason the papacy must be love or it is not tending [the sheep]. And wherever the little word, "Tend my sheep," institutes the papal see, it follows that there there are as many popes as there are people who love Christ and tend the sheep. This is true, for in former times all bishops were called popes, [a title] now applied only to the bishop of Rome.

But look what our Romanists are doing here: they cannot overcome these words of Christ and must admit, with great reluctance, that no one can tend the sheep unless he loves Christ—as the written words of Christ here clearly express. Oh, how they would like to charge him with lying, or to deny him! But listen to what they say when they have knocked their heads against a wall so hard their heads swim; they say that Christ certainly demands love from the office of the pope, but not the high love they call "meritorious to eternal life"; instead, ordinary love is enough, the same as a servant loving his master.[66]

Now look! They make these babbling comments about love out of their own head and without Scripture; and yet, they still insist on showing off as the ones who argue with me about Scripture. Tell me, dear Romanists, all of you melted together into one mass, where is there a single letter in Scripture about the love you dream up? If the Rastrum beer[67] of Leipzig could talk, it would easily overwhelm such swimming heads and speak better about love.

But let us look further. If there must always be some love in the papacy, where is it if a pope does not love Christ at all and seeks only his own profit and honor in the papacy—as many of

[66] Alveld wrote in his German tract, "The Lord did not ask Peter whether he loved him meritoriously to eternal life, for Peter did not know this. Instead, Christ asked him whether he loved him as a shepherd loves his master when he faithfully protects and looks after his sheep for him." Cf. *WA* 6, 319, n. 1.

[67] Cf. above, p. 76, n. 38.

them, indeed almost all, have done since the time it began? You have not escaped me yet! You must confess that the papacy has not always existed, but fell many times due to the lack of love. If it had been instituted by divine order in these words of Christ, it would not have fallen. You may turn where you will—these words do not produce a papacy. Or must the papacy cease to exist in Christendom whenever there is no love in the pope? Now you yourself have said that although the person may be evil, the office can remain. Here again you confess, and have to confess, that the office is nothing when the person is evil. Otherwise, you have to let "tending" be something other than papacy. This is true. See what you can do against that!

But let everyone beware of the poisonous tongues and devilish glosses which invent such a love. Christ speaks of the highest, strongest, and best love that can ever be. He does not want to be loved with a false love and a half-love. Here one must either love completely and as much as possible, or not at all. Christ's intention is to instruct all preachers in the person of St. Peter as to what their mission should be. It is just as though he said, "Look Peter, if you should preach my word and thus tend my sheep, then hell, the devil, the world, and everything in the world will rise against you. You will have to risk body, life, possessions, honor, friends, and everything you have. You will not do this unless you love me and steadfastly cling to me. Now if you should start to preach, and if the sheep were being tended, and if the wolves were to break in on you and you wanted to flee like a hireling, not risk your life, and leave the sheep to the wolves without tending them, you would have done much better never to have started to preach and to tend sheep." For if he who preaches the word falls, when he should be standing at the head, everyone is offended, the word of God is completely disgraced, and more evil is done to the herd than if they had had no shepherd. Christ seriously cares about the tending of the sheep. But it makes no difference to him how many crowns the pope wears and how he elevates himself in all splendor over all the kings of the world.

Let anyone say, if he can, whether the papacy has such love, or whether Christ, with such words, instituted a superfluous authority like the papacy. No doubt whoever preaches with such love is a pope. But where are such [popes]? I know no saying which troubles me more in my preaching than this one, "I feel little love, but I am overburdened with preaching." They accuse me of being snappish and vengeful. I am afraid I have done too little to them! I should have pulled even more [at the sheep's] clothing of these raving wolves, who do not cease to tear up Scripture, to poison it, and to pervert it, to the great injury of the miserable and poor sheep of Christ. If I loved them enough I should really have behaved differently toward the pope and his Romanists who, with their laws and prattling, their indulgence letters and much other tomfoolery, destroy for us the word of God and faith. They impose laws on us as they please so that they can capture us and afterward sell us these same laws for money. They could weave ropes of money with their mouths, and yet they boast of being shepherds and "tenders," while in reality they are wolves, thieves, and murderers, as the Lord says in John 10 [:8, 12].

I know very well that the little word "love" deadens, tires, and weakens the pope and his Romanists. Nor do they like it if one really insists on it, for it knocks down the papacy. It also made Dr. Eck weak at Leipzig.[68] Who would not be weakened by it, when Christ so directly orders Peter not to tend sheep at all unless there is love? He wants love, otherwise tending amounts to nothing. I certainly want to wait a little longer and see how they plan to heal this particular stab wound. If they stab me with "tend," I stab them even harder with "love." Let us see which penetrates more! This is the reason why some popes are so skilfully silent about the word "love" in their canon laws and blow up the word "tend" so much, thinking that they have thus preached to the drunken Germans who would not notice how the hot mush burns their mouth. This is also why pope and Romanists cannot tolerate questioning and research into the foundation of papal power, and whoever investigates this foundation, not satisfied with their miserable words, must be acting offensively, blasphemously, and heretically. But if one questions whether God is God and investigates all his mystery with unbearable sacrilege, it pleases them and does not concern them. Where does this perverted game come from? From the fact that, as Christ

[68] At the Leipzig Debate in 1519. Cf. above, p. 56, n. 4.

says in John 3 [:20], "Everyone who does evil fears the light." Which thief or robber likes to be thoroughly investigated? Thus no evil conscience can stand the light, but truth loves the light and hates the darkness, as Christ also says, "He who does what is true comes to light" [John 3:21].

Now we see that Christ's two sayings addressed to Peter, on which they build the papacy, oppose the papacy more strongly than any other. Furthermore, the Romanists cannot come up with anything which does not put them to shame. I shall let the matter rest here and will ignore the other things the miserable Romanist spits out in his booklet, since I and a few others[69] have strongly knocked them down many times before in Latin. I find nothing in it except that he uselessly vents his spleen against Holy Scripture, just like a sniveling child. Nowhere is he master of his words, nor does he understand himself.

This then is my opinion about the papacy: Since we see that the pope has full authority over all our bishops, and he has not arrived at this power without God's providence—although I think he arrived at it not by the gracious but more by the angry providence of God which permits men to elevate themselves and to suppress others as a punishment of the world—I do not want anyone to oppose the pope. Rather, everyone should fear divine providence, honor such power, and endure it with all patience, just as though the Turks ruled over us; in that case it is harmless. I fight for only two things: First, I will not tolerate it that men establish new articles of faith and scold, slander, and judge as heretics, schismatics, and unbelievers all other Christians in the whole world only because they are not under the pope. It suffices that we let the pope be pope. It is not necessary for his sake to slander God and his saints on earth. Second, I shall accept whatever the pope establishes and does, on condition that I judge it first on the basis of Holy Scripture. For my part he must remain under Christ and let himself be judged by Holy Scripture. But the Roman knaves come along and put him above Christ, make his a judge over Scripture, and say that he cannot err. They want to make everything he dreams about in Rome,

[69] John Lonicer and John Bernhardi published replies to Alveld shortly before Luther wrote his tract. Cf. the Introduction, above, pp. 52-53.

and indeed everything they might ever think of, into articles of faith for us. As if this were not enough, they want to establish a new way of faith, namely, that we should believe in those things that we can see with our eyes, although by its nature faith consists of things which no one either sees or feels, as St. Paul says in Hebrews 11 [:1]. The Roman authority and community is indeed physical, as everyone can see. If the pope ever came to that—may God forbid!—I would freely say that he is the true Antichrist of which all Scripture speaks. If these two things are granted, I will let the pope be; indeed, I will help to elevate him as high as they please. If they are not granted, then to me he shall be neither pope nor Christian. Whoever cannot do otherwise may make an idol of him. But I will not worship him.

Moreover, I would certainly let kings, princes, and all the nobles try to keep the knaves of Rome from their streets and to keep episcopal capes[70] and benefices out of their land. How could Roman avarice get the idea of annexing all the religious foundations, bishoprics, and benefices of our fathers? Who has ever heard of or read about such unspeakable robbery? Do we not also have people who need them, instead of having to make ass-drivers and stable-boys, and indeed the whores and knaves of Rome, rich from our poverty—especially when they regard us as nothing but arrant fools and also slander us in the worst possible way? It is known everywhere that the Russians wanted to come into the Roman assembly.[71] But the holy shepherds in Rome tended these sheep in such a way that they refused to receive them unless they first committed themselves to pay an eternal tax of I do not know how many hundred thousand ducats. They [the Russians] could not eat "grass" like this, and so they stayed as they were, saying that if they had to buy Christ they would save their money until they came to Christ himself in heaven. That is the way you act, you scarlet whore of Babylon, as St. John calls you [Rev. 17:4]. You put our faith to shame before the whole world, and yet want to be known as someone who makes everyone a Christian. It is a pity that kings and princes have so little respect for Christ and are so little moved by

[70] Cf. above, p. 60, n. 14.

[71] Cf. above, p. 58, n. 11.

his honor that they let such a horrible disgrace of Christendom gain the upper hand. Yet they see that the people in Rome think of nothing but becoming more and more senseless and increasing all misery, so that there is no more hope on earth except with worldly power. I shall say more about this if the Romanist comes again. Let this be enough for a start. God help us finally to open our eyes. Amen.

I shall spare my dear Romanist an answer to the slanders and malicious words with which my person is being attacked, although they are numerous. They do not affect me. I have never meant to take revenge on those who slander my person, my life, my work, or my nature. I myself know very well that I am not worthy of praise. But that I am more cutting and passionate when defending Scripture than some can stand—no one can deny me that, nor do I intend to stop. Let anyone who pleases slander, curse, and judge my person and my life—it is already forgiven him. But let no one expect grace or patience from me when he wants to make liars out of the Holy Spirit and my Lord Christ, whom I preach. I am not concerned about myself, but I shall defend Christ's word with a joyful heart and renewed courage, without regard to anyone. To this end God has given me a joyful and fearless spirit, which I trust they shall not harm in all eternity.

No one should think that when I mentioned Leipzig, I wanted to shame this honorable city and its university. I was forced to do so by the boisterous, arrogant, and imagined title of the Romanist, who boasts of being the public reader of all Holy Scripture in Leipzig[72]—a title which all of Christendom in the whole world never ascribed to itself—and by his dedication of it to the city and its council.[73] If he had not put his apelike book into German to poison poor laymen, he would have been much too insignificant for me to bother with. This crude miller's beast still cannot sing his hee-haw and yet, all on his own, he embarks on a matter which the Roman see itself, as well as all the bishops and scholars, could not clarify in a thousand years. Moreover, I would have thought that Leipzig is too precious in his eyes to smear his drivel and snivel on

[72] Contained in the title of Alveld's Latin tract. Cf. the Introduction, above, p. 51.
[73] In the German tract.

this honorable and famous city. But he does not think he is such a bad guy.[74] I can see clearly that if I were to permit these crude heads their presumptions, in the end even the bath maids would write against me! I only ask that whoever wants to get at me should be armed with Scripture. What good does it do when a poor frog puffs itself up?[75] Even though he bursts, he will never be like an ox. I would like to leave this matter, but they force themselves into it. I hope that God may grant both our prayers, namely, to help me get out of it, and to keep them in it. Amen.

Honor and praise be to God alone to eternity. Amen.

---

[74] The proverbial German reads, *ein schlechter fritzsch,* meaning "a bad Fritz" (Frederick).

[75] A reference to one of Aesop's fables, "The Conceited Frog." Cf. Ennis Reed (ed.), *Fables of Aesop* (New York: Oxford University Press, 1966), p. 62. Cf. also below, p. 163.

TO THE GOAT IN LEIPZIG

1521

Translated by

Eric W. and Ruth C. Gritsch

INTRODUCTION

Jerome Emser (1477-1527),[1] the "goat of Leipzig"—Luther's designation because Emser's coat of arms, a shield and helmet adorned with a goat, was displayed on the title page of his writings—had pursued a variegated career before engaging Luther in a bitter literary feud. After studying law and theology at the universities of Tübingen and Basel, he became secretary to Cardinal Raymund von Gurk, papal legate in the matter of indulgences until 1505. While traveling with the cardinal in Germany and France, Emser became acquainted with humanists and edited the writings of the Italian philosopher Pico della Mirandola in Strassburg. In 1504 he matriculated at the University of Erfurt for the Master of Arts degree, lecturing on humanism at the same time. He stated later that Luther had been among his students.[2] Probably recommended by Cardinal Raymund, he transferred to Leipzig, where he became secretary and court chaplain to Duke George of Saxony and an occasional lecturer at the university until 1510. In a short time he received the baccalaureate degree in theology and a degree of Licentiate of Canon Law. When Duke George urged him to research the life of Benno of Meissen, a revered Saxon bishop (d. 1106), to aid the process of canonization, Emser collected material from various sources and published a biography of Benno in 1517. He even went to Rome in 1510 to plead for Benno's canonization in the name of Duke George, who awarded him prebends in Dresden and Meissen for his efforts. Emser's work was not in vain, since Benno was pronounced a saint in 1523.

When Luther was invited to preach at the Castle Church in Dresden on July 25, 1518, Emser invited him to a banquet at his home. Even though Luther engaged in heated debate with one of the guests, the Leipzig Thomist Magister Weissestadt, he had no

[1] Cf. Gustav Kawerau, *Hieronymus Emser. Ein Lebensbild* ("Schriften des Vereins für Reformationsgeschichte," 61 [Halle, 1848]), and *RGG* 2, 462.

[2] Cf. Ludwig Enders, *Luther und Emser. Ihre Streitschriften aus dam Jahre 1521* (2 vols.; Halle, 1889-1891), II, 179.

direct theological encounter with his host at that time.[3] Their controversy began a year later when Emser, who had attended the Leipzig Debate, defended Luther's "orthodoxy" in an open letter, dated August 13, 1519, addressed to John Zack, administrator of the archbishopric in Prague and provost of Leitmeritz.[4] Emser assured Zack that despite the heretical Hussite support for Luther—some Hussite leaders had corresponded with Luther and offered their spiritual support[5]—Luther himself did not identify his cause with theirs. As an eyewitness to the Leipzig Debate and "truthful priest of Christ," he, Emser, was convinced that Luther had in no way whatsoever agreed with the errors of the Hussites. Emser closed the letter with his expressed hope that Luther would never sink so low in his controversy with Eck—Emser called Eck "a very brave theologian" (*fortissimus theologus*)—as to rely on the prayers of heretics rather than on Holy Scripture.

When Luther read Emser's open letter to the Bohemian Catholics, he became convinced that it was a clever device to continue the intrigue Emser had launched at the Dresden banquet. On that occasion Emser had lulled Luther into making statements conservative Roman theologians could later use against him to substantiate their suspicion of heresy.[6] Now Emser used his eyewitness account of the Leipzig Debate to create the impression that Luther had never agreed with the heretic Huss, even though he had made some statements in Leipzig to that effect.[7] Accordingly, to Luther Emser's falsification of the record of his debate with Eck was but another trap for him. If he accepted Emser's "defense," he would appear to have silently recanted his statements on Huss; if he rejected Emser's interpretation, Emser would be justified in accusing Luther of heresy, since the Leipzig statements could then no longer be regarded as the emotional outbursts of a debater in trouble.

---

[3] Cf. the interesting account by Schwiebert, *Luther and His Times,* pp. 340-341.

[4] The title of Emser's Latin letter to Zack is quoted in *WA* 2, 655. A German translation is found in *St. L.* 18, 1479-1489.

[5] Cf. *WA,* Br 1, 419-420, and Smith (ed.), *Luther's Correspondence,* I, 197-199. On Luther's relationship to the Hussite Brethren, cf. Harrison S. Thompson, "Luther and Bohemia," *Archiv für Reformationsgeschichte,* 62 (1953), 160-181.

[6] Cf. Schwiebert, *op. cit.,* p. 341.

[7] Cf. Luther's own account of the debate in *LW* 31, 322.

Luther decided to take the "goat" by the horns and published his response to Emser's intrigue under the title *An Addition to Goat Emser* in the latter half of September, 1519.[8] Mocking Emser's attempt at defense as a "Judas kiss," he told Emser that it would have been much better to call him a "Bohemian heretic," as Eck had, than to write such a deceitful letter. In reality, Luther argued, Emser only wanted to condemn him but was too cowardly to do so. "From now on," Luther closed his letter, "I prefer to debate those who love the truth more than their own honor."

As soon as John Eck read Luther's response to Emser, he decided to join the debate once again. On October 28, 1519, he published a reply to Luther's charges against Emser in the form of an open letter to the bishop of Meissen, John von Schleynitz, entitled *An Answer for Jerome Emser Against Luther's Mad Hunt.*[9] In it he charged that Luther was responsible for all the malice associated with the Leipzig Debate. But Luther refused to be drawn any further into a debate which appeared to be useless. Although Emser retorted with another pamphlet, *Assertion of the Goat Against Luther's Hunt*[10]—his chief argument was that Luther had opposed the papacy in Leipzig because his Augustinian Order did not share in the profits from the sale of indulgences—Luther could not be moved to reply. "Emser pours out his fury," he wrote to his friend Spalatin on November 20, 1519, "but in such a way that he confirms my letter. I regret that such coarse, stupid, gross bullies interfere in this business."[11]

But the real controversy between Emser and Luther was still to come. In December, 1520, Emser renewed his attack on Luther with a lengthy treatise written against Luther's famous address *To the Christian Nobility of the German Nation*[12] of August 18, 1520, entitled *Against the Un-Christian Book of the Augustinian Martin Luther, Addressed to the German Nobility.*[13] It prompted an

[8] *Ad Aegocerotem Emserianum Additio. WA* 2, 656.

[9] *Pro Hieronymo Emser contra malesanam Luteri Venationem responsio. WA* 2, 657

[10] *A. Uenatione Luteriana Aegocerotis assertio. WA* 2, 657.

[11] Cf. *WA*, Br 1, 556-557; Smith (ed.), *op. cit.*, I, 252.

[12] Cf. *LW* 44, 115-217.

[13] *Wider das unchristenliche buch Martini Luters Augustiners, an den Tewtschen Adel aussgangen.* Enders, *op. cit.*, I, 1-145.

immediate reply from Luther. Without awaiting the full content of Emser's printed version, Luther jotted down his answer, *To the Goat in Leipzig,* responding to the first part of Emser's treatise given to him by friends who seemingly had access to it in Leipzig.[14] Luther, together with Philip Melanchthon, was convinced that Emser had already written a similar attack in Latin under the pseudonym of Thomas Rhadinus in October, 1520. Published in Rome by a Dominican monk under this name and reprinted in Leipzig by Melchior Lotther soon afterward, it had infuriated Luther because he assumed Emser's malice behind the name. Melanchthon had written a rebuttal of it shortly after its appearance in Wittenburg in November, 1520.[15] In reality, Emser was not the author. "You burden me with the lie that I was to have written the booklet of Thomas Rhadinus against you and to have had it printed secretly in Rome," Emser retorted later.[16] But neither Luther nor Melanchthon accepted Emser's statement as true, even though their friends Spalatin and Agricola did.[17]

Luther's *To the Goat in Leipzig* is the first of a series of four treatises he wrote against Emser. All four provide significant insights into the formation of Luther's doctrine of the church and his new, radical understanding of the ministry. We shall describe the historical origins of each treatise in subsequent introductions to give the reader an opportunity to retrace Luther's theological affirmations in the context of the controversy. The following translation is based on the first German edition of the treatise, entitled *An den Bock zu Leyptzck,* printed by Melchior Lotther in Wittenberg and available in *WA* 7, 262-265. Jerome Emser's German treatises have been reprinted in Enders, *Luther und Emser.* There are English translations of Luther's first three German treatises by Augustus Steimle in *PE* 3, 275-401.

[14] *WA* 7, 260, and Enders, *op. cit.,* I, v, suggest that Luther received the first printed pages as they came off the press.

[15] Melanchthon also used a pseudonym, Didymus Faventinus. Cf. *WA* 7, 260.

[16] Cf. *To the Bull in Wittenberg.* Enders, *op. cit.,* II, 6.

[17] Cf. *WA* 7, 259.

TO THE GOAT IN LEIPZIG

My greeting to the goat in Leipzig.

If I had called you a goat, my Emser, you would certainly have written a book or two about it, swamping me with all kinds of lies, slander, and invective, as is your custom. But since you have described yourself as a goat in such glaring letters that everyone must see it, and since you threaten no more than to butt, saying, "Beware, the goat will butt you," I trust I may as well receive you as a goat with your own favor and grace. It was necessary for you to put it down on paper; your entire nature certainly reveals you to be a goat. Furthermore, your booklets and speeches prove beyond any doubt that you can do no more than butt. Did you think I could not answer your frivolous threats and would say, "Dear ass, do not kick"?[1] May God protect from the billy goat those nanny goats whose horns are wrapped in silk; God willing, I do not need such protection.

Have you never heard the fable about the roaring match between the ass and the lion? When some animals fled at the sound of the ass's braying, the lion turned to him, saying, "If I didn't know you are an ass, I myself would have been afraid of you." Every day you can see that I am not afraid of those who have more skill and intelligence in one hair than you have in your whole body and soul together, and yet you dare defy me and try to scare me! Thus you really prove that you confuse stupidity with reason and have changed from a man into a goat.

What do you, stupid goat, want to accomplish with Holy Scripture? [How can you] interpret it, not according to the letter which kills, but according to the Spirit which gives life [II Cor. 3:6], as you boast in this little book of yours? You can hardly express what is on your mind in German, for your words roam about so clumsily, so helterskelter, and in such disorder. Moreover, as far as I can

[1] *Leck nit.* Luther's translation of Acts 9:5, *wider den Stachel lecken.*

see, you do not know and will not learn in a long time what "letter," "Spirit," "death," and "life" mean in Scripture. Your canon law is not going to teach it to you, and your goat's brain will not discover it either. This is one more indication that you have put off the man and put on the goat: you are a "licentiate of canon law" and a "prohibitor of Holy Scripture,"[2] and this you will certainly remain.

But I think I detect your real reason for writing. I shall disregard the fact that you are doing so presuming a skill and intelligence your own conscience undoubtedly denies you. I shall clearly demonstrate this to you when you finish butting and when it is my turn to clip the horns of the goat.[3] But ever since you knew my name you have had such a hatred for me within yourself, through no fault of mine, that I have often wondered how a man can bear such hatred and live, although your body does begin to show it. And this hate has made you almost a byword and an example to all other haters.

This same spirit of malice induced you to write the first book to the Bohemians[4] against me, in which you dealt with me in your fashion. I answered you[5] and, quite unknowingly, struck your scabs and sores. At that time, God knows, I knew nothing of your goatlike nature. Then you got really furious and wrote the second book, on account of which all scholars became your enemies, as you know. Because you poured out so many evident lies and whole bundles of invective I had pity on you and did not intend to answer.

Ever since then your unspeakable hatred cannot be sated; it cannot stop and cannot cease revenging itself. You wrote many malicious letters as well as a third book against me, under the name of Thomas Rhadinus.[6] You had it printed in Rome under a pseudonym so that no one might know your poisoned heart. I am really afraid that your hatred, and nothing but that, might kill you,

---

[2] *Prohibitat Sacrae Scripturae.* A pun on Emser's title *Licentiat sacrorum Canonum,* "licentiate" meaning "licensed" in papal laws.

[3] Proverbial German, *dem bock die horner schaben,* meaning "to rebuke" or "to put someone in his place." Cf. Thiele, *Luthers Sprichwörtersammlung,* No. 396.

[4] Cf. the Introduction, above, p. 108.

[5] Cf. the Introduction, above, p. 108-109.

[6] A Dominican monk who wrote a tract against Luther from Rome in 1520. Luther was incorrect in ascribing the book to Emser. Cf. the Introduction, above, p. 110.

particularly when you discover that you accomplish nothing and that I despise you. You miserable man, in view of your inhuman and unresting hatred, how could anyone believe that you can understand pure and good Scripture, since you neither read nor study it? O God in heaven, how deeply deluded you are! Will you not ever think that God is your Lord and judge and change your bitter and hateful heart?

Since I have not answered your lies and slander up to now, you fancy that you have won and that I am unable to answer you. Maybe you are putting your trust in the bull[7] and are encouraged [to hear] that I cannot write any more. You think that you alone will remain on the field with your masks[8] and that you will be able to defend yourself without danger and win without opposition. Moreover, you boast that as a priest of God you would suffer my barking,[9] which I have now endured from you three times in silence. Yet you do not see that in all your books there is one slanderous word after another, so that everyone says there is no more slanderous writing than yours. You even want to be famous for it because you call such mad and senseless fury "patience" and "suffering." You are able to pervert everything and give it a new name. Is it surprising, then, that you make of Holy Scripture what you please? But beware, from now on I shall not be silent and I shall not allow you to soil Holy Scripture with your goatish snout, as you have begun to do. Perhaps we shall soon settle the accounts you have owed for so long.

I ask only one thing: Quit your lying and write the truth. I am not surprised that you know nothing about Scripture. But your love of lying is not fitting for a priest of God and makes answering you an unpleasant task. To be sure, I shall let you slander and curse, for I know very well that your nature and your hatred do not let it stop.

---

[7] The papal bull, *Exsurge, Domine,* of June 15, 1520, signed by Leo X, granted Luther sixty days of grace to recant. It also prohibited the publication of his books. If he refused he was to be declared a heretic and cut off from the church as a "withered branch," together with his followers. For details, cf. Schwiebert, *Luther and His Times,* pp. 484-486.

[8] *Larven,* a reference to Emser's pretensions.

[9] *Holheypellen,* a word related to *bellen,* meaning a dog's angry barking.

My goat, you should not interpret this first sexto[10] to mean I could not wait for the end of your first little book. Rather, because you write that I have fled before you, and because you are so very certain that I will do nothing but let you triumph, you should know that it will turn out quite differently, God willing. For if you had anticipated my answer you undoubtedly would not have presented such a shoddy piece of work. Therefore, since your assurance has made you so negligent and careless that you yourself no longer notice what you are prattling and spewing out, and since I intend to answer not just you (you are not worth it) but also to take the occasion to present some Christian instruction regarding the Spirit and the letter (of which you do not understand one iota), I want to rouse and admonish you finally to wake up and take the sword—not by the blade as you are doing now with such great assurance, but by the hilt, with both hands. [I also admonish you] to confer with your fellow-spirits and write something serious and worthy of an answer at the end of the booklet. Let your best come forth so that it is not necessary to write many useless books and thus waste people's time. Dear goat, you are not far from where you want to go!

If you should tell me that the teaching of Scripture hangs by goose feathers, whereas the ideas which you have spun out of the [scholastic] teachers, who have erred many times, and out of your own head, hang by chains, I shall tackle this too, God willing, and answer your slanderous mouth which so frivolously defames and defiles the word of God. So be alert, and take up both small and large swords. For you have to defend three books, several letters, and especially some un-Christian lies. This [task] should exhaust your butting or else make you lie some more. I too shall take a vacation for a change and let my mind run freely against you. Therefore, dear goat, do not think you are alone on the field.

I certainly know that it is not easy to deal with a shameless slanderer and liar, for according to the proverb, "This I know for

[10] *Sextern.* Luther refers to his book as a sexto because it was printed on pages one-sixth the size of a full printer's sheet. Quartos, sextos, and octavos were originally printed sheets folded two, three, and four times. These designations came to refer to books printed on pages one-quarter, one-sixth, and one-eighth the size of a full printer's sheet.

sure: if I fight against filth, I shall not remain pure, whether I win or lose."[11] But, for the sake of truth, I must endure your excessive and endless slander and blasphemies. If you knew something different perhaps you would write it. Therefore, I have to be patient and let you carry on[12] as your unrelenting hatred directs you. I, too, have sounded off[13] many times, but for the most part I have written good things without doing so. You, however, can do nothing but curse and slander. Never mind, dear goat. It does not help to look for anything good in you.

Let the will of the Lord be done. Amen.[14]

---

[11] A Latin distich, *Hoc scio pro certo, quod si cum stercore certo vinco vel vincor, semper ego maculor.*

[12] Luther used a proverbial German expression, *her schlacken unnd schneyen lassen,* which literally means "let rain and snow fall." *Schlacken* is of Low German origin and refers to precipitation that is half rain and half snow. Cf. *WA* 7, 265, n. 2.

[13] *Rumoren.* Cf. *LW* 32, 8.

[14] Luther switched to Latin here: *Fiat voluntas domini, Amen.*

CONCERNING THE ANSWER OF THE GOAT IN LEIPZIG

1521

Translated by

Eric W. and Ruth C. Gritsch

INTRODUCTION

Emser immediately countered Luther's *To the Goat in Leipzig* with a very brief and angry pamphlet entitled *To the Bull in Wittenberg.*[1] "You should have listened to my words," he chided Luther for his heated reply, "before you judged them. But your haughty spirit, which collects my quartos before the ink is dry on them, cannot endure anyone's speaking or writing against it."[2]

When Luther received the pamphlet, probably in the last days of January, 1521, from his friend Haugold von Einsiedel, who resided in the territory of Duke George of Saxony, he was particularly angered by Emser's reference to a statement he had made at the Leipzig Debate. "Three times I have warned you like a brother," Emser wrote, "and have asked you, for God's sake, to spare the poor people whom you have so clearly offended by this affair. But you have given me your final answer in these words: 'The devil may care! This affair did not begin in God's name, and it will not end in God's name.' "[3]

Luther wrote his brief reply, entitled *Concerning the Answer of the Goat in Leipzig,* at the end of January or the beginning of February, 1521, and dedicated it to H. E., who is probably Haugold von Einsiedel.[4] It anticipates Emser's announced attack on Luther's address *To the Christian Nobility of the German Nation* and explains his statement regarding the Leipzig "affair."

It should be mentioned that Emser wrote a brief and satirical *Reply to the Answer of the Raging Bull in Wittenburg.*[5] Calling Luther a notorious heretic and mocking him in a Latin poem, it only discloses Emser's desire to leave nothing unanswered.

[1] *An den stier zu Uuiettenberg.* Cf. Enders, *Luther und Emser,* II, 3-8.

[2] *Ibid.,* p. 4.

[3] *Ibid.,* p. 5.

[4] H. E. could also mean Hieronymus Emser. The editor of *WA* 7, Paul Pietsch, accepted the conjecture of several scholars that Haugold von Einsiedel was meant. Cf. the evidence on this conjecture in *WA* 7, 266-267.

[5] *Auff des Stieres tzu Wiettenberg wiettende replica.* Cf. Enders, *op. cit.,* II, 27-44.

The following translation is based on the first German edition of Luther's pamphlet, entitled *Auff des bocks zu Leypczick Antwort,* printed by John Grünenberg in Wittenberg. The text is found in *WA* 7, 271-283.

CONCERNING THE ANSWER OF THE GOAT IN LEIPZIG

Dr. Martin to the Worthy and Honorable H. E.,[1] My Very Kind Lord and Friend, with My Good Wishes.

Honorable and worthy lord and friend: I have received, together with your own writing, Emser's quarto *To the Bull in Wittenberg*[2] and, although many people are dissuading me from replying to him[3] because he is such a well-known liar and blasphemer, I wanted to show him his lies so that he would not get too puffed up.[4] For even though he is such a crude head that he believes he is right and has won (even though he only comes up with sheer lies and not one good thing), I did not think it right to remain silent when he uses all his lies to put my own teaching to shame. I did not want to keep all of this from your kind concern. And so—God be with you.

First, he intends to show what kind of bird I am.[5] He really needs to do this, for even though I am not pious, God has so far protected my life so that no one has been able to reproach me honestly, and in the last two years I have put so many lies and liars to shame that Emser's demonstration will cost him much skill and effort. I have one advantage over him: no one has to show what kind of bird he is. He can be recognized by his song and by his

---

[1] Haugold von Einsiedel. Cf. the Introduction, above, p. 119.

[2] See the Introduction, above, p. 119.

[3] An allusion to the German proverb, *Ein offenbar lugen ist keiner antwort wert,* that is, "An obvious lie does not deserve a reply." Cf. Thiele, *Luthers Sprichwörtersammlung,* No. 28.

[4] Proverbial German, *dass der saw der pauch nit zu gross wurd;* literally, "so that the sow's belly would not get too big." Cf. Thiele, *Luthers Sprichwörtersammlung,* No. 266.

[5] A reference to the German proverb, *Man kennet den fogel bey den feddern.* Cf. Thiele, *Luthers Sprichwörtersammlung,* No. 167. Emser stated in *To the Bull in Wittenberg* that in the larger work he was about to publish *(Against the Un-Christian Book of the Augustinian Martin Luther Addressed to the German Nobility),* "I shall show our lay brethren what kind of bird you are." Cf. Enders, *Luther und Emser,* II, 3.

feathers. His little books read just the way his reputation smells. It is indeed a blessing when liars and knaves curse me.

Twice he had it printed, in Latin and in German,[6] and in addition blabbed around that I supposedly said, "I did not begin this game[7] in the name of God, and it will not end in the name of God either." What would he do if he really knew something about me? How fervent a Christian love (of which he boasts) would he have toward me, since he is so busy [spreading] this poisonous, invented, and impertinent lie, whereby he imagines and hopes that he is dealing me a deathblow and in a single moment dishonoring all my books and teachings and consigning them to the devil. But you missed, and the blade has cut your own fingers! You miserable man, how dare you testify and swear by God's holy name that you do not oppose me out of hatred, envy, and lies, when your heart and conscience certainly know otherwise? Hold still; I shall spread your feathers a little so that you can see yourself. Other people already know what kind of bird you are.

It was in Leipzig, in the chancellery of the castle (I have a lively and good memory of the occasion), that, in accordance with Eck's[8] practice, the debate was arranged to his advantage and to my disadvantage. We saw that the opposition sought honor rather than truth. I had hoped until then that they had begun in God's name just as I had. Then I said plaintively and with a sad heart the words, "This matter did not begin in God's name, and it will not end in God's name either"—which the results have proved. Everyone can see how my prophecy has now been fulfilled. For it is as plain as day what kind of fruit the debate has yielded.

I can verify these words of mine not only through the people on our side who were there, but through Emser's own conscience as well, since he stood there too, his face burning with envy and glittering with great malice.

That is why I disregarded this notorious lie and intended never to reply, thinking this holy priest of God and Christian lover might one day be ashamed of such a notorious and shameful lie and be

---

[6] Cf. the Introduction, above, p. 119.

[7] The Leipzig Debate in the summer of 1519. Cf. Luther's own account of it in *LW* 31, 307-325.

[8] John Eck, Luther's opponent at the Leipzig Debate.

afraid that, although I and those on my side are silent, the table, stove, and ceiling of the chancellery might yell at him, "Emser, don't lie yourself to death! That lie is too much even for a rhymester and poetaster." For I do not like to write against those whom I know to be convicted through their own conscience and who knowingly put forth stinking lies.[9]

Furthermore, this holy priest of God and everyone else know very well that it was Eck and not I who started the debate. How then could the remark about the beginning be applied to me? For I can boast—and even prove—that in all these matters I have never started anything with anyone. Instead, I was always reluctantly torn and driven away from useful and wholesome affairs, so that many godly people pitied me and I had to defend and protect myself at the cost of much precious time against my lying and malicious assailants, who wantonly challenged me so as to win their honors at my expense; and when they failed, they wanted to drive out the guest with filth. But, God willing, they shall have me as a guest against their will, for they invited me. Or else they shall have to let me go honorably and suffer and pay for the malice they exhibited toward me at the instigation of the devil. Thus I hope to God that the game shall not be spoiled for me and, before the next decade, Emser, Eck, and the pope, with all his liars and seducers, will find out whether they or I have started in the name of God, even if they burn my books and me in the bargain.[10]

My words, therefore, did not refer to me but to Eck, Emser, and the Leipzig theologians. This holy priest of God perverts them in the same manner as the Jews interpreted Christ's word about the tribute to Caesar [Luke 23:2] and about the construction of the temple [Matt. 26.61]. He wants to prove his Christian love by writing that I had said I did not begin the matter in the name of God. Moreover, he testifies and swears that he did not do so out of envy and hatred, and thus the holy name of God must serve his poisonous lies and must be put to shame. Do you not know your

[9] Proverbial German, *stincken und liegen.* Cf. Thiele, *Luthers Sprichwörtersammlung,* No. 349.

[10] According to the injunction of the papal bull *Exsurge, Domine* of June 15, 1520, Luther's books were to be burned. Cf. Schwiebert, *Luther and His Times,* pp. 484-492.

feathers at all, you noble bird? Who will believe that you write a single word of truth when you not only lie so impertinently and maliciously—despite my extreme efforts in asking you not to do so—but also fearlessly undertake to drive such poison into innocent hearts with your un-Christian testifying and swearing and bring so much death to so many Christians with your lies, under the living name of God? How you would rage and stink if you had so bravely caught me with a single letter as I have caught you in this lie!

It is a piece of this same truth of yours when you write that I said, "The devil may care if the poor and simple folk are offended by my teaching!"[11] My Emser, who wants to make me out to be a coward, should not attack me with lies. Many lies have been invented about me in the last three years, as you well know, and they were all put to shame. Since you, too, deal with lies, I have no fear of your coming away with honor, even though your lies might persist for a while.

May God be praised and blessed that you, Eck, the pope, and the whole Behemoth[12] are offended by my teaching. But I have heard, through the writing and testimony of many pious people, only that my teaching is consoling, useful, and wholesome to simple, sad, and captive consciences; and they have expressed heartfelt gratitude to me, unworthy as I am, and have praised God that they have lived long enough to hear such words. Christ says, "A disciple should not be better than the master. If they have called the master of the house Beelzebub, they will also call the household the same thing" [Matt. 10:24-25]. "If they hear my word, they will hear yours also" [John 15:20]. His Ecks, "points,"[13] Emsers, goats, wolves, serpents, and other raging stupid animals were also offended by him; but the sheep heard his voice. My Annases, Caiaphases, Herods, Judases, Pharisees, scribes, and pious, noble, and delicate folk must also be offended by me—that is the way it goes! Christ says, "Let them alone; they are blind guides of the blind" [Matt. 15:14]. It would not have been a mortal sin if someone had said what you

[11] Cf. the Introduction, above, p. 119.

[12] A legendary monster. Cf. Job 40:15. It is Luther's favorite designation for the "Romanists."

[13] *Spitzen,* a pun on Eck, meaning "corner" or "point" in German.

lie about me, you assassin, [namely,] that the devil may care if you and villains like you are offended—although I do not say it.

Therefore, dear liar, I did not say, as you attribute to me, that I so disregard the offense taken by simple folk that for my part they can go to the devil. You invent this so as to brand me a proud and arrogant man, as you put it. My joyous and great spirit hurts you in your heart. But I am and, God willing, I shall remain a stable, proud, and fearless spirit in my defiance of you, Eck, the pope, and your mob, even the devil. With God's help I shall defy and despise you as senseless and blind minds and poisonous liars. I wish that your hateful eyes would be forced to see my joyous spirit every day, although even hearing about it almost grieves you enough. All your envy, pain, rage, and whatever evil you might intend shall not help you at all. As long as I do not humble myself before you raging and bloodthirsty tyrants and do not accept your lies and poison, I must remain proud. So, too, Christ and John must have possessed the devil in the opinion of the Jews [John 8:48; Matt. 11:18].

But if I knew that my teaching were injurious to any simple man (which cannot be, since it is the gospel itself), I would rather suffer ten deaths than allow such teaching to go forth or let it go unrecanted. It would have to be a villain even worse than Emser himself who would not truly be sorry about offending the poor, common people. It would also have to be a non-Christian who would sympathize with the offense of tyrants and Pharisees. But I refuse to debate very much about whether I am a proud man, since this concerns not my teaching but my own person. I have said more than once that anyone may attack my person in any way he pleases. I do not pretend to be an angel. But I let no one attack my teaching without a counterattack, since I know that it is not mine but God's. For in it lies my neighbor's and my own salvation in the praise and honor of God. But I think one should believe my Wittenbergers, who see my daily life and associate with me, rather than the absent and lying Emsers. Indeed, I know very well that I am warned every day, not only by my neighbors but also in writing from many other countries, not to be so free to everyone. They scold my spirit which is all too common and offers itself to anyone, even at the peril of my life. No one has attributed to me an arrogant spirit except Emser alone, whom I should really believe as an enemy telling me the truth as they say—if only he had not made himself such a palpable liar. Moreover, I think that the matter with which I alone am burdened should certainly humble an arrogant spirit, even if there were no more to me than nature alone. Many people consider it impossible for me to live under such circumstances. Indeed, I have so much work to do that three of me would not be enough to do it in six years. Thus I am now, by God's grace, vigorous, healthy, joyous, and courageous, and I even have a little leisure—which, no doubt, my Lord Christ provides in answer to the prayers of godly people and without any merit of my own—thereby defying and offending all the enemies of the divine word so that they, in their annoyance, God willing, become like their Jewish fathers of whom it is written, "They have provoked me with a strange God, so I will provoke them with a strange people," Deuteronomy 32 [:21].

Again, you also write that I have forbidden obedience to the pope and the authorities, and, according to your kind of hardened lying, you do not even blush at the many books in which I clearly teach differently, particularly in the book *The Babylonian Captivity of the Church,*[14] which is supposed to be the worst. You also lie about my presence, my absence, my books; you are a liar from every angle. I have burned the books of the pope[15] for the sake of this same article, namely, that he deprives the authorities of their [rightful] obedience—and you say I prohibit it. I said that pope and bishops do not have the power to burden Christians with their laws, but that those who are under them should endure and bear as much of their illegal tyranny as can be done without sin or danger to themselves. I have written this not once but many times.

Further, dear liar, you cannot deny the book of Thomas Rhadinus.[16] Your drivel and snivel cannot be hidden in this way. The skill therein, which you readily boast to be your own, looks like you, copied from your mind, which is crude and makes no sense in philosophy and theology, as you shall soon know. If there

---

[14] Cf. *LW* 36, 3-126.

[15] On December 10, 1520, Luther burned the bull of excommunication, together with canon law and other papal books. Cf. *Why the Books of the Pope and His Disciples Were Burned by Doctor Martin Luther*, 1520. *LW* 31, 379-395.

[16] Emser denied authorship in *To the Bull in Wittenberg*. Luther is mistaken here. Cf. above, p. 110.

were skill in it, I would not attribute it to you. Who will believe you that you seriously intend to attack the abuses of the spiritual estate? Why have you been silent, and are still silent to this very day, about the abominable abuse of indulgences and Roman knavery? Besides, you do not attack any of my books except those in which I only attacked vices, not any estate. How can you revel in such lies of yours? You admit the vices and evil habits of the estates, and yet you mumble something to the effect[17] that you want to be acclaimed a pious man and an enemy of vice.

I can see it very well: while the water rises above the ribs[18] and evil habits are drowning together with incapable men, you pretend to save the estate. But you really strengthen vice and evil habits, as happened at the Council of Constance.[19] We shall no doubt be instructed about this in your precious and skilful booklet,[20] which started with lies and will probably end with lies as well. I could point out many more such lies that I have ignored up to now. Do not swing your ax too high, otherwise the chips might fall into your eyes in great heaps.[21] I therefore ask you once again, my Emser, for God's sake restrain yourself in lying and recant the lies you have already told so that you do not tempt God too much. I know well that you cannot hurt me, and I would rather see you getting well than being ruined. I do not want to leave anything undone that a Christian is obligated to do for his enemy. Since I see that you intend to put your soul on the line and give up life just like an angry bee, I want to give you the freedom and the choice in these writings (as I previously did to one of my enemies) to be

[17] *Heltist dennoch den brey im maul,* a proverbial German expression which literally means, "you keep your mouth full of porridge." It refers to a person who mumbles or equivocates. Cf. Thiele, *Luthers Sprichwörtersammlung,* No. 135.

[18] *Das wasser will ueber die koerbe gehen.* Although it is difficult to determine accurately the meaning of the word *koerbe,* there is sufficient evidence to show that it is derived from *korve* or *korbe,* an expression used by sailors to refer to the ribs of a ship. Cf. *WA* 7, 891, notes to p. 276, n. 2.

[19] The Council of Constance did not succeed in reforming the church and burned John Huss at the stake in 1415.

[20] Emser's *Against the Un-Christian Book of the Augustinian Martin Luther, Addressed to the German Nobility.* Luther had just read the first pages; the book appeared later. Cf. the Introduction, above, p. 110.

[21] From the German proverb, "He who swings the ax above his head will have his eyes full of chips" *(wer uber sich hewet, dem fallen die span ynn die augen).* Cf. Thiele, *Luthers Sprichwörtersammlung,* No. 29.

angry or to laugh. Moreover, I want to admonish you and encourage you, just in case your last hour arrives (for none of us is sure of any given moment), not to be frightened or to despair of my image and memory. Whatever you have done to me shall not hurt you. You can certainly count on that! I shall have done my part for the salvation of your soul. And even if you, incited by the evil enemy, despise such an offer, if you laugh at it and even make the sign of the cross against it, as I fear you might, just remember it when the time comes and the need arises, and do not despair. I also want all my other enemies to know this, if they do not yet know or have not yet experienced the lessons of ultimate despair and anxiety. I know what I am talking about now. The time will come when they too will know, may God grant it, without being destroyed by it. Moreover, do not ever think that I will recant a single iota of my teaching, even if it were God's will that you become my cousin,[22] sister, or brother-in-law, or whether you become a sheep or remain a goat. It is not a question of recanting, but of staking life and limb on it, my Emser—either that, or nothing. For that may God grant me his grace. Amen.

So that you yourself may grasp how you lie and how you write against me, not prompted by love for truth but by sheer raging hatred, I shall say further: If I really were so possessed, God forbid, as to say that I did not begin this matter in God' name, why do you attack that? Especially since you scream that you wanted to attack only my teaching, without any hatred? How many are there who still teach the truth for the sake of money, property, and honor? Did you not read, Matthew 7 [:22-23], that some will say to Christ on the Last Day, "Lord, did we not preach in your name, and do many mighty works"; and then he will say to them, "Depart from me, you evildoers"? Thus he proves to them that they did not act in his name, as they boasted. Look out that you, too, are not one of them, you who boast and swear so mightily that you have begun it [this matter] in God's name.

Again, Balaam, Numbers 24, uttered the noblest prophecies, not in the name of God, but for the sake of the good. Christ said, Matthew 23 [:1-3], that one should listen to the scribes who sit on

[22] Emser's *To the Bull in Wittenberg* concluded: "I admonish you, out of Christian love and faithfulness, to desist from this folly. . . . If you recant, we might still become cousins and I shall help you attack the abuses." Enders, *op. cit.*, II, 8.

Moses' seat, even if they are malicious, and you must undoubtedly admit that they did not teach in the name of God but for [their own] advantage and honor. Is it not true that you and all the other papal hypocrites and liars rely on this foundation, all of you saying that one should not despise avaricious, unchaste, and ambitious prelates and teachers? In short, one should not look at the life but at the teaching. Now it is impossible for these same people to be able to rule and to teach in God's name; rather, as St. Paul says about them, "They all look after their own interests" [Phil. 2:21]. If you want to wipe out all those who do not teach and rule in God's name, how many of the spiritual estate can you preserve? And where will you be? I hope that you do not want your teaching to be read or obeyed according to your holiness either. For what else would it be but sheer knavery?

St. Paul boasts and rejoices in Ephesians 1 [Phil. 1:15] that the gospel was preached by some out of envy and rivalry, and even by enemies of the gospel for the sole purpose of destroying it. But you, who are so much holier and more precious than St. Paul, think you can suppress my teaching whenever you can bring up a single evil word about me. Thus you want it to be known that in your delusion you no longer recognize your own hatred and malice. Meanwhile you despair of the cause, are unable to cut off my teaching, and turn your snout and jaw toward my personal life to disgrace it with such scrutiny that you are watching every word of mine since you cannot criticize any action. Thus you intend to write against my teaching and actually write against my life. I think you got into the carnival[23] and have become the poet of whom Horace writes that he intended to make a wine cask but the result was a jug,[24] just like the preacher who intended to preach on love and then preached about a goose.[25] To be sure, you do not have

[23] *Fassnacht,* Shrove Tuesday.

[24] "That was a wine jar when the molding began; why, as the wheel turns, does it turn out a pitcher?" Horace (55-8 B.C.), a Roman poet, in *Ars Poetica,* 21. See H. Rushton Fairclough (trans.), *Horace: Satires, Epistles and Ars Poetica* ("The Loeb Classical Library" [Cambridge: Harvard University Press, 1947]), p. 453.

[25] John Mathesius (1504-1565), a friend of Luther, collected *Sermons on Luther's Life (Luthers Leben in Predigten),* which was published in Nürnberg in 1570. Sermon No. 7 contains various anecdotes about preachers who told such stories from the pulpit to relieve the Lenten sadness (*ibid.,* p. 64). A sermon on "A Blue Duck" is contained in Thomas Murner's (1475-1537) *Guild of Fools (Schelmenzunft)* of 1512 (ed. Spanier; Halle, 1912). A Franciscan priest, Murner later became Luther's enemy. See Luther's attack on Murner below, pp. 215-224.

the ears of an ass, as you yourself say,[26] but take care you do not have an ass's brain and heart when you act in such an imprudent and senseless manner.

If I had wanted to attack your life, do you not think I, too, could have found something to write about? I could prove, from your second book *Assertion*,[27] that you admit to having hated me and to having written your first book of praise to the Bohemians[28] with hatred for me; that in this same book you very frequently lie; that again and again you talk of nothing but your own opinions, and that you write nothing without lies. But I wanted to have nothing to do with your own or with anyone else's life, and I do not want to have anything to do with it now. I do not deal with [someone's] life, I deal with his teaching. An evil life is most harmful to itself. But evil teaching is the greatest evil on earth, and it leads souls to hell in large numbers. I do not care whether you are godly or evil. I shall attack your poisonous and deceitful teaching, which opposes God's word, and, with God's help, I shall counter it well.

And so that your profound skill and great holiness may be shocked and cross itself at the sight of such a poor sinner and great fool as I am, I say further and confess that I do not boast of having begun something in God's name, as you boast with such solemnity. How do you feel now, Emser? Now let your pen splutter, ring all the bells, and cry aloud that everything in me is the devil's work, as you would so dearly have liked to do in your murderous stab. Dear Emser, my heart is so affected that I hope I have begun it in God's name. But I am not so bold as to pass judgment on it and loudly proclaim that it surely must be so. I do not want to suffer God's judgment for it. Instead, I crawl to his grace and hope that he has let it be started in his name. And, since I am a sinful man of flesh and blood, if something unclean has mingled with it, I hope he may graciously forgive me and not deal severely with me in his judgment.

---

[26] Cf. *To the Bull in Wittenberg:* "Although I do not have ears like an ass, since Aristotle, Thomas, Bonaventure, popes, cardinals, and bishops, be they dead or alive, must be your asses, I would rather stay in the asses' stable (in which Christ, too, was born) than be in your crow's nest." Enders, *op. cit.*, II, 3.

[27] Cf. the Introduction, above, p. 109.

[28] Cf. the Introduction, above, p. 109.

It is St. Paul who makes me such a coward when he says in I Corinthians 4 [:4], "I am not aware of anything concerning myself, but this does not justify me. Nor do I judge myself; it is the Lord who judges me"; and David, "Lord, enter not into judgment with me; for no living man is righteous before you" [Ps. 143:2]. But you, you insolent and intrepid hero, far above St. Paul and all the saints, with neither flesh nor blood, being only Spirit and God—you calmly appeal to God's last judgment, do everything without hate and in the name of God, and quickly defy God's terrible judgment. You should rather snap your fingers at him and pull his beard as well. It might perhaps be correct, whenever you go out into the streets of Leipzig, to have all the bells rung and roses strewn in the path of the new saint. If you have defeated me, in your writings, I ask that you [now] attack the terrible and divine last judgment as something that does you an injustice since it does not allow your cause to be undertaken in the name of God. Moreover, command God, as you do, not to enter into judgment upon you. For you alone, among all men, have already judged yourself and have awarded yourself the crown, and you alone will be found righteous.

What are you trying to do, Emser? Do you not see how your hatred is blinding you so much that you no longer understand your own words and actions? I have never read more horrible and abominable words—my ears ring when you thus take God's last judgment on yourself.[29] And if I had no other reason to believe that you lie and play the hypocrite in everything you say, this abominable appeal of yours to the last judgment would be more than enough [reason] for me. For that cannot come from a really truthful heart, or all of Scripture would have to be false. High oaths are signs of deep lies. You thought that you could win trust by lying. But you only managed to put that trust to the utmost shame. Who will ever believe anything from you after you have appealed with a false heart and lying words to divine judgment? If you are not lying, then it is your blindness that eliminates trust in you. For what good could you accomplish in divine Scripture when you are

[29] *To the Bull in Wittenberg:* "I attest on my honor as a priest, just as I would under oath, that envy or hatred of your person has had no room in my heart and has not now, and in this matter I appeal to the last judgment of God, who will pass sentence upon you and me." Enders, *op. cit.*, II, 5.

so stupid and blind that you no longer understand your own words or your own heart, not to mention God's judgment, and when you babble away like a madman and a drunkard?

Therefore, my advice to you is that you remain a rhymester and write your shabby doggerel.[30] It would do no harm if you lie or err in them. The word of God and Scripture are too much for you. You do them too much violence. I shall add still another example to toast your booklet: You begin with the complaint that my teaching has spread so far that there is no home in which there is not unrest and division because of me.[31] My Emser, who asked you to give such noble testimony against yourself and in favor of my teaching? How could my teaching be strengthened more than through this testimony of its worst enemy? God drives you like Caiaphas [John 11:49-50], so that even your hatred produces the best testimony for me just at the moment you think to produce the worst. My hope, that I began in God's name and teach the true word of God, has no stronger support or more miraculous sign than the fact that my teaching has spread so fast into all the world and has created such disunity without my effort and intention and in spite of great opposition and persecution by all the powerful and learned. If it had not done so, I would have despaired and grown tired a long time ago.

The real nature of the divine word is to produce such deeds and disturbance, which is proven by Psalm 147 [:15], "God's word runs swiftly," and by Christ, "I will give you a mouth and wisdom, which none of your adversaries will be able to withstand or contradict" [Luke 21:15], and Matthew [10:34-36], "Do not think that I have come to bring peace on earth; I have not come to bring peace, but the sword and dissension. For I have come to set a son against his father and a daughter against her mother. And a man's foes will be of his own household."

---

[30] Emser's ability as a poet was acknowledged by some humanists. Erasmus of Rotterdam, for example, praised him for writing a brief poetic commentary to his work. Cf. Gustav Kawerau, *Hieronymus Emser* (Halle, 1898), pp. 19, 31.

[31] Luther had just read the first pages of *Against the Un-Christian Book of the Augustinian Martin Luther, Addressed to the German Nobility:* "There has never been anything worse, more damaging, or more poisonous than Luther's teachings, his books, and his writings, which in a short time caused such strife, disorder, and violence that there is not a country, not a city, village, or house undivided and not opposing each other." Enders, *op. cit.*, I, 7.

If then my teaching has such an effect in the world, as the enemy himself confesses, what could be better for me than hearing this? Is it not a wonderful God who turns Balaam's malediction into a benediction [Numbers 24], the threats of my enemies into my consolation, and their defiance into my strength? Do you see how well you have hit upon the nature and work of the divine word, you precious dealer in Holy Scripture? You want it to be peaceful, to cause no dispute, and to offend no one. But Christ says, "No"; it cannot and it will not be so. If your first sexto begins with such crude foolishness, what will the next twenty do?[32] I think whatever you write will be nothing but sheer tomfoolery and blasphemy. You want to write books and do not know where to start. You undertake to deal with God's word and you do not even know its nature, its direction, or its intention. Where do you think you butted me so well, dear goat? I hope you will butt me like this in everything!

The reason why I firmly believe that the books of the pope and of all the sophist theologians are, for the most part, the devil's teaching is this: They entered the world in peace and honor, without opposition, and they have been feared more and considered higher than the holy gospel. If they had come from God they would have pleased fewer people, have caused disunity in families, and created martyrs. But you holy priest of God and lover of Christianity claim to write peaceful teaching which should not offend, and you appeal to the last judgment—and do so without hatred and in the name of God! You should rather call St. Simeon a liar when he says, Luke 2 [:34], that Christ "is set for the fall and rising of many, and for a sign that is spoken against." All the quarrels and wars of the Old Testament have prefigured the preaching of the gospel, which must and should cause quarreling, disunity, dissension, and disturbance. Such was the condition of Christianity at the time of the apostles and martyrs, and that was its best time.

The discord, dissension, and disturbance produced by God's word are blessed events. With them a true faith begins and struggles against false faith. Suffering and persecution also begin again, as does the true nature of the Christian people. To avoid such an

[32] Cf. *To the Bull in Wittenberg:* "If the first sheet already throws you into such a rage and you already show how you feel the goat's butting, what will the other twenty that follow do to you?" Enders, *op. cit.*, II, 3.

occurence, so Emser argues, one should preach something else, something peaceful. The Antichrist in Rome has long desired the same thing and unfortunately has achieved it, something which St. Paul calls "working of error,"[33] [that is,] strong preaching and belief in error. John Huss and Jerome of Prague were burned at Constance for the sake of such preaching.[34] For their teaching also butted the heads of goats and wolves and created a rebellion. When Emser's idols, pope and cardinal, consulted with each other as to how they should oppose their teaching, especially concerning both kinds in the sacrament, the Florentine cardinal[35] burst out, "Oh, well! Let these beasts eat and drink whatever they please. But if they want to reform us and teach us what to do, then let us fight them." And the game was indeed played according to this counsel.

My cardinal of St. Sixtus[36] did the same thing at Augsburg, pretending that if I but recanted regarding indulgences, the rest would cause no trouble. They probably wanted to find some nice "distinction" and a way out. This is the way they seek God's honor and the truth. Therefore, if Emser produces Aristotle and crowds me with the names of Huss and Jerome, I would rather share Huss's disgrace than Aristotle's honor. I would rather let him have the knave and liar Aristotle, whether he finds him in the pigsty or the asses' stable,[37] so that I may have Huss, who, by the grace of God, is again coming to life and tormenting his murderers, the pope and the popish set, more strongly now than when he was alive. If the pope and all papal liars should burst with malice they still have to hear John Huss say to their faces, "Although you Christian murderers might shed innocent blood, you will never be able to hide it." Abel, who was too weak for his brother when he was alive,

---

[33] II Thess. 2:11. Luther incorporated the words from the Vulgate translation, *operationem erroris,* into the text.

[34] John Huss (*ca.* 1369-1415), Bohemian reformer, and Jerome of Prague (d. 1416), his friend and disciple, were martyred while the Council of Constance was in session.

[35] Francis Zabarella, archbishop of Florence, cardinal from 1411 to 1417. He died in Constance in 1417.

[36] Cajetan, who tried to make Luther recant at Augsburg in 1518. Cf. above, p. 56, n. 3.

[37] Cf. above, p. 130, n. 26.

really tormented him when he was dead [Gen. 4:10-14]. I hope that it also happens to me that I, like Samson, bring them more misfortune with my death than with my life [Judg. 16:30]. For Christ's death, too, did more than his life, as he says in John 12 [:24], "Unless a grain of corn falls into the earth and dies, it remains alone; but if it dies, it bears much fruit."

It does not vex me when he says that there is a prophecy about a monk who will pervert the world.[38] St. Paul and St. Peter are strong enough on my side, against all false prophets. They both proclaimed the perversion coming through the pope and his followers. Moreover, when I have clear Scripture on my side I do not care about any prophet, even if he comes from heaven, because St. Paul said, Galatians 1 [:8], that we should not even believe an angel from heaven if he teaches differently than the gospel. But it is clear that the pope and those who rule as tyrants with him have taught differently. Huss proved it; so did I and many others; and I shall prove it even better, so help me God.

You, Emser, have frivolously taken this matter upon yourself, although it is no concern of yours, and have meddled in it unnecessarily. I shall see how you get out of it, for you have ruffled my feathers again; you shall indeed stay through the end of the game, and your name shall be mentioned in many more books, no matter how you complain. But if you want to recant your error and quit your hypocrisy, you shall very soon render me peaceful and silent. If not, then do what you can. May God help his truth. Neither to me nor to you, but to God alone, be honor and praise. Amen.

---

[38] Cf. *Against the Un-Christian Book of the Augustinian Martin Luther, Addressed to the German Nobility*: "Many years ago it was prophesied that a German monk would fall into great error in our time. . . . It is to be feared that he [Luther] is not far from being this monk. Perhaps he really is the one of whom the prophecy speaks." Enders, *op. cit.*, I, 6.

ANSWER TO THE HYPERCHRISTIAN, HYPERSPIRITUAL, AND HYPER-LEARNED BOOK BY GOAT EMSER IN LEIPZIG—INCLUDING SOME THOUGHTS REGARDING HIS COMPANION, THE FOOL MURNER

1521

Translated by

Eric W. and Ruth C. Gritsch

INTRODUCTION

The controversy between Luther and Emser reached its climax with the publication of Emser's lengthy treatise, *Against the Un-Christian Book of the Augustinian Martin Luther, Addressed to the German Nobility.*[1] Emser's "Preface to the Common German Nation"—Luther entitled his treatise *To the Christian Nobility of the German Nation*[2]—announced his strategy for the bout with the "fencing master" from Wittenberg, as he put it:[3] he would use as his weapons the "sword," Holy Scripture, the word of God; the "long spear," ancient, authentic Christian tradition and ecclesiastical usage; and the "short dagger," the scriptural interpretation of the church fathers who assisted the church in its understanding of the word of God. The bout itself would consist of three rounds, corresponding to the three parts of Luther's treatise. The first round would deal with the divine right (*Recht*) of the pope and the clergy, which Luther attacked as the "three walls of the Romanists"; the second round would tackle the matter (*Handel*) of ecclesiastical abuse and corruption, which Luther listed as matters to be dealt with in a general council; and the third round would take up the question of change (*Wandel*), which Luther suggested in his proposals for a reform of the church. Using the form of a dialogue between himself and Luther, Emser quoted sentence after sentence from Luther's treatise and closed his refutation with the prayer that the triune God himself, with the Virgin Mary and the heavenly host, should lead the church from sinful schism to blessed unity.[4]

Luther was not too eager to reply. "Emser is vomiting his poison at length to please Duke George," he wrote to George Spalatin on February 17, 1521, after receiving Emser's complete treatise. "I am obliged to answer the man only on account of his most impure lies."[5] He was pleased to hear that friends of his cause had tied a

[1] On Luther's initial reaction, cf. above, pp. 109-110.

[2] Cf. *LW* 44, 115-217.

[3] Cf. Emser's preface in Enders, *Luther und Emser,* I, 5-16.

[4] Cf. *ibid.,* pp. 143-145.

[5] Cf. *WA,* Br 2, 266; Smith (ed.), *Luther's Correspondence,* I, 465.

copy of Emser's treatise to Magdeburg's public pillory, flanking it with two whips and adorning it with the inscription, "This is the place where the book belongs."

When friends urged him to reply to Emser, Luther went to work. On March 29, 1521, he sent the literary product to his friend John Lang in Erfurt, under the title *Answer to the Hyperchristian, Hyperspiritual, and Hyperlearned Book by Goat Emser in Leipzig –Including Some Thoughts Regarding His Companion, the Fool Murner.*

Although Luther clearly exhibits his contempt for Emser in the treatise, he also deals with the fundamental issues raised in the controversy: the primacy of the pope, the priestly estate, and the relationship between Scripture and tradition. With theological sagacity Luther gets to the heart of the fundamental difference between his definition of authority and that of Emser, who represents the traditional view. While Emser subjects the word of God to ecclesiastical authority, Luther regards the word of God as the judge of ecclesiastical tradition—a principle he elaborates in the section entitled "Concerning the Letter and the Spirit." By applying this principle to such questions as the primacy of the pope and the priestly estate, Luther arrives at new definitions of church and ministry.

In his appendix to the treatise, Luther quickly responded to the attacks of Thomas Murner, a Franciscan friar from Strassburg.[6] Murner had written three treatises against Luther during November and December, 1520:[7] the first attacked Luther's *Treatise on the New Testament, That Is, the Holy Mass;*[8] the second defended Alveld against Luther's *On the Papacy in Rome;*[9] the third joined Emser's attack on Luther's address *To the Christian Nobility of the German Nation.*[10] Luther, who had been informed of Murner's intentions by his friend Wolfgang Capito, a humanist in Mainz,[11] did not

[6] Cf. the biography by Waldemar Kawerau, *Thomas Murner und die deutsche Reformation* (Halle, 1891), and *RGG* 4, 1192-1193.

[7] The titles of the three German treatises are found in *WA* 7, 615-616.

[8] Cf. *LW* 35, 75-111.

[9] Cf. above, pp. 49-104.

[10] Cf. *LW* 44, 115-217.

[11] Cf. Capito's letter to Luther, written December 4, 1520, *WA*, Br 2, 233; Smith (ed.), *op. cit.*, I, 407.

bother with an extensive reply. He was extremely busy with lectures, preaching, and the preparations for his trip to the Diet of Worms.[12] Besides, friends had begun to defend Luther against Murner, whose satirical language gave rise to mocking poems such as the one sent to Luther from the Rhineland.[13] Thus Luther limited his reply to the two principal points Murner attacked: that the church is a spiritual, "Platonic" community and that the primacy of the pope cannot be derived from Matt. 16:18.

The following translation is based on the first German edition of Luther's treatise, entitled *Auff das ubirchristlich, ubirgeystlich und ubirkunstlich buch Bocks Emszers zu Leypczick Antwortt D.M.L. Darynn auch Murnarrs seynsz geselln gedacht wirt,* printed by John Grünenberg in Wittenberg and found in *WA* 7, 621-688. Occasionally significant passages from Emser's treatise are cited to provide the reader with some insights into the temper and significance of the controversy.

---

[12] For the story of Luther's appearance in Worms, cf. *Luther at the Diet of Worms. LW* 32, 101-131, and Schwiebert, *Luther and His Times,* pp. 493-512.

[13] Cf. below, p. 223.

ANSWER TO THE HYPERCHRISTIAN, HYPERSPIRITUAL, AND HYPER-LEARNED BOOK BY GOAT EMSER IN LEIPZIG—INCLUDING SOME THOUGHTS REGARDING HIS COMPANION, THE FOOL MURNER[1]

Dear Goat, Do Not Butt Me! [2]

Preface

Look here, goat Emser: Are you the man with the long spear and the short dagger? May God guard us against pitchfork stabs which make three holes! Goat Emser, you seem to me to be a strange warrior. St. Paul described four divine weapons in Ephesians 6 [:11-17]: a sword, a helmet, a breastplate, and a shield. But you need only one of them, the sword. And since St. Paul did not teach enough, you improve the armor with a long spear and a short dagger, and then you rush at me with uncovered head, uncovered chest, and uncovered stomach, as though I would do no more than kneel before you, let the naked knight stab me, and say, "Have mercy, Sir Goat, and let me live!" Moreover, you swear by your priesthood, as Hannibal did by his god,[3] that you will not cease to write against me. Goat Emser, if you had improved your oath as you did the armor, swearing by your horns and beard, as Socrates did by

[1] *Murnarr,* a pun on the name Murner.

[2] Luther's reply to the statement on the title page of Emser's tract against Luther, *Against the Un-Christian Book of the Augustinian Martin Luther,* "Beware, the goat will butt you!" Cf. Enders, *Luther und Emser,* I, 1.

[3] According to Roman tradition, Hannibal took an oath as a child "never to be afraid of the Romans." Polybius (*ca.* 200-130 B.C.), *Hist.,* III, 11. Cf. W. R. Paton (trans.), *Polybius: The Histories* ("The Loeb Classical Library" [6 vols.; Cambridge: Harvard University Press, 1922]), II, 29.

his dog,[4] it would have been a true philosophical oath almost frightening to me, since you recently found Aristotle in the asses' stable with Christ,[5] as you boast. I can see very well that the situation will get serious because the long spears and short daggers are coming, against which I have not guarded myself up to now because St. Paul did not mention them.

In such a serious situation I have to stick to the breastplate, helmet, and shield which Emser leaves behind—not because he despises them, as everyone knows, but because he does not need them, since he has above all a thick hide, a hard head, and an obstinate chest with which he can oppose not only me but also the Holy Spirit. But St. Paul defines the weapons in such a way that he calls the helmet "a helmet of salvation," the breastplate or cuirass "a breastplate of righteousness," and the shield "a shield of faith." Emser does not need any of them; he is content with the most holy father, the pope, just as a creature should really be content with its creator. That is why he also introduces the holy fleshly law more than the divine law, takes up the sword with the long spear and the short dagger and thus naked attacks an armed cuirassier, that is, the heretic Martin Luther. What do you think? I really think the goat is a man and a big hero. He may truly dare to do it.

Well, I put on my armor in the name of God. Paul calls the breastplate or cuirass of righteousness the righteous, guiltless life which does no one an injustice, or, as one says in German, "a good cause and a good conscience."[6] For St. Peter teaches [I Pet. 4:15-16] that a Christian should live so that he cannot be persecuted justly, suffering persecution only because of his innocence. Just as the cuirass or breastplate protects the chest and gives one courage against stabs, so someone who has a good cause, a good conscience, and is righteous, is fearless, relies on his armor, and is courageous when facing his enemies. St. Paul in II Corinthians 1 [:12] says,

---

[4] Socrates (470/69-399 B.C.) said during his trial, "I swear to you Athenians, by the dog I swear!" according to Plato in *Apology*, 21, C. Cf. Harold N. Fowler (trans.), *Plato: Apology* ("The Loeb Classical Library" [Cambridge: Harvard University Press, 1960]), p. 83.

[5] Cf. above, p. 130, n. 26.

[6] *Eyn gutte sache und gutte gewyssen.*

"Our reliance or boast is our good conscience, that we have behaved in the world with sincerity," etc. The goat does not find this armor necessary, for it is too heavy for him, and he likes to go without a breastplate, a good cause, or a good conscience. He is content with the long spears and short daggers of blasphemous words and lies.

But now the evil spirit is furious with godly, innocent people and is out to pierce their good causes with long spears and short daggers, that is, to rebuke them with great, poisonous, and cunning lies and false interpretations and to disgrace them in public, as goat Emser is doing to me. Nor is any cause so good that one could boast about it before God, before whom no one is guiltless (Exodus 34 [:7]). Thus one needs the shield of faith to retain one's trust in God. And even though everyone has been repulsed because of the poisonous tongues, if he keeps from becoming fainthearted and weary, and puts his trust not in human assistance or in his own right but in God alone, he will bring everything to a good end. That is why Paul says, "Above all taking the shield of faith, with which you can quench all the flaming darts of the evil one" [Eph. 6:16] (he could almost have referred to Emser's short dagger). He does not say "flaming darts of the evil one" and "quench" in vain, for the lies and false declarations of the evil ones are so maliciously hot and poisonous that, if they could, they would set the whole world on fire. And their hearts nearly burn up because of their great hatred, so that one says of them in German, "Oh, how bitterly evil his intention is!"[7] That is why the righteous one must put his cause in God's hands and trust him, and in this way quench the fiery darts with the shield of faith. Paul often tried this, and he experienced it from the Jews. I have experienced it from none of my enemies except Eck and Emser, who are both well armed—not with bad darts, but rather with poisonous, fiery ones. But so far they have not been able to do me any harm. If there were no faith these fiery darts would truly burn up one's heart, which has happened to many people. Nor does Emser need such a shield, for he knows that I have never attacked anyone with lies. But I need it, for in all my life I have neither read nor heard more fiery and malicious lies than those of goat Emser, as we shall see.

[7] *Ey wie bitter boss meynet erss.*

Furthermore, one needs the helmet of the Savior—the Savior or salvation is Jesus Christ. He becomes a helmet if we console ourselves with and act according to his example and keep him before our eyes. St. Paul says, Hebrews 12 [:3], "Consider him who endured from sinners such hostility against himself, so that you may not grow weary in your faith." He made himself into a helmet when he said, "Remember the word that I said to you, 'A servant shall not be greater than his master.' If they persecuted me, they will persecute you" [John 15:20]. Just as the helmet gives the heart security and peace, so does a Christian feel secure and peaceful when he thinks of his Lord Christ and of how the same things happened to him. He lets things take their course and joyfully says, "Well, whoever wants to have a better life than his dear Father and Lord must be a rogue." Goat Emser does not need this helmet either, but he draws a picture of it at the end of his book, placing it at his feet and diligently begging people who do not know him to take him seriously. But his head remains uncovered so that the princes of the air [Eph. 2:2] might have free access to it.

He takes the sword, the word of God, and claims to strike not with the sheath, that is, with the letter, but with the blade,[8] that is, with spiritual understanding. Since he is a regular young Aristotle, he can probably do better "spiritually" than he can in German and Latin! But I certainly would take this same sword from him with my armor if I knew where he left it. I see nothing in his whole book but the long spears and short daggers of a bareheaded, naked, and open liar and blasphemer. It must have been a clever witch who told him this dream that the sheath is called "letter" and the blade "Spirit." But I think that his holy priesthood found this and everything else in the asses' stable with Aristotle.

Well then, since this ass's skin is itching and he feels too well,[9] let us go to the heart of the matter. He has shown three great bits of wisdom in his delicate, noble little book.

---

[8] *Scheyden-schneyden* are the words Emser used in his tract *Against the Un-Christian Book of the Augustinian Martin Luther.* "Therefore, when Luther wants to fight with the sheath *(scheyden)* in order to prove his cause only with the letter or literal meaning, one must strike him with the sword, the blade *(schneyden),* that is, one must use the true understanding of Scripture as the Christian teachers have developed it." Cf. Enders, *op. cit.*, I, 10.

[9] *Jucket dich die hawt* and *Es ist yhm zu wol.* Cf. Thiele, *Luthers Sprichwörtersammlung,* Nos. 187, 324.

First, that he does not attack any of my books in which I deal with Scripture and teaching, but rather the one in which I offer, with very little Scripture, merely my loyal advice to the German nobility. As they are intelligent enough, they did not need my teaching but only my good opinion and admonition.[10] "Here I want" (said the goat) "to grab the monk in his bath and win some honor, for I am afraid to attack any of his other books."[11]

The second is that since he did not yet trust his advantage, he thought he would write a thick book including many quotations which would be difficult to answer. He thought, "If I write a small one, then Emser might be found out quickly, just as has happened to me before," for it is difficult to hide a great deal of foolishness under a little paper. "But if I write much and quote much, everyone will have to say, 'Oh, how learned is the goat in Leipzig! I think he really gave it to the monk and fought a little bout with this famous fencer.'" Once upon a time there was an ape who saw a shoemaker cut leather. When the shoemaker left the workshop, the ape ran in and, as is his manner, cut some leather too, and ruined all of it. Likewise, when my goat saw that I quote Scripture and teachers in some books, he thought, "I can do that too," thinking it would be enough to pile up whatever he found, just as people of his kind have hacked and martyred many writings.

The third is that since this was not sure enough either, he first of all diligently uses the spiritual understanding of the true Emser and cuts out my words whenever he pleases, smears them with his own poison, and leaves whatever precedes and follows, so that my meaning and his poison should not be noticed. He does all this out of hyperchristian love and an elevated spirit. In addition, he calls upon the precious blood of Christ, praying for me and saying that he wishes to save me from the error Emser imposes upon me and which I absurdly teach. He wants everyone to say, "O God forbid! Does Luther teach such poison? O blessed be the goat in Leipzig who shows us what kind of bird he is!" These are the fiery darts and daggers of the evil one, as St. Paul calls them, with which

[10] Cf. *To the Christian Nobility of the German Nation*, 1520. *LW* 44, 115-217.

[11] An allusion to the German proverb, *Er beisst des fuchses nicht*, literally, "he does not bite the fox." It means to lack courage. Cf. Thiele, *Luthers Sprichwörtersammlung*, No. 218.

he would like to inflame the world against me. But this will not help him, for God has built up too great a courage in me against it and has given me a fine shield, which I shall now try out in the following way.

Where I said[12] that much misery resulted from forbidding priests to marry, he interprets my words as though I had taught that God punishes the world for the sake of chastity. Here he proves his hyperchristian wisdom, quoting much Scripture to show that God punishes unchastity, as though no one had read this. Thus he wants to claim that I teach unchastity and curse chastity. His raging hatred is so blind that he cannot imagine that no one will believe him. Nor does he see or hear that my books are publicly available, from which even a child could make him out a liar and a scoundrel.

Again, he interprets the fact that I recommend founding fewer rather than more religious foundations[13] as though Luther had taught that one should not keep monastic vows, that one should throw off cowls and run away from the monasteries. If these are not fiery and malicious darts, then I do not know what fire, malice, and darts are! Again, where I have taught Christian freedom[14] and advised how to be courageous, he interprets it to mean that I have taught haughtiness and pride. He manifests his skill by showing that Holy Scripture teaches only humility so that, if Emser had not appeared, no one would have known that Scripture teaches humility. Thus, according to the hyperchristian and hyperspiritual interpretation of goat Emser. Luther teaches sheer unchastity, haughtiness, disobedience, and similar vices. This is also the place to mention that he charges me with saying that I did not begin the matter in God's name, and the devil may care if the common people are annoyed by my teaching.[15]

The whole book is full of such items and spiritual interpretations; therefore, I cannot help thinking that what I have feared so long has actually happened to him: his unbearable hatred has made him so raving and mad that he has neither wit nor sense left. He cannot believe that there are still people on earth. It has certainly

[12] Cf. *To the Christian Nobility of the German Nation. LW* 44, 176.

[13] Cf. *LW* 44, 172-173.

[14] Cf. *The Freedom of a Christian,* 1520. *LW* 31, 327-377.

[15] Cf. above, p. 119.

happened before that a frantic hatred has made a man wild and raving, as the poets have sung about Hecuba.[16] But if he is not insane, then I should not call him a lying knave who lies intentionally and out of sheer malice, which he knows has been recognized by everyone else. Thus he scolds himself in public before everyone in this book. All of my own books are available, and I appeal to them.

This is the same way that John Huss and Jerome of Prague were burned at Constance.[17] No one there could honestly contradict them, so false opinions were ascribed to them, as can be seen clearly from the writings and books of both of them. Likewise Christ, when he says, "Render to Caesar the things that are Caesar's" [Matt. 22:21], should really have said that one should not pay Caesar any interest. And St. Stephen, Acts 8 [7:48; Isa. 66:2], when he preaches that the temple of Jerusalem is not the true house of God but that Christ makes a true house of God through faith, says, "God does not live in houses made by men, as he says through the prophet Isaiah, 'Heaven is my throne, and the earth is my footstool; what is the house which you would build for me? My spirit will rest on a quiet, humble heart.' " Since they could not in any way contradict this clear passage, they hired false witnesses who said he had blasphemed against God and the holy temple and that he should therefore die [Acts 6:13].

My goat does the same thing, filled with the same Jewish spirit, because he could not deny that much misery has come out of forbidding marriage in the spiritual estate, as I have said,[18] so that even children in the street sing and speak of it. I included the clear statement of St. Paul, I Timothy 4 [:1-3], with which I proved that with such a law the pope has been the apostle of the devil. This must silence everyone, not just Emser; they are completely unable to respond to it—yet he steps out of line, strikes me with the blade of his spiritual understanding, charges me with teaching that God

[16] The mother of Hector and other Greek mythological heroes. Euripides' play *Hecuba* (424 B.C.) shows how her desire to avenge the deaths of her two children fills her with such hatred and animal ferocity that she is supposedly transformed into a bitch. She also appears in Homer's *Iliad.*

[17] Cf. above, p. 134, n. 34.

[18] Cf. above, p. 148, n. 12.

punishes the world for the sake of chastity, and commands me and my Greeks,[19] who have refused to accept the pope's devilish commandments, to stay at home. This is supposed to serve as an answer to me. Is not the world strange? If I were ever discovered to be such a liar, cheater, and crude fool, all my teaching and honor, my faith and trust, would be finished; everyone would consider me a knave and a dishonorable villain (and rightly so). Even though my enemies uninterruptedly and ceaselessly lie about me in a crude and cruel way and publicly disgrace themselves, they have the luck that no one turns away from them, and everyone is still waiting to see whether they catch me sometime. One can certainly tell by their wilful lying that their attack on me is not of God. Thus, even if I were filled with devils, their cause would not be valid because they intend to exorcise the devil not with the finger of God but with the devil [Luke 11:18-20]. Everything is forgiven them, no matter how much they lie and fool; but if I should waver by a hairsbreadth, everything I ever said must be heresy. And when they cannot do this, they nevertheless cling to me and urge themselves on with my sharp and biting writings; they cannot forget the speck in my eye, but no one wants to perceive the log in his own eye.

Therefore I truly need God's help. I, a single man (who certainly cannot live without weakness) should close a round circle without a single crack and should not stumble at all, although I have been driven into the game against my will. But they, the big mob who push themselves into it, have a better chance of prevailing, even though their case is full of flaws and holes and consists of loose pieces. Nevertheless, it has to be as the Song of Solomon 2 [:2] says, "As a rose among thorns so is my love among maidens"; and Psalm 110 [:2], "You are to rule in the midst of your foes." I stand alone in the midst of them; they are a ring around me, many against one, so that it may be seen how easily the strong and invincible truth increases its honor from the lie, and how much effort and labor it takes for the weak lies to acquire their disgrace from the truth. Thus my goat would certainly have acquired enough disgrace with joy and pleasure from other things, but he had to get it with great raging and raving from the truth.

[19] A reference to the Greek church, which broke with Rome in 1054 and does not accept the authority of the pope.

This should be answer enough to the goat, since it is clear from his un-Christian lying and perjury with what kind of attitude and spirit he has written—for one should not fight the recognized devil; rather, one should cross oneself and flee. However, there comes a time to expose and bring to light the evil spirit who does not stop lying and blaspheming God's truth through goat Emser's snout, so that his dishonor is brought home to him. And Emser and his kind should be informed about the meaning of Isaiah's saying, "You are pregnant with a fire and bring forth nothing but stubble" [Isa. 33:11]. The poets write that the big mountains, too, were once supposed to give birth to a child; everyone expected a child as large as a mountain, and when it turned out to be a mouse, everyone laughed. That is the origin of the proverb, "The mountains are pregnant, but will produce a mouse."[20]

My goat Emser, too, has made horrible threats to butt and has sharpened long spears, short daggers, and swords. The great bloody war was waged on the poor paper, which thus increased the supply for the privy and the dispensary. Even such an honor is too great for the un-Christian lies, blasphemies, and perjuries which were made against God's holy word.

Since I had proven so clearly, with strong and well-founded Scripture, that all Christians are spiritual and are priests,[21] so that not even Emser dared to invent a lie (which really surprises me) to slander it and was unwillingly forced to let it stand, nevertheless he demonstrated his mastery by dividing the interpretation of Scripture into two parts, saying that I strike with the sheath but he would strike with the blade. Well, let us watch, for he will display an unusual masterpiece. He claims for himself St. Paul's saying in II Corinthians 3 [:6], "The letter kills, but the Spirit gives life." He then teaches us that he who understands Scripture according to the letter and not according to the Spirit should rather read Virgil[22] or

[20] The saying originates in Phaedrus (*ca.* 40 B.C.), a Roman writer of fables. Cf. Ben E. Perry (ed.), *Babrius and Phaedrus* ("The Loeb Classical Library" [Cambridge: Harvard University Press, 1965]), p. 339 (IV, 24).

[21] *To the Christian Nobility of the German Nation,* 1520. *LW* 44, 127-128.

[22] Virgil (70-19 B.C.), a famous Roman poet.

some other heathen fable, for he reads his death. This is what Luther does, who obeys the letter, strikes about with the sheath, and does not teach the Spirit.

Let us rather note carefully that this is the chief article of the Emserian theologians, and on this field it will be "win or lose." It follows from this, and God's holy priest must conclude from it, first of all, that St. Peter taught the letter and death, since he says, I Peter 2 [:9], "You are a royal priesthood and a priestly kingdom." With this saying I proved that all Christians are priests, for Peter said it to all Christians, as the words clearly state and mention the people by name. So if I teach the letter and death and fight with the sheath by quoting these words of St. Peter, this insult does not apply to me but to St. Peter. Therefore, I desire from this highly spiritual priest of God that he kindly point out to me, in these words of St. Peter, which is the letter and which is the Spirit—unless he wanted to say that they contain neither letter nor Spirit, which he certainly does not do.

He says, "He who interprets the words of St. Peter to mean that all Christians should be priests to the extent that they are consecrated by bishops strikes with the sheath, takes the letter, and follows a deadly reasoning. For St. Peter speaks of the inward spiritual priesthood which all Christians possess, and not of the consecrated priesthood." Here I answer: It is true that St. Peter speaks of the spiritual priesthood. Indeed, I go further and say that he does not utter even a syllable about the consecrated priesthood. That is why his words cannot be either a sheath or a deadly letter, as Emser imagines. Instead, whoever applies St. Peter's words to consecrated priests retains neither sheath nor letter. He is wrong and everything he does is worthless. St. Peter's words have only one simple meaning which encompasses both letter and Spirit. But Emser does not know what "letter" means. That is why he makes "sheath" and whatever he pleases out of God's word. In addition, he allows himself to imagine that there are two kinds of priesthood, a spiritual one and a churchly[23] one which he calls "ecclesiastical" (*ecclesiasticum*). Thus he thinks that the words of Peter could fit both and that all that

[23] *Kirchisch.* Luther coined his own word to distinguish his definition of "ecclesiastical" from that of Emser.

matters is to give them their proper sense—and he accuses me of not giving them their proper sense.

All this is sheer error and blindness, and Emser should have stayed home with such hopeless attempts.[24] For I have never said that St. Peter's words refer to his invented priesthood, which he calls *ecclesiasticum* and which I shall call "churchly" from now on. Furthermore, I did not say that all Christians are churchly priests. Therefore, if this holy priest of God had put his glasses on his nose and taken a better look at my booklet, he would not have needed to ascribe such lies to me. Even if the silly dream remained, according to which St. Peter's word meant two kinds of priesthood, one with the letter and sheath and the other with the Spirit and blade, the whole churchly priesthood would still be a deadly and harmful thing. For, as Emser himself says, it implies on the basis of the dead letter that St. Peter is only talking about the spiritual, living priesthood. For whatever is not Spirit does not live and is dead. Again, since he gives me the dead letter and yet calls my priests the living ones of whom Peter speaks, he calls the living ones dead and his dead ones living. Thus he fools himself, does not know what he babbles, declares his own priesthood dead, and disgraces it more than anyone ever did. This is what happens to those blind leaders of the blind who want to deal with divine Scripture and to wield the sword of the Spirit, which is too heavy for them. Clearly, as they say, the sword is bigger than he is.[25]

Therefore, to avoid the foolish dream of Emser, one should know that Holy Scripture, especially the New Testament, which no longer contains figures,[26] writes of no more than one spiritual priesthood, just as I wrote when discussing the papacy that it [the New Testament] writes of no more than one spiritual church.[27] The priesthood of which Emser dreams and the church of which the

[24] Proverbial German, *Bleib daheymen mit deinen blinden griffen.* Luther generally preferred the version, *Bleib daheymen mit deinen faulen fisschen,* meaning literally, "stay home with your foul fish." Cf. Thiele, *Luthers Sprichwörtersammlung,* No. 104.

[25] The German proverb, *Wer hatt hie den man anss schwerd bundenn,* says literally, "Who has tied the man to the sword?" It refers to a person who undertakes a task that goes far beyond his capabilities. Cf. Thiele, *Luthers Sprichwörtersammlung,* No. 192.

[26] *Figur.* Cf. above, p. 68, n. 30; p. 77, n. 42.

[27] Cf. above, p. 65.

papists write agree with Scripture as life agrees with death. And here I offer this challenge: If Emser brings me one letter from Scripture which calls his churchly priesthood priesthood, he will have won. But [if not] he must grant me victory!

Scripture makes all of us equal priests, as has been said, but the churchly priesthood which we now separate from laymen in the whole world, and which alone we call priesthood, is called "ministry" [*ministerium*], "servitude" [*servitus*], "dispensation" [*dispensatio*], "episcopate" [*episcopatus*], and "presbytery" [*presbyterium*] in Scripture. Nowhere is it called "priesthood" [*sacerdocium*] or "spiritual" [*spiritualis*]. I have to say this in German: Scripture, I say, calls the spiritual and priestly estate a service, caretaking, an office, an elder, an attendant, a guardian, a preaching office, and a shepherd. We intend to prove this thoroughly. St. Paul says to St. Timothy, "A servant of God must not be quarrelsome" [II Tim. 2:24]. Here he calls Timothy a servant of God in the special sense of preaching and spiritually leading the people. Again, in II Corinthians 12 [11:23], "If they are servants of Christ so am I." And in I Corinthians 4 [:1], "Dear brethren, we do not want people to regard us as more than servants of Christ and stewards of his spiritual goods." And Christ, in Matthew 24 [:45-51], talks much about the same stewards.

Now, the little word "priest" stems from the Greek language in which *presbyteros* means *senior* in Latin and "the elder" [*eldist*] in German. That is why in former times the spiritual rule was always held by the elders, just as the councilors of a city, *senatus* in Latin, derive their name from their age. Young people have never been very good rulers. Thus priest indicates age, not status; nor does it make one a cleric or a spiritual man. St. Peter says, in I Peter 5 [:1-2], "I, the elder, exhort you, my fellow elders, to tend the flock of Christ that is in your charge." Again, "You young people are to be subject to the elders" [I Pet. 5:5]. Here one has to say in German "priests or ministers" [*priester odder geystlichen*] because of the wrong use of the words.

"Bishop" too stems from the Greek language. For he whom they call *episcopus* is called *speculator* in Latin and "a guardian or watchman on the tower" [*warttman odder wechter auff der Wart*] in German. This is exactly what one calls someone who lives in a tower to watch and to look out over the town so that fire or foe do not harm it. Therefore, every minister or spiritual regent should be a bishop, that is, an overseer or watchman, so that in his town and among his people the gospel and faith in Christ are built up and win out over foe, devil, and heresy. Thus St. Luke, in Acts 20 [:17-18, 28] says, "Paul called to him the priests of the church," that is, the elders of the Christians in Ephesus, "and said to them, 'See to yourselves and to all the flock of Christ, over which the Holy Spirit has set you as bishops, to feed the church of God, which he has acquired with his own blood.' " Here it is clear that the elders are called bishops, that is, overseers of God's church—of the Christians who are God's people.

Thus Emser too certainly knows from St. Jerome[28] that priest and bishop are one and the same thing in Scripture. For St. Paul says in Titus 1 [:5], "You should appoint a priest in every town" (that is, an elder over them); and soon afterward he says about the same priest, "But this same bishop must be a blameless man" [Titus 1:7]. He clearly calls the same man priest, bishop, elder, and watchman. But no one should be surprised that bishop, pastor, priest, chaplain, cathedral dean, monk, and many similar names have different meanings now, since no word of Scripture has retained its true meaning. That is why God and his Scripture do not know the present bishops. The spiritual estate has been established and ordered by men's laws and regulations in such a way, and has become so deeply entrenched in the course of time, that one thinks it is founded on Scripture, even though it is more than twice as worldly as the world itself while calling itself and pretending to be spiritual. Yet there is nothing behind it.

That is why I have called this same priesthood churchly, since it stems from the order of the church and is not founded on Scripture. For in previous times this matter was handled as follows, and this is the way it should still be done: since in every Christian town they were all equally spiritual priests, one of them—the oldest or rather the most learned and most godly—was elected to be their servant, official, caretaker, and guardian in regard to the gospel and the sacraments, just as a mayor in a city is elected from among the common mass of all citizens. If tonsure, consecrations, anoint-

[28] Cf. *Commentary on Titus (Commentariorum in Epistolam ad Titum)*, Titus 1:7. *MPL* 26, 600-602.

ments, and vestments make priests and bishops, then Christ and the apostles would never have been either priests or bishops.

Now come on, Emser. If you prove with a single passage or even one letter that our priests are called *sacerdotes, ecclesiastici,* or *religiosi spirituales,* I shall gladly approve of and praise your jugglery with the sheath and blade of two kinds of priesthood. Indeed, you are obliged, before you become a defender, to show what you want to defend and where it originates—although this time your great spiritual brain has become shamefully forgetful, and you are defending something not knowing what, how, or where. You are a "licentiate of canon law" and a "prohibiter of Holy Scripture";[29] you have a "license" to babble whatever you please but you have a "prohibition" against proving anything.

But you know very well that when you drag in by the hair some passages of the fathers to apply to your dreams, it does not move me at all. Even if they agreed with you, it is not enough. I want to have Holy Scripture because I fight against you with Scripture. Moreover, the fathers do not count with me at all unless you have first proven that they have never erred. That you will do when the ass gets horns and the goat turns into a sheep! And when you have done that, I shall still say that no holy father has the power to command and to make an article of faith or a sacrament that Scripture did not command or make. I shall disregard your long straw spear of usage and your short wax dagger. Christ did not say, "I am Emser's long spear and short dagger." Nor did he say, "I am usage and custom," nor "I am Ambrose, Aristotle, this or that teacher." Instead, he said, "I am the truth" [John 14:6]. Since Emser dares to wage the whole quarrel with three main items, spear, dagger, and sword, I shall attend to these three, and first of all to the spear.

Concerning Emser's Long Spear

Your long spear is Goliath's spear [I Sam. 17:45], and your short dagger is Joab's dagger [II Sam. 20:8]. If usage were sufficient, the heathen would have the very best excuse, since for more than four thousand years they have been used to worshiping idols.

[29] See above, p. 112, n. 2.

You should first prove that usage is right and comes from God; you think it is enough to appeal to usage. So that I may lay before you something from philosophy, O new philosopher, [let me suggest] that you should not prove the antecedent (*prius*) through the consequent (*posterius*) and beg the question (*principium petere*).[30] I attacked the priestly estate which was a cause and instigator of this usage, not vice versa. And you answer me with usage. This is just as though I said, "The coat should make the tailor and the shoe should make the shoemaker." You see, you have such a fine clever philosophy that Sir Thomas Rhadinus,[31] Emser's sister's only brother, could have said it, for he, too, philosophizes in this manner.

Who doubts that from the beginning until now the churchly priesthood has had different vestments, manners, and works than other common Christians, and that thereby a public usage has come down to us and is maintained? Should this same constant usage therefore be sufficient to create two kinds of priesthood in Christendom? Why does not the variety of priesthood create a variety of practices and usages in cathedrals and monasteries, since none is in concord with the other, and yet constant usage is maintained in all of them? Therefore learn, dear goat, that no usage can change or reinterpret anything in Scripture or in articles of faith. Instead, usage applies only to external, changeable works and manners, in which neither the Christian nor the priestly estate, but only offices, services, and similar works are indicated and realized. Thus consecration does not make a cleric, but it does make servants out of clerics; tonsure, chasuble, mass, and sermon are not the signs of a priest but rather of a servant and official of the common priesthood.

All of us in the whole mass of people are priests without the consecration of the bishop. But through consecration we become the stewards, sevants, and administrators of the other priests who may be deposed and changed, just as a priest in cathedral churches is provost, dean, cantor, custodian, and holder of similar offices for the others. Canon law almost does no more than to make such officials priests and spiritual (for which it is called "spiritual law");

[30] Luther ridiculed Emser's bad logic: Emser proved the priestly estate *(prius)* through its long historical tradition *(posterius)* or usage, thus begging the question of its cause, or foundation *(principium).*

[31] See above, p. 126.

this elevates and emphasizes such a matter too much and masks the words of Holy Scripture. The fact that no one is any longer called a priest and spiritual except such servants of priests does not argue against me. Indeed, this is precisely why it [cannon law] should be burned and destroyed.[32] Human traditions [*traditiones hominum*] and human laws have at all times damaged and obscured divine laws, as Christ teaches in Matthew 15 [:3-9] and as Paul teaches everywhere. That is why you, goat, should have saved your lead dagger until you could cut butter or soft cheese.

It is true that the holy fathers called the churchly priestly estate priesthood. What else should they have called it? It was already the custom to separate the laymen and rulers of the masses, so that each had to be called by his own name. Thus, if I were to preach today about the rulers of the church, who would understand me if I did not call them, in the usual way, priests, clerics, spiritual? The practice of calling our rulers *sacerdotes* started very early, on the basis of Hebrews 5, for it is written there, "Every high priest [*sacerdos*] chosen from among men," etc. This refers to the Old Testament, but is also applied to the New Testament because of the same expression. But if the dear fathers would have had to write about this they certainly would have done it differently and according to Scripture; they would not have defended it with desecrations.

But, just so that you can try your own spear and dagger to see whether they stab you or me harder, give me an answer to this: You all say with one voice that the priest celebrates mass and blesses the bread, not in his own person but in that of the whole church. This is where truth, your conscience, necessity, and the common statement and faith of the whole world drive you, so that Christendom might maintain itself and be worthy even if the priest is not pious, faithful, and worthy (since no saint is worthy enough). But then who is the true priest? He who does it as a servant, or the one in whose name he does it? Who is the cleric? He who does the work and sends it, or the servant who carries it and brings it? The

[32] Luther had burned the canon law in December, 1520. Cf. *Why the Books of the Pope and His Disciples Were Burned*, 1520. *LW* 31, 379-395. Emser attacked Luther for it in his tract *Against the Un-Christian Book of the Augustinian Martin Luther*. Enders, *op. cit.*, I, 3.

priest is a messenger and servant in this work, so someone else must be the true priest. I really think it has been proven clearly enough that we are all priests. And these priests are not a different kind of priest; they are servants and officials (as was said above)[33] of the common priesthood. So there are not two kinds of priesthood in Christendom, as you have dreamed. See, this is what happens to drunken fighters who hold the sword by the blade and the spear by the point and let out ridiculous grunts.

As I have written several times by now,[34] it was through the pope's damned law and rule that the precious, customary terms "church," "priest," "spiritual," and the like were taken away from the community and applied only to the smallest group, which we now call the spiritual and priestly estate and whose affairs we call the affairs of the church. Yet all of us are in a common church; we are all spiritual and priests, to the extent that we believe in Christ. They are only stewards, servants, officials, caretakers, shepherds, guardians, and watchmen. Therefore, I think that goat Emser's dream of two kinds of priesthood lies in sand and mire.

I am surprised that you, wise man and victorious knight, are not ashamed to fight against me with the argument of usage in matters concerning Christian faith and the word of God. You juggle with long spears and daggers even though usage is, also in worldly dealings, the weakest and usually the most ridiculed argument. Everyone expects you to attack me with Scripture, so you let Scripture go and fall upon usage. But I certainly sense that the cider of the holy burned law, of which you are an unworthy licentiate and in which much is decreed regarding usage, was unable to stop fermenting and kicked the bottom out of the barrel,[35] so that you, together with Elihu [Job 32:2-22], who also mocked the saintly Job, suffocate from your great [rhetorical] skill. What can you teach us—that this priesthood has maintained itself until now through usage? What peasant or child does not see and grasp this? Take a spoon and taste what you are saying! If the priesthood developed and has remained through usage, then one can, through

[33] Cf. above, p. 157.

[34] Cf. especially *On the Papacy in Rome*, above, pp. 49-104.

[35] A German proverb, *dem fass den poden auss gestossen*. Cf. Thiele, *Luthers Sprichwörtersammlung*, No. 335.

human power and will, replace it with another custom and abolish it. This can happen to all customs. Thus it surely follows that it is not of divine order, for divine order does not depend upon any wavering custom and cannot be changed by men. It is also true, and I have said it before and still say it, that such an external priesthood has no foundation in Scripture, but rather has been called this and has been maintained through long usage. See how nicely your spear stabs me! You intend to write against me and end up writing for me and against yourself. This is what your haughty art of warfare does: you carry the spear by the point [and hold it] against yourself, attack with the shaft toward me, and run yourself through.

But tell me, Emser, do you yourself consider it a Christian custom to call yourselves something different from what Scripture calls you? Are you ashamed of your names? Or is the Holy Spirit not good enough to name you? Are you not satisfied with his naming you? You despise his names and invent your own names so that whoever reads Scripture cannot recognize you and has to ask, "Where do these strange people come from?" St. Paul calls the minister of each town a bishop [Titus 1:5, 7], that is, a guard, priest, elder, servant, steward, and not a *sacerdos.* But you call bishops, who are now no more than worldly princes, *sacerdotes,* who celebrate mass and pray the hourly prayers. You twist and turn God's word as you please. And just as you have discarded the works, so are you also ashamed of the names; and to cover it up you attach to yourselves the glorious and worthy titles *sacerdos* and *ecclesiasticus* and the like.

Not satisfied that God and we permit such evil and perverted usage and wink at your faults,[36] you claim to force us to consent to it and sanction it as though it were right and the work of the Holy Spirit himself. In fact, it is your own arbitrariness and your despising of the Holy Spirit. You want to make a long spear and a short dagger out of it. This is supposed to be right for no other reason than that you have invented it, and the Holy Spirit must be wrong, must give in to you, and must have been your fool. At the

[36] Proverbial German, *durch die finger sehen,* literally, "to look through one's fingers." It means to overlook deliberately or to pretend not to see. Cf. Thiele, *Luthers Sprichwörtersammlung,* No. 331.

top of your voice you scream and lie that I blasphemously attack and disgrace the head of the church the pope and the priesthood, which I certainly have never done. For I have taught that we should suffer and honor even the power of the Turks (whom you want to devour) and all other unjust powers. But I am to call you gracious squires, admire you, and submissively thank you when you and your pope blaspheme Christ, God, and his Holy Spirit, pervert all their words and works, and play around with them just like jugglers with their heaven.[37] I must be acting out of hate because I refuse to preach your new and invented way as being based on Scripture, and it is not enough for me to leave it alone and to let it have its own dignity outside Scripture. But you act out of love when you usurp God's Scripture as your own property and add or subtract from it whatever you please. God must obey you and must let himself be mockingly made into an idol[38]—and I thought you should obey God and should let yourselves be made his children! Not only are we supposed to allow you to degrade our Lord, but we, together with you and the Jews, should say to him, "Hail, rabbi of the Jews" [Matt. 27:29] and hold this terrible mockery to be the highest honor to God. Woe to you, Antichrist, and to all your apostles and clerics!

Thus you yourself must confess with me that this priesthood did not come out of Scripture. For whatever exists on the basis of usage is already known without Scripture and is without God's order. Likewise, if it is confirmed by the teachings of the fathers and men, it is known to be not from Scripture because usage and human teaching are something different from Scripture. This is the answer to the long spear and to the argument of usage which, if it were Christian usage, should really have some basis in Scripture and should have just a tinge of the Spirit's sword. But since it is pure usage, what else is it but a carnival play? However, I do not want to ridicule you yet, as I am tempted to, because perhaps you could not find the sword for Shrove Tuesday, and so I shall excuse you until we get to it in the third part.[39] Meanwhile I am giving you as

---

[37] The canopy erected over the juggler's booth at a fair was called "heaven." Cf. *LW* 32, 30-31, and *WA* 7, 349, n. 1.

[38] *Putzen.* Luther frequently used the word as a synonym for *goetz,* meaning "idol" or "dummy." Cf. *WA* 9, 513, n. 1; 670, n. 1.

[39] Cf. below, pp. 203-206.

much time and space as you wish, and not only to you alone but to your whole papal sect, you who call yourselves the only church of God. You had better use diligence and—may St. Aristotle and the holy cremated law assist you—search for the sword, then take it up and vigorously swing it at the heretic Luther and really strike him with the blade. But be careful not to strike your own cheek! I am afraid you will not find it and will meanwhile swing with sacks of straw. It will probably have to do for this Shrove Tuesday. I ask everyone for God's sake to excuse my abuse. Who can handle with constant, courageous seriousness these childish, foolish, and blind heads who dare everything and accomplish nothing? They are those of whom Christ says in Matthew 11 [:17], "If we sing to them, they do not dance; if we wail to them, they do not cry." No matter how one treats them, neither seriousness nor abuse will help. This crude goat's head pretends to fight with the sword and the moment he has mentioned it he says, "Now we shall put down the sword and take up the spear." He has never picked it up in the past, nor will he pick it up again in the future. Who can tolerate such crude tomfoolery in such serious matters, since they really intend to lead people around by the nose[40] and deceive them?[41] I mock with justification (I hope) those who mock my God and his word and work, just as Elijah mocked the prophets of Baal [I Kings 18:27].

To come to an end: No one doubts that the sword of the Spirit, God's word, is valid in every quarrel. But Emser should first prove that usage—even if it is good usage—and human teaching are valid. But he lets the sword lie, which is valid there, and introduces usage and human teaching, which are not valid. Where then is this high and mighty philosopher, Sir Thomas Rhadinus, who found Aristotle in the asses' stable? Did not Aristotle teach that it is not right "to prove the proposition which is to be proven by the same proposition and to beg the question" (*probanda per probanda probare unnd petere principia*)? These are the wizards who lure our dear young people into philosophy and themselves know as much about it as they do about theology. They take money from them only to let

[40] *Bey der nassen zufuren,* that is, to fool someone and lead him around like a bear in a circus. Murner used the phrase in one of his adjurations for fools. Cf. Spanier (ed.), *Thomas Murner, Narrenbeschwörung* (Halle, 1894), p. 54.

[41] *Das maul schmieren,* that is, to deceive someone with smooth words. Cf. Thiele, *Luthers Sprichwörtersammlung,* No. 255.

them go away knowing less than when they came. It would certainly be a virtue for you crude asses to know your own philosophy, which you praise so highly. To me this is a ridiculous guild, where no one really knows his own craft. Thus the dagger too cuts into your fingers.

Concerning the Lead Dagger of Goat Emser

In order not only to blunt and refute his spear and dagger, but also to destroy them completely, I shall show that he was like a dreaming man who in his sleep finds a spear and dagger and fights vehemently. When he wakes up, it was a dream. I have found out that all who write and intrigue against me have in them a stupid heart and a cowardly conscience. They fear Scripture since they well know that it is unknown to them. That is why they make such a great effort, why they writhe and twist, to avoid the necessity of attacking me with Scripture and of themselves getting beaten with Scripture. So they invent a new lie, discover daggers, spears, and similar tomfoolery, and say that Scripture is so obscure that we cannot understand it without the interpretation of the holy fathers and that therefore we have to follow not the text but the glosses of the fathers. This is what Emser calls striking not with the sheath but with the blade. When they finally do bring up a passage of the fathers against me, they ring all the bells, beat all the drums, and vehemently scream that they have won; they stuff their ears and cover their eyes and thus believe they have clogged and muffled all of Scripture for me.

When I detect such cowardice and flight from light, how can I be afraid of such blind moles who fear the light? By their cowardice they force me to think that they know nothing in Scripture. That is why they are like the old frog to whom the young frog lamented how a big animal, an ox, had come and trampled all the other little frogs to death. The old frog was furious, blew itself up, and said, "Well then! Am I not as big?" "No, dear mother," said the little frog, "not even if you burst."[42] This is how my goats, too, blow themselves up with their own breath, wind, and spirit, and if I come with the foot of the ox, of which Scripture speaks, I shall step on them so that they squeak.

[42] One of Aesop's fables. Cf. above, p. 104, n. 75.

So that such deceptive chatter may be recognized, I ask them again: Who told them that the fathers are clearer than Scripture and not more obscure? How would it be if I were to say that they understand the fathers as little as I understand Scripture? I could stuff my ears against the sayings of the fathers as well as they can against Scripture. But this is not how we shall reach the truth. If the Spirit spoke in the fathers, he spoke even more in his own Scripture. And whoever does not understand the Spirit in his own Scripture—who will believe that he understands him in the writings of someone else? This means precisely to use the sword in its sheath. If one does not grasp it as it is by itself, but rather through human words and glosses, it will soon be blunt and more obscure than before. Yet Emser insists on calling this striking with the blade. The naked sword gives him the shivers. But there is no help for it, he has to like it.

Therefore, one must know that Scripture without any glosses is the sun and the whole light from which all teachers receive their light, and not vice versa. This can be seen from the following: when the fathers teach something, they do not trust their own teaching. They are afraid it is too obscure and too uncertain; they run to Scripture and take a clear passage from it to illumine their own point, just as one puts a light into a lantern, as Psalm 18 [:28] says, "Lord, you light my lantern." In the same way, when they interpret a passage in Scripture they do not do so with their own sense or words (for whenever they do that, as often happens, they generally err). Instead, they add another passage which is clearer and thus illumine and interpret Scripture with Scripture, as my goats would certainly discover if they would read the fathers correctly. But since they run around everywhere and look at neither Scripture nor the fathers correctly, it is no wonder that they do not know what Scripture or the fathers teach.

I cannot tolerate their slandering and blaspheming Scripture and the holy fathers. They accuse Scripture of being obscure, although all the fathers attribute the brightest light to it and draw from it, as David says in Psalm 119 [:105], "Your word is my light." Again, they attribute to the fathers the light with which to illumine Scripture, even though all the fathers confess their own obscurity and only illumine Scripture with Scripture. That is the real art, to gather Scripture correctly. The father who can do this best is the best father. One should read the books of all the fathers with caution, not believing them but rather watching out whether they also cite clear passages and illumine Scripture with clear Scripture. How could they have overcome the heretics if they had fought with their own glosses? They would have been regarded as fools and senseless people. But since they cited such clear passages, which did not need glosses, that all reason was captivated by them, the evil spirit himself, along with all the heresies, had to retreat before them.

It is a different study of Scripture to interpret obscure Scripture and figures; it is called hunting, because one seeks and hunts some interesting reasonings as one would hunt game. But the kind of study useful to battle is that one is learned in Scripture, as Paul says [Titus 1:9]. It means to fight powerfully and with many clear passages, as with a drawn and naked sword, without any glosses and interpretations. This was the significance of the golden spears in Solomon's temple. Thus the opponent, overcome by the bright light, must see and confess that God's sayings stand alone and need no human interpretation. The foe who does not believe clear Scripture will certainly not believe the glosses of any of the fathers either.

It follows from this that one should not believe any teacher and that Emser's dagger is only a foolish invention. Instead, one should see whether they cite clear Scripture and obey it so that nothing more than the naked sword, the word of God, rules everyone. St. Paul taught us this when he wrote, "Test every doctrine; hold fast to what is good" [I Thess. 5:21]. He did not say that one should hold fast to everyone's teaching, but that one should test them all and hold fast to what is good. But Emser, together with his sophists, thinks, just as Eck also foolishly pretended in Leipzig,[43] that one should not test or try the fathers' teaching but rather accept it in every detail, even though everyone knows that they all erred many times. If, however, we should test them, as St. Paul says here, what kind of touchstone should we use other than Scripture? It must really be clearer and more certain than the fathers' teaching, for how else could we use it as a test to judge what is right or wrong? This is what the goat, so much more learned than St. Paul, intends

[43] Cf. *The Leipzig Debate*, 1519. *LW* 31, 321-322.

to reverse, claiming that we should not obey the mere text but rather the interpretation of the fathers. He thus makes the fathers the judges and testers of God and God's word to prove how true it is that no foolishness stands alone. Such juggling has never been heard of among the ancient fathers; it is a new invention of the pope and his sects, the mighty schools, to try to grasp Scripture not alone but through the interpretation of the fathers, so that they may escape the sword.

Since the goat has become a new philosopher, I must present him his Aristotle and prove to him how learned his Rhadinus is therein. Aristotle had written—and nature, without Aristotle, also teaches it to the peasants—that one cannot prove something obscure and uncertain with something obscure and uncertain, even less, light with darkness. Instead, whatever is obscure and uncertain must be illumined with something clear and certain. Since, then, all the fathers prove their point with Scripture, it is incredible that they could have been so mad and nonsensical (as follows from Emser's philosophy and short dagger) as to consider Scripture an obscure fog (as Emser scolds and blasphemes) with which they clarified and illumined their teaching. Rather, they most certainly considered Scripture the principal light and the greatest clarity and certainty, to which they appealed and upon which they relied as upon the most obvious and the clearest teaching to judge and to test all teaching.

St. Augustine did the same thing, and writes that he would believe no teacher, no matter how godly and learned he might be, unless he proved his teaching with Scripture or clear reason.[44] From this we learn how the fathers should be read, namely, that we should not consider what they say but whether they use clear Scripture or reason. But Emser and the pope's sects should not be blamed for fearing to do and to suffer such things and for inventing other ruses. For if they really would allow themselves to be pressured into proving their point with clear Scripture—God help them—then the abomination would be discovered and they could no longer deny that their sect is the rule of the Antichrist seducing the whole world in the name of "church" and "priesthood," as I shall bring to

[44] Cf. *Letter to Jerome. MPL* 33, 277; *PNF* 1, 350.

light someday,[45] if God grants it. That is why they are almost forced to blaspheme and to disgrace Scripture, to sweep it under the rug,[46] and to pretend that it is an obscure fog and that one should follow the interpretation of the fathers and seek the light in the darkness. One should not use the fathers' teachings for anything more than to get into Scripture as they did, and then one should remain with Scripture alone. But Emser thinks that they should have a special function alongside the Scriptures, as if Scripture were not enough for teaching us.

But to get a better look at the hypermiraculous art of the dear goat: even if Scripture is an obscure fog, how dare you fight me with it and pretend to strike me with the blade? Can you blow both hot and cold out of one mouth?[47] Is Scripture both an obscure fog and the brightest light in your head at the same time? For since you use three different weapons, the sword, the spear, and the dagger, then the sword cannot be either spear or dagger. Therefore, when you use the sword, namely, God's word, you must not use the dagger, namely, the fathers' interpretation. How quickly you changed your mind, you who say that the word of God is an obscure fog and that we should not work with our reason! But you work with it when you wield the sword! Indeed, I see clearly that in this matter you have taken leave of your senses. That no one is able to do what you do is because you no longer possess any reason which would make you resemble a rational being. I am sure you know what I mean, you noble goat. How cautious you are in your writing!

It also follows from these three weapons that you intend to make us spiritual with human words and teachings. For since spear and dagger are something different from the sword, and the sword is God's word which alone is the truth, spear and dagger must be human words and lies. For whatever is not God's word, is a lie, as Psalm 116 [:11] says, "All men are liars." That is why I said that

[45] A few weeks later, Luther pursued the theme in his response to an attack by the Dominican Ambrosius Catharinus. Cf. *WA* 7, 705-778.

[46] Proverbial German, *unter die banck stossen,* literally, "to put under the bench." Cf. Thiele, *Luthers Sprichwörtersammlung,* No. 468.

[47] An allusion to the statement in Sebastian Brant's famous *Ship of Fools* (Basel, 1494), quoted in *WA* 7, 641, n. 2: "He who wants to please everyone must have breath which is both cold and warm."

your spear is Goliath's spear and your dagger is Joab's dagger. But if the dagger should also be God's word interpreted by the fathers, and the spear the interpretation of God's word, then they are not three different weapons but only one, namely, the sword which is contained in all three. For all kinds of things could happen with you, not to mention a sword sticking in a dagger. I think you went to a school of dolts and the ass read better than you. I wish you would stay home with your dreams and ruses and practice such reckless juggling in your own verses, leaving alone God's word, which cannot tolerate such frivolous poems. To fight against the enemy we have no more than one word, which is spear, sword, dagger, and every other weapon: that is the holy word of God. Thus I hope you see your sheer monkeybusiness about these three weapons. Next time take on things you can prove with Scripture or reason. Then there will be less ridicule for you at your carnival. No one except your own dream has anything to say about the spear and the dagger. This then is my answer to you and all the teachers you may want to quote, whether it be the first one you mentioned, Aristotle, or Gerson and Scotus[48] in addition. If they do not suffice, take a calendar[49] and increase the number, so that meanwhile no one notices how you fear Scripture and flee from it as the devil flees the cross.

To fortify this spear and dagger, they even invented a foundation for themselves so that they would not have to stay with Scripture and be revealed as more unlearned than laymen. They know no shame when one wants to deal with Scripture. Although they know very well that with their usage and human teachings they survive like butter in the sun, they keep saying, "Not everything one must do in the church is written in Scripture. Rather, Christ commanded the apostles and their successors to teach and to arrange these things, as is written in the last chapter of St. John [John 21:25], 'But Jesus performed many more signs which are not written in this book; were every one of them to be written, I suppose that the world itself could not contain the books that would be

[48] Duns Scotus (1270-1308), famous scholastic theologian who opposed Thomas Aquinas and influenced the Franciscan theological tradition. Cf. Luther's critique of this tradition in *Against Latomus*, 1521. *LW* 32, 153.

[49] Since saints were generally listed on calendars, Luther was urging Emser to increase his own list.

written.' " Just look at these fine interpreters of the saints—how prettily they could weave a tassel and excuse for their dishonor from the leaves of this holy fig tree and gospel [Gen. 3:7]! They come along just as though they had done everything written in Scripture, and as though too little were written, even though no one (except Christ) has ever fulfilled completely one iota of Scripture. John says that not all the miraculous things Christ did are written down; he does not say that not all the things we should do are written down. Indeed, he clearly states soon afterward[50] what we should do, saying, "But these signs are written that you may believe," [John 20:31]. This faith is also the work we Christians should do, as he himself says in John 6 [:29]. Now these interpreters come along and say, "Not everything we should do is written down." John speaks of the things Christ did, but they apply it to human laws and works. Christ's miraculous signs and our work are supposed to be one and the same thing. Thank you, you fine fellows! You really know how to interpret Scripture, especially Emser, who never hits the mark of the letter here, and cuts me with the blade of the Spirit, just as he proves the elevation of the saints through the words of the psalm, "Praise the Lord in his saints."[51] If only God would command you someday to blaspheme Scripture! How miserably you ape us!

Even if it [John 21:25] were said about human laws and works, which cannot be, should one therefore seek to write so many books that the world could no longer contain them, and therefore do precisely what the apostle wants to leave undone? Truly, there is more than enough written in Scripture so that there is no need for more commandments and laws. Indeed, there is no longer any power on earth to make Christian laws, as I have proven many times.[52] And if those who pretend to do so had the Spirit in them,

[50] Luther is mistaken here, since the passage he quotes precedes John 21:25.

[51] Ps. 150:1. Luther is quoting the Vulgate, which reads, *Laudate dominum in sanctis eius.* Modern translations substitute "sanctuary" for "saints." Cf. Emser's statement in *Against the Un-Christian Book of the Augustinian Martin Luther:* "[Luther] departs from his mother, the holy Christian church, which, in accordance with God's will, commandment, and revelation, has had the custom from the beginning of the church until today of canonizing and exalting the saints. There is much scriptural evidence that this is the will and commandment of God, such as Psalm 150 [:1], 'Praise God in his saints.' " Enders, *op. cit.*, I, 115.

[52] Cf., for example, *The Babylonian Captivity of the Church*, 1520. LW 36, 70.

they would certainly not pervert this saying of St. John so blasphemously for their own false argumentation. This perversion presents clear evidence of the kind of spirit out of which they intend to be lawmakers.

They have still another passage, John 14 [:26], where Christ said during supper, "The Holy Spirit, whom the father will send in my name, will teach you all things and remind you of what I have said to you." Here they pretend that Christ did not let everything be written down in the gospel. They do not look at the clear words of Christ. For he says, "The Holy Spirit will remind you" not of "what you should institute and command" but of "what I have commanded and said to you." So once again Christ's commandment is made the same as a human commandment. The disciples could not grasp and bear everything he said to them at the time. That is why he said that the Spirit should tell them again the parts they might have forgotten or not understood, which then actually happened. Christ was so diligent in taking precautions against the erection of any man's law in his church that he wanted to say everything beforehand, even though it was neither remembered nor understood. Now the sects of the pope turn it around and want to attribute to human law what Christ preached against human law. And yet they do not want to be heretics but the masters of all Christians!

In this matter the sects of the pope are up to their necks in the Manichaean heresy.[53] They [the Manichaeans], too, claimed that the Holy Spirit, who was to teach more than is written in Scripture, was promised; St. Augustine overcomes this masterfully and proves in *Against Felix*[54] that everything the promised Holy Spirit should teach was fulfilled and written down by the apostles.

Again, when Christ says to the disciples, "He who hears you hears me" [Luke 10:16], they interpret it to mean that they can make laws as they please. They drive us into their own law, indeed, into their own net of money, with this same word, even though Christ speaks only of the gospel which he commands the apostles

[53] Named after Manichaeus, a Persian religious philosopher who was executed in Persia *ca.* 275. It was a syncretistic cult teaching the incompatibility of spirit and matter. Augustine was a Manichaean until 384.

[54] Felix was a Manichaean. The passage is found in *MPL* 42, 519.

to preach and us to hear. When he says to Peter, "Whatever you bind shall be bound" [Matt. 16:19], they again come along saying that the pope may make laws as he pleases, even though Christ only says the word about binding and loosing of sins. Thus they base all their points not only on their own invented lies, but also (which is unbearable) on the perversion, poisoning, and shameful use of the holy divine word. And yet they still want to be the masters of all Christians and declare everyone a heretic who does not worship their abomination and blasphemy.

That is why it is really an abominable and un-Christian blasphemy of Emser that he wants Roman usage and law kept just as though they were written in Scripture, although universal Christendom neither affirms nor keeps them since the Greeks and Orientals, who are also Christians (even though it annoys Emser and the pope's sects), have not accepted them. And even if they were to belong to universal Christendom, it would still not be an error of faith not to keep them. To obey human laws does not make a Christian; not to obey them does not make a non-Christian. Even though it is not right to despise wilfully and without reason what the masses believe and do, it is tyrannical and inhuman, indeed, devilish, on the other hand, to burden, drive, and impose human laws without cause upon a single Christian, to say nothing [of coercing] a whole or large mass of them.

That is why I would let everyone who wants to do so, keep the papal and human laws, wherever it is possible for faith and God's word not to be crowded out by them. But I will not keep silent when fear and despair are created with them and all those who do not obey them are accused of being damned heretics even if they keep all the other articles of faith. That is what Emser does here; he admits that I do not violate a single article of faith but nevertheless refuses to let me be a Christian. In baptism we have sworn allegiance and paid homage not to the pope but to Christ. If he leads us to imperial human law, violence, tyranny, prison, death, and every kind of suffering, we are obliged to follow. The pope has also sworn to him to teach us not his own but Christ's word, and to be our example. If he does not do so he is a murderer and a thief, as Christ himself calls such wolves in John 10 [:1, 8] Now let us hear some of his lies.

His first lie is that I intend to cut off the head of the church and then heal the body.[55] In this case his own idea pleased him as much as did the spear and dagger. For in that particular book[56] I did not write anything about the papacy [as such], only about its improvement and offense. It is true that in other books,[57] impelled by their driving and hunting, I have been forced to write that the pope does not derive from God's order. I trust that I have proven [my point]—without any assistance from Emser. But in so doing I have not rejected him, as the liar Emser lies. My books clearly prove this. If that had been my intention at the time, why should I have suggested that the papacy be reformed? This suggestion proved that I wanted to retain and hold on to it; otherwise, I would have had to say that one should destroy it instead of reforming it.

Even if the pope should become equal to other bishops, which will not happen until the Last Day (for Christ himself has to remove this enemy of his whom we could not reform), it would not remove the church's head, as Emser lies. He thinks he has won the point that the pope is the head of the church; he has a long way to go. Christ is the head of the church. The pope is often a heretic and knave, and it is absolutely disgraceful to hear from Emser that he gives the church a heretic and knave as its head. It is much worse than having him cut off its head. Even the pope dies, like everyone else. Yet the church does not live without a head, for just as it lives forever so must its head also live forever.

Emser's second lie is that I wanted the hands of the laymen washed in the blood of the priests.[58] His holy priesthood and Christian love seek nothing but fire.[59] If I were dead he could

---

[55] Cf. Emser's statement in *Against the Un-Christian Book of the Augustinian Martin Luther:* "He would not be a physician but a knave and murderer who, when called to help a patient, would first cut off his head. Thus all other medicine for the rest of the body would be worthless. You see, my dear Germans, Luther acts just that way and his very first aim is to cut off the head of Christianity." Enders, *op. cit.*, I, 18.

[56] *To the Christian Nobility of the German Nation,* 1520. Cf. *LW* 44, 115-217.

[57] *On the Papacy in Rome,* 1520. Cf. above, pp.49-104.

[58] Cf. Emser's statement in *Against the Un-Christian Book of the Augustinian Martin Luther:* "Until now Luther urged the common people, in his other books, to wash their hands in the blood of the priests." Enders, *op. cit.*, I, 16.

[59] That is, to burn Luther like John Huss.

spread such lies as truth, just as happened to Huss. This is the way I have written against Sylvester, "in contrast,"[60] as this noble poet and rhetorician well knows: if heretics are burned, why should we not much rather attack the pope and his sects with the sword and wash our hands in their blood, if he teaches what Sylvester writes, namely, that Holy Scripture has its power from the pope. But since I dislike burning heretics,[61] or killing even a single Christian, and since I know full well it is against the gospel, I merely indicated what they deserve if heretics deserve the fire. Nor is it necessary to attack you with the sword. The nobility and worldly powers, if they just despise your tyrannical shamming and false ban, can certainly advise you womanish and childish people with a single letter and command. They can say to you, "This is the way it must be," and you have no choice but to obey. The way you react to it, with burning, banning, raging, and raving against the clear truth, it seems you would really like to have a Bohemian example made of yourselves and fulfil the prophecy which says that the priests should be slain. If this should happen to you, you cannot blame me. Just continue as you are, you are on the right track! Where advice is not possible, help is not possible.[62] You will very soon find out if you can end the game in that way, even if it rains and snows nothing but bishops, Emsers, Ecks, and popes. I trust you have foreseen that no one will destroy the pope but you yourselves, his own creatures, as the prophet says.

But tell me, dear Emser, if you may write that it is necessary and right to burn heretics and think you do not thereby soil your hands with Christian blood, why should it not also be right to strangle you, Sylvester, the pope, and all your sects in the most scandalous way? For not only do you write in the manner of a heretic and of the Antichrist, but you also say what all the devils are not allowed to say, namely, that the gospel is confirmed by the pope, its power is dependent on the pope's power, and the church

[60] *Per contentionem,* a term used in rhetoric to describe the method of contrasting two arguments by printing them side by side. Luther used this method by reprinting Prierias' polemic treatise, adding a foreword, a postscript, and marginal glosses. Cf. *The Abridged Response to Martin Luther (Epitoma responsionis ad Martinum Luther),* 1520. *WA* 6, 347, 326.

[61] Cf. *Defense and Explanation of All the Articles,* 1521. *LW* 32, 87.

[62] A German proverb, *Wo nit zu radten ist, do ist nit zu helffen.*

has done what the pope does? What heretic has ever so completely condemned and destroyed God's word in one stroke? That is why I still say, "If heretics have deserved the fire, you and the pope should be killed a thousand times." Still I do not want it to happen. Your judge is not far off. He will find you in good health and nimble. Do not get bored in the meantime. Yet I would prefer you to come before him with remorse and penance. God help you to do this, Amen. Nevertheless, I would like the Roman courtiers to be repelled with force just like other thieves and robbers, if they cannot be stopped in any other way.

So that I may not be ridiculed along with you I shall ignore your babbling that I put the priesthood to shame and your claim that St. Paul was consecrated by the apostles and St. Peter had a tonsure; I shall also ignore all the useless talk you spew forth about consecration and priestly estate and the threefold meaning of "spiritual"—*spirituale, ecclesiasticum, religiosum*—and that not all Christians are spiritual, *spirituales*. You probably also would like to say that the laying on of hands on the head meant more than consecration. Who can stop you if you intend to do nothing but lie and preach, as some do, that St. Bartholomew prayed the rosary and the psalter of our dear lady? I do not need any logic here: I call spiritual *spirituales,* devout Christians *ecclesiasticum,* and do not know *religiosum* in this context. I thought that for once the naked sword would strike me with the blade, but neither sheath nor sword nor man is at hand. You also lie that I have made all laymen bishops, priests, and spiritual in such a way that they may exercise the office without a call. But, as godly as you are, you conceal the fact that I added that no one should undertake this office without a call unless it be an extreme emergency. And what shall I say, since there is almost one lie after another in your book? I am afraid you will lie, blaspheme, hate, and rave yourself to death. In previous times it was easy to write against heretics. For even though they erred, as honest people they did not need to lie and stuck to the heart of the matter. My persecutors let the matter drop and, like knaves, rely solely upon lies. But to keep you from being displeased at hearing nothing but your lies, let us deal again with something good—the Spirit and the letter, which is the main theme of your book.

Concerning the Letter and the Spirit

St. Paul says, in II Corinthians 4 [3:6], "The letter kills, but the Spirit gives life." My Emser uses and interprets this to mean that Scripture has a twofold meaning, an external one and a hidden one, and he calls these two meanings "literal" and "spiritual." The literal meaning is supposed to kill, the spiritual one is supposed to give life. He builds here upon Origen,[63] Dionysius,[64] and a few others who taught the same thing. He thinks he has hit the mark and need not look at clear Scripture because he has human teaching. He would also like me to follow him, to let Scripture go and take up human teaching. This I refuse to do, even though I too have made the same error. I intend, in precisely this example, to give reasons and to show clearly that Origen, Jerome, Dionysius, and some others have erred and failed in this matter, that Emser builds upon sand, and that it is necessary to compare the fathers' books with Scripture and to judge them according to its light.

First, if their opinion were correct that the spiritual meaning gives life and the literal one kills, we would have to confess that all sinners are holy and all saints are sinners. Indeed, Christ himself, together with all the angels, would have to be simultaneously alive and dead. We intend to make this so clear that even Emser with all his lying powers cannot fight against it. We shall consider the passage from Paul in Galatians 4 [:22], "Abraham had two sons, Isaac and Ishmael, by two women, Sarah and Hagar." This is said according to the literal meaning and the letter. Now this is the meaning Christ has. God the Holy Spirit and all angels and saints hold fast to it and insist that it is as the literal meaning and the letter say, and this is truly the way it is. What now, Emser? Where is your Origen? If you are really the man who does not

[63] Origen of Alexandria (*ca.* 184-253), a Greek church father whose principles of allegorical exegesis were the source of many lengthy controversies. Cf. *The Babylonian Captivity of the Church,* 1520. *LW* 36, 30.

[64] Dionysius (*ca.* 500), the "Areopagite" (a pseudonym based on Acts 17:34), is associated with Christian neo-Platonism and mystical ideas about the church. Cf. *LW* 36, 109.

strike with the sheath and wounds only with the blade, you had better say now that the letter and literal meaning kill Christ and the Holy Spirit together with all the angels and saints. What can anyone say more blasphemously than that the truth in all of Scripture is deadly and harmful, as Emser rages here?

Again, (as you say) the spiritual meaning is that Abraham is Christ, the two women are the two testaments [Gal. 4:24], the two sons are the people of the two testaments, as St. Paul interprets. Now not only the saints but also the worst sinners, indeed, even the devils in hell, hold to this same meaning. So step onto the battlefield, my Emser, strike out merrily with the blade, and say that all the devils and knaves are alive and holy since the Holy Spirit gives life. Now admit it: is it not true that if you take this piece of Origen, Dionysius, Jerome, and many others, you have taken almost all their skill? Is not Scripture here clearer than all of them put together? With what do I test, judge, condemn, and defeat them all so that no one can deny it, other than with the same passage of St. Paul which they take as their basis, namely, "The letter kills, the Spirit gives life" [II Cor. 3:6]? What kind of glosses do I add? Is not the text itself so clearly against them that everyone is forced to say Yes?

This is the way one should deal with the whole Scripture, even with the ancient figures like the one prohibiting Jews from eating either pork or rabbit since pigs and rabbits do not ruminate [Lev. 11:6-7]. This was the literal meaning and letter. This is the way David, all the holy prophets, and Christ himself with his disciples have understood it and obeyed it. If they had not understood and obeyed it in this way they would have been in opposition to God. Then why did the letter not kill them? On the other hand, great deadly sinners and, above all, devils may understand that the pig means carnal teaching, or whatever one wants to interpret here spiritually; so why does the Spirit not give them life? Where are you now, man from Leipzig with the cutting sword? Better go and write even more about me, that I have praised ceremonies as being "holy, just, and good, given by a good God." You yourself must now see and confess that the result is as I said it would be. Did I not tell you that you do not know even one jot about what Spirit and letter are in Scripture? You should mind your own business and leave Scripture in peace. Do you see now what good it does to refer to many teachers and to rely on their writings?

St. Paul says further in Romans 7 [:14], "Divine law is spiritual but I am carnal," and he cites one of the Ten Commandments, "*Non concupisces,* you shall not covet!" [Rom. 7:7]. He argues here with rich words and wisdom that this same spiritual law kills. What do you intend to do here, Emser? Where are you, man with the spear, dagger, and cutting sword? St. Paul says here, "The spiritual law kills"; you say, "The spiritual meaning gives life." Start whistling; let us hear your skill: which is the literal and which is the spiritual meaning in this commandment, "You shall not covet"? You certainly cannot deny that no other meaning can be understood here but the one given by the letters themselves; and he speaks here of the evil lusts of the flesh. Yet St. Paul still calls the law spiritual and says it kills. And you say that it would be better to read a poetic fable than such a meaning of Scripture. St. Paul thinks that anyone who understands a meaning different from this literal meaning in regard to the evil lusts does not understand anything at all in this commandment. How nicely Emser harmonizes with St. Paul, just like the ass with the nightingale. This is the way one must deal with all of God's commandments, be they ceremonial or other commandments, small or great. Thus it is quite obvious that Emser fails miserably here and knows less about Scripture than a child.

Moreover, his erroneous and false understanding leads to the humiliation of all of Scripture as well as to his own great disgrace. For the diligence and efforts of all teachers are directed solely to discovering the literal meaning which alone is valid for them too. Thus Augustine also writes that "figures prove nothing."[65] This means that Emser's spiritual understanding counts for nothing; but the other one [the literal one] is the highest, best, strongest, in short, the whole substance, nature, and foundation of Holy Scripture. If one abandoned it, the whole Scripture would be nothing. But the spiritual one, which Emser inflates, counts in no dispute and does not stand the test; it would not matter at all even if no one knew it, as I have proven in my book on the papacy.[66] For it

[65] Cf. *On the Unity of the Church,* I, 5, 8. *MPL* 43, 396.

[66] Cf. above, p. 70.

would not matter if no one knew that Aaron is spiritually Christ, nor can it be proven. One must let Aaron be just Aaron in the simple sense, unless the Spirit himself interprets him in a new sense, which then would be a new literal sense—as when St. Paul makes Christ out of Aaron for the Hebrews [Hebrews 9–10].

Why are you so bold now, Emser, that you dare to say that this literal meaning is deadly? You babble on, not knowing yourself what you are saying, when you claim it is better to read one of Virgil's fables than such a meaning in Scripture. This means to condemn the whole Scripture and to prefer the devil's lies or fables to the holy word of God, especially since it [Scripture] has no other meaning that counts but the one you teach as deadly and to be avoided. This is called striking with the blade and a true Emserian spiritual interpretation! This is the way to strike the heretic Luther! Turn the leaf over, Emser, and you will find that the meaning you call spiritual and alive is precisely the one which, if one adheres to it alone and lets the literal meaning go, would better be replaced by the mere fables of poets. For it is dangerous, and Scripture can exist without it. But Scripture cannot exist without the other meaning. That is why Origen received his due reward a long time ago when his books were prohibited, for he relied too much on this same spiritual meaning, which was unnecessary, and he let the necessary literal meaning go. When that happens Scripture perishes and really good theologians are no longer produced. Only the true principal meaning which is provided by the letters can produce good theologians.

The Holy Spirit is the simplest writer and adviser in heaven and on earth. That is why his words could have no more than the one simplest meaning which we call the written one, or the literal meaning of the tongue. But [written] words and [spoken] language cease to have meaning when the things which have a simple meaning through interpretation by a simple word are given further meanings and thus become different things [through a different interpretation] so that one thing takes on the meaning of another. This is true for all other things not mentioned in Scripture because all God's creatures and works are sheer living signs and words of God, as Augustine and all the teachers say. But one should not therefore say that Scripture or God's word has more than one meaning.

The fact that a painted picture signifies a living man without any words or writing should not cause you to say that the little word "picture" has two meanings, a literal one, signifying the picture, and a spiritual one, signifying the living man. Likewise, even though the things described in Scripture mean something further, Scripture should not therefore have a twofold meaning. Instead, it should retain the one meaning to which the words refer. Beyond that we should give idle spirits permission to hunt and seek the manifold interpretations of the things indicated besides the words. But they should beware of losing themselves in the hunt or the climb, as happens to those who climb after chamois, and as also happened to Origen. It is much more certain and much safer to stay with the words and the simple meaning, for this is the true pasture and home of all the spirits.

Now see how well Emser rides along with his twofold Bible. The result [of his effort] is that nothing remains certain. When St. Peter says, "We are all priests" [I Pet. 2:9], he says this is said in the spiritual sense and not in the literal one. But when I ask why it is not the literal sense, he answers, because the literal sense kills. He does not understand a jot of what he says. He does not see that he himself now really disgraces his own priesthood by teaching clearly that it is not the living and spiritual, but rather the literal, deadly, and harmful priesthood, and that it would really be better to be a poet-priest than such a literal priest. If whatever is not Spirit does not live and cannot be understood according to the spiritual meaning, then it must certainly be understood according to the letter as dead, harmful, and worse than pagan, if the high and hyperspiritual theology of Emser is to endure. That is why it would be good if a smith remained a smith, a verse-maker a verse-maker, and let those who have power and marrow in their fists and arms wield the spiritual sword. Scripture does not tolerate the division of letter and Spirit, as Emser so outrageously [divides them]. It contains only a simple priesthood and a simple meaning.

Those who have called the letter a veiled and hidden word, as Augustine also did for a while, have committed a more reasonable error. For example, if I said, "Emser is a crude ass," and a simple man following the words understood Emser to be a real ass with long ears and four feet, he would be deceived by the letter, since through such veiled words I wanted to indicate that he had a crude and unreasonable mind. One teaches such flowery words to boys in school, calling them *schemata* in Greek and *figurae* in Latin, because one dresses up and ornaments speech with them just as one ornaments a body with a jewel. Scripture is full of such flowers, especially in the prophets. For example, John and Christ in Luke 3 [:7] call the Jews "a brood of vipers." And St. Paul calls them "dogs" in Colossians 2 [Phil. 3:2]. Psalm 110 [:3] says, "The dew of your children will come from the womb of the morning." Again, "The Lord will send forth from Zion the scepter of your power" [Ps. 110:2], that is, Christ's children will not be born from the womb of a physical woman or mother, but rather without the work of a man, like the dew from the sky, from the womb of the morning of the Christian church. Again, Christ, in Matthew 5 [:13-14] says, "You are the salt of the earth, and the light of the world." But St. Paul does not mean a letter like this; this belongs to grammar and to elementary school.

If you can humble yourself and not despise me completely, then listen to me: I shall do my Christian duty toward you as I am bound to do it to my enemy; and I shall not withhold from you God's gift to me. In this matter I shall teach you better (to speak without boasting) than you have ever been taught by any other teacher, with the exception of St. Augustine—if you have read his *On the Spirit and the Letter*.[67] None of the others will teach you this. You will not find a single letter in the whole Bible that agrees with what you, along with Origen and Jerome, call the "spiritual meaning." St. Paul calls it *mysteria*, that is, veiled and secret meaning. Therefore, the earliest fathers called it *anagogas*, that is, "the more withdrawn meanings, separate knowledge" (*remotiores sensus, separatas intelligentias*). At times they also called it "allegory," as St. Paul himself does, Galatians 4 [:24]; but this is not yet Spirit, although the Spirit grants this as well as the letter and all gifts. As we read in I Corinthians 14 [:2], "The Spirit utters the hidden meaning." Some people, out of ignorance, therefore,

[67] *De spiritu et litera, ad Marcellinum* (412). *MPL* 44, 199-246; *PNF* 5, 83-114.

attributed a fourfold meaning to Scripture: the literal, the allegorical, the anagogical, and the tropological. But there is no basis for it.

Thus "literal meaning" is not a good term, because Paul interprets the letter quite differently than they do. Those who call it "grammatical, historical meaning" do better. It would be appropriate to call it the "meaning of the tongue or of language" as St. Paul does in I Corinthians 14 [:2-19], because, according to the sound of the tongue or speech, it is understood in this way by everyone. For the language or tongue which hears that Abraham had two sons from two wives retains this same meaning and does not think beyond the meaning [given] by the tongue or language until the Spirit leads it on and discloses the hidden understanding about Christ, about two kinds of testaments and peoples. These are called *mysteria*, just as Paul, Ephesians 5 [:32], calls [the unity of] Christ and the church in one body *mysterium*, although Scripture and the letter speak of husband and wife—Genesis 2 [:24]. But here it is necessary that no one invent mysteries on his own, as some people have done and are still doing. The Spirit himself must do it—or else one must prove it with Scripture, as I have written in the book on the papacy.[68]

That is why Paul's saying, II Corinthians 4 [3:6], "The letter kills, but the Spirit gives life," harmonizes with these two meanings, the literal and the spiritual, as well as Emser's mind harmonizes with philosophy and theology. At the moment I shall ignore how and why Origen, Jerome, and some other fathers have stretched and misused this passage. Certainly they stretched more passages in the same way to fend off Jews and heretics, as everyone well knows or is able to know. They should be excused for this, but we should not follow them in this as these unclean animals are doing who have no judgment with regard to the work and teaching of the fathers; they gobble up everything they find until they obey the fathers only in those things in which the dear fathers slipped as men. And they drop them when they did well, as I could easily prove with regard to all the teachings and lives now held to be the very best.

[68] Cf. above, p. 73.

Let us deal now with the passage concerning the Spirit and the letter. In this passage [II Cor. 3:6], St. Paul does not write one iota about these two meanings, only about two kinds of preaching or preaching offices. One is that of the Old Testament, the other is that of the New Testament. The Old Testament preaches the letter, the New [Testament] preaches the Spirit. And, to avoid the kind of dreaming goat Emser does, let us hear the Apostle's own clear words spoken about the servants or preachers of the New Testament. They are written in II Corinthians 4 [3:3-6]: "You are a letter from Christ made through our preaching and written not with ink but with the Spirit of the living God, not on stone tablets but on tablets of human hearts. That is why we need no other letter of recommendation. Such is the confidence we have through Christ in God. Not that we are sufficient in ourselves to claim anything as coming from us; our sufficiency is from God, who has qualified us to be servants and preachers of the New Testament, not of the letter but of the Spirit; for the letter kills, but the Spirit gives life," etc.

Are not these clear words about preaching? Here we see clearly that St. Paul names two tablets and two sermons. Moses' tablets were made of stone in which God's finger inscribed the law, Exodus 20 [:1-17; 24:12; 31:18]. Christ's tablets, or (as he says here) Christ's letters, are the hearts of Christians in which not letters, as in Moses' tablets, but the Spirit of God is inscribed through the preaching of the gospel and through the office of the apostles. What does all this mean? The letter is nothing but divine law or commandment which was given in the Old Testament through Moses and preached and taught through Aaron's priesthood. It is called "letter" because it is written in letters on stone tablets and in books. It remains letter, and does not yield more than that, because no man improves through the law; he only becomes worse. Thus the law does not help, nor does it grant grace; it only commands and orders something done which man is neither able nor willing to do. But the Spirit, the divine grace, grants strength and power to the heart; indeed, he creates a new man who takes pleasure [in obeying] God's commandments and who does everything he should do with joy.

This Spirit can never be contained in any letter. It cannot be written, like the law, with ink, on stone, or in books. Instead, it is inscribed only in the heart, and it is a living writing of the Holy Spirit, without [the aid of] any means. That is why St. Paul calls it Christ's letter and not Moses' tablets, for it is not written with ink but with God's Spirit. Through this Spirit or grace man does what the law demands. He pays what he owes the law, and thus becomes liberated from the letter which kills him, living now through the grace of the Spirit. For everything which does not have the grace of the living Spirit is dead, even though external obedience to the whole law glitters. That is why the Apostle says of the law that it kills, gives no one life, and holds one eternally in death if grace does not arrive to redeem and give life.

These then are the two ways of preaching: the priests, preachers, and sermons of the Old Testament deal with no more than the law of God. The Spirit and grace are not yet openly preached. But in the New Testament only Spirit and grace, given to us through Christ, are preached. For the New Testament preaching is but an offering and presentation of Christ, through the sheer mercy of God, to all men. This is done in such a way that all who believe in him will receive God's grace and the Holy Spirit, whereby all sins are forgiven, all laws fulfilled, and they become God's children and are eternally blessed. Thus St. Paul here calls the New Testament preaching the "ministry of the Spirit" [II Cor. 3:6], that is, the office of preaching whereby God's Spirit and grace are offered and put before all those who are burdened by the law, who are killed, and who are greedy for grace. He calls this law "a ministry of the letter," that is, the office of preaching whereby no more is given than the letter or law. No life flows from it, the law is not fulfilled by it, and man can never satisfy it. That is why it remains letter, and in the letter it can do no more than kill man, that is, show him what he should do and yet cannot do. Thus he recognizes that he is dead and without grace before God and that he does not fulfil the commandment, which, however, he should fulfil.

From this it is now clear that the words of the apostle, "The letter kills, but the Spirit gives life," could be said in other words: "The law kills, but the grace of God gives life." Or, "Grace grants help and does everything that the law demands and yet is unable to do by itself." St. Paul therefore calls the law of God a law of death and of sin, saying in Romans 8 [:2-4], "The law of the Spirit of life in Christ has set me free from the law of sin and death. For it was impossible for the law to help me; indeed, it only made things worse because of the malice of the old flesh. That is why God sent his Son in our likeness and let him put on our sinful flesh. Thus he destroyed our sin through the sin Christ took upon himself in his suffering, in order that the just requirement of the law might be fulfilled in us." Thus we see that in a masterful way St. Paul teaches us how to understand Christ, God's grace, and the New Testament correctly—namely, that it is nothing but [the story] of how Christ stepped into our sins, carried them on the cross in his flesh, and destroyed them, so that all who believe in him are set free from sin through him and receive the grace to enable them from now on to satisfy the law of God and the letter that kills, and to live in eternity. You see, this is "ministry of the Spirit and not of the letter," the preaching of the Spirit, the preaching of grace, the preaching of true indulgence, the preaching about Christ. This is the New Testament about which there would be much to say if the evil spirit had not blinded the world through the pope and had not led human teaching into the abyss of utter darkness.

Now we see that all commandments are deadly, since divine commandments are also deadly. For everything that is not Spirit or grace is death. Therefore, it is a crude misunderstanding to call allegories, tropologies, and the like "Spirit," since all of them are contained in letters and cannot give life. Grace has no other vessel than the heart. Now just as not all men accept the life of this Spirit—indeed, the majority let this Spirit's servants present and preach this rich grace in vain, and do not believe the gospel—so too, not everyone takes up the ministry of the letter or the preaching of the law. They do not want to let themselves be killed; that is, they do not understand God's law, and they go on without receiving either the letter or the Spirit. But let us set forth goat Emser's blind mind even more clearly: he thinks the letter should be avoided and the death of the letter should be escaped. This is what happens to those who read only the books of the fathers and leave Scripture aside. They juggle with their spears and daggers, making an obscure fog out of Scripture and a light out of the teaching of the fathers.

The Apostle does not want us to avoid the letter or to escape its death. Indeed, he complains in the same passage [II Cor. 3:7] that there was a veil hanging over the law for the Jews, just as over the face of Moses (Exodus 34 [:33-35]), so that they failed to see the letter, its death, or its brilliance. He wants us to preach and make the letter clear and to lift the veil from Moses' face. This is how it happens: he who understands the law of God correctly and looks it in the face—without the veil—will find that the works of all men are sin and that there is nothing good in them unless the grace of the Spirit enters into them. This then is the end of the law and its meaning, of which Paul speaks in II Corinthians 4 [3:13], "They did not see the end of Moses." For it [the law] wants to make everyone a sinner and all that is ours into sin; in this way it wants to show us our misery, our death, and our merit, and lead us into true knowledge of ourselves. As St. Paul says, Romans 7 [:7], "If it had not been for the law, I should not have known sin"; and Romans 3 [Gal. 3:22], "Scripture consigned all men to sin," so that the whole world's mouth might be stopped and it might know that no man can be upright before God without grace, even though he does works of the law.

Those who want to emphasize their good works and boast about free will do not allow all human works to be sin. They still find something good in nature, just as the Jews and our sophists, together with the pope, do. They are the ones who do not want to let Moses' face shine clearly. They put a veil over the law and do not really look it in the face. They refuse to let everything belonging to them be either sin or death before God; that is, they do not really want to know themselves or to be humble. They only strengthen their pride. They flee the letter and a true understanding of it, just as the Jews fled the face of Moses. That is why their mind remains blind and they never come to the life of the Spirit. Therefore, it is impossible for someone who does not first hear the law and let himself be killed by the letter, to hear the gospel and let the grace of the Spirit bring him to life. Grace is only given to those who long for it. Life is a help only to those who are dead, grace only to sin, the Spirit only to the letter. No one can have the one without the other. Therefore, what Emser calls the letter and death is, in reality, nothing but the veil, the harmful misunderstanding of the letter, and the damnable flight from this blessed death. In fact, it is not even this good an understanding. So far away is this poor and blind man from Scripture, and he pretends to hit the mark with the sword blade! I think he has only struck his own cheek!

My good advice to such unlearned minds would be to give up writing books. For while they madly cite the words of a few fathers, they thumb their noses at the poor people so that they fall for it and accept this error, perhaps for life. Thus such books are not without harm, and their insane author is guilty before God because of such corruption. Who will give Emser the grace to eradicate, as he ought to, the errors and lies resulting from his book? It would have been better for him, as Christ says, to have a millstone fastened around his neck and to be drowned in the depth of the sea [Matt. 18:6]. For not only does he write erroneous, harmful, and scandalous teaching, but he also blasphemes the very best teachings of Christ and completely poisons the poor people and drives them away. Woe to you, Emser! If you had waited until God called you and drove you, he would have worked with you too and given you his Spirit to write something useful. But now you do as Jeremiah says, "I did not send the prophets, yet they ran; I did not speak to them, yet they prophesied" [Jer. 23:21]. The hateful and deceitful spirit has driven you. That is why you do not write anything but lies and error. I can do no more than to warn everyone against your poison. And if I were not afraid for these poor people I would not have considered you worth answering, just as I did not before,[69] for in these matters you are ignorance itself!

But to return to our topic: it is certainly true that wherever the law alone is preached and only the letter is dealt with, as happened in the Old Testament, and where the Spirit is not preached afterward, there is death without life, sin without grace, misery without consolation. This creates miserable and imprisoned consciences who in the end despair and are forced to die in sin. They are thus condemned to eternity through such preaching. In our day the murderous sophists have done this kind of thing and are still doing it with their "systems" [*summae*] and "confessionals" [*confessionales*],[70] in which they drive and torture people

[69] Cf. above, pp. 105-115.

[70] Systems of theology and manuals of confession.

with commands to do penance, to confess, to repent, and to make satisfaction. After this they teach good works and preach good doctrine, as they say. But never once do they hold the Spirit and Christ up to the sorrowful consciences, so that Christ is now unknown in the whole world and the gospel is pushed under the rug.[71] The whole New Testament office is silenced and only the very best people explain Moses and the commandments, and even they are quite rare. The majority deals only with tomfoolery, teaching canon law, papal laws, human teaching, and their own statutes. To these things they cling, these they keep, these they teach daily; and they no longer have an opportunity to know the truth, as St. Paul says [II Tim. 3:7].

If God's commandment, preached and explained as well as possible, is harmful and damning, as St. Paul says here, why then do the sophists and the goat pretend to make people godly with human teachings, with their own laws and an increase in good works? Indeed, since the law kills and condemns everything which is not grace and Spirit, they do no more with their many laws and works than to give the law much to kill and to condemn. Thus all their labor and effort is in vain, and the more they do the worse they become; for it is impossible to satisfy the law with works and teachings. Only the Spirit can satisfy it. That is why Scripture calls their nature *aven* and *amal* [in Hebrew], that is, "trouble" and "effort" [Ps. 10:7]; and it calls this same lost crowd *Behaven,* that is, the "church or crowd of trouble" [Hos. 4:15]. Again, Amos 7 [:16] calls it *Beth-Ishac,* that is, the "church of deceit," because everyone under it is deceived by their false teaching, work, and life.

That is why I advised, and still advise, that one should not pretend to institute a reformation to better such human teaching and canon law as Emser foolishly suggests, for that is impossible. Rather, they [human teaching and canon law] should be burned, eliminated, destroyed, and reversed. Or else they should be reduced as much as possible and the two offices of the letter and the Spirit advanced once again, which can only be done if human teaching is left far behind. It is only fair that they give way to the letter and the Spirit of God, since they hinder it and are detrimental to it. We

[71] Cf. above, p. 167, n. 46.

have more than enough to preach on the letter and the Spirit, even if we preached from the beginning of the world until the end of it.

But even though we are already in the New Testament and should have only the preaching of the Spirit, since we are still living in flesh and blood, it is necessary to preach the letter as well, so that people are first killed by the law and all their arrogance is destroyed. Thus they may know themselves and become hungry for the Spirit and thirsty for grace. So [the letter] prepares the people for the preaching of the Spirit, as it is written about St. John [the Baptist], that he made the people ready for Christ through the preaching of repentance [Matt. 3:1-12]. This was the office of the letter. After that he led them to Christ, saying, "Behold, the Lamb of God, who takes away all the sins of the world" [John 1:29]. This was the office of the Spirit. These then are the two works of God, praised many times in Scripture: he kills and gives life, he wounds and heals, he destroys and helps, he condemns and saves, he humbles and elevates, he disgraces and honors, as is written in Deuteronomy 32 [:39], I Kings 2 [I Sam. 2:6-8], Psalm 112 [:7-8], and in many other places. He does these works through these two offices, the first through the letter, the second through the Spirit. The letter does not allow anyone to stand before his wrath. The Spirit does not allow anyone to perish before his grace. Oh, this is such an overwhelming affair that one could talk about it endlessly! But the pope and human law have hidden it from us and have put up an iron curtain in front of it. May God have mercy! Amen.

On the basis of this [discussion] everyone can easily understand what St. Paul means when he says, Romans 7 [:12], "The law is good, just, holy, and spiritual," and yet, it is still a killing letter. For it shows how man should be truly good, just, holy, spiritual, and in harmony with all things. But, as the law discloses, things are quite different with man; he is evil, unjust, sinful, carnal, and out of harmony with the law in every measure. This disharmony brings him eternal death, God's wrath, and disgrace before God, who wants his law fulfilled (as is only right) to the last letter and iota. Thus man recognizes himself in the mirror and in face of the letter or the law—how dead he is and in what disgrace he is with God. This knowledge makes him afraid and drives him to seek the

Spirit, who makes him good, godly, holy, spiritual, brings all things into accord with the law, and leads him to God's grace. The law then becomes dear to him, and the letter never kills him. Instead, he lives in the Spirit as the law demands; indeed, he no longer needs any law to teach him, for he knows it now by heart. Everything the law demands has become his nature and essence through the Spirit.

Thus we want to finish this [discussion] now with St. Augustine's fine comment regarding Psalm 17, in which he defines nicely and briefly what the letter is. He says, "The letter is nothing but LAW WITHOUT GRACE."[72] We, on the other hand, may say that the Spirit is nothing but GRACE WITHOUT LAW. Wherever the letter is, or the law without grace, there is no end to making laws, to teachings, and to works. And yet they are of no avail; no one becomes better through them, everything remains dead in the letter. On the other hand, wherever the Spirit of God exists, there is freedom, as St. Paul says [II Cor. 3:17]; there no teaching or law is needed; everything happens as it should happen. It is just like the man who has healthy, good vision; he does not need anyone to teach him how he should see. His vision is unhindered, and he has more than any teaching could help him get or give to him. But if his vision is not healthy, he is no longer free, and there is not enough teaching to help and protect him. He will have to worry about every single glance and have a rule about it in order to see. Thus it is St. Paul's opinion, I Timothy 1 [:9], that "the law is not laid down for the just," for the Spirit gives him everything that the law demands. Thus when he says, "God has made us preachers of the Spirit and not of the letter," he means that in the New Testament only grace and not law should be preached, so that men become truly godly through the Spirit.

Where are you now, Goliath Emser, with your spear and sword? You have buckled on this sword and let your own head be cut off with it. You could not have found a passage in the whole Bible which serves me as well against you as does this one on which you base your argument and comfort. You boast to strike with the blade, but you do not even get to the point of touching

[72] Luther's quote reflects the core of Augustine's commentary. Cf. *Expositions on the Book of Psalms*. *MPL* 36, 448-454; *PNF* 8, 49-50.

either sheath or hilt! Do you see now how you torture this saying spiritually, dragging it to the point that the letter means literal meaning and the Spirit means spiritual meaning? And you say that one should flee the letter and death. What a fine fencer you are! What a fine round you have fought with the famous fencer! Now then, since I have unbuckled your sword and have beheaded your arrogance, we shall come back again to your spear, your dagger, and your whole armor. I hope I shall uncover a dead Goliath, hold up his head, and show everyone your abomination, your threat, and your Goliath-like blasphemy. Let us see where your idol the pope will be with his laws, and where the entire army of these Philistines will be with their human teachings.

If the pope, with his bishops and priests, is a pious and loyal follower and heir to the apostolic see, I hope he is also obliged to execute their office and to preach the Spirit, in accord with these words of St. Paul. But if he is to preach the Spirit, he is not to preach any law but rather freedom from even the laws of God, as was said. Thus I ask: Where do this pope and priesthood come from? Not only do they never preach this Spirit, indeed, they do not even explain the letter correctly. Instead, they [preach] their own law, canon law, and nothing but human teaching—consecrated salt, water, vigils, masses, and whatever other tomfoolery like this you can name. They fill the world with them, obscure the law of God, and replace the veil of Moses which the apostles had lifted. Furthermore, they imprison the world in their law, destroy Christian freedom, ruin the Spirit, and drive away grace. [In return] for such abominable evil they steal, rob, and take all our money and property. St. Paul says that even the brilliance of Moses, that is, the law of God, is annulled through the preaching of the Spirit, so that only the brilliance of the Spirit shines in the church. But the pope does not only reintroduce Moses (which would still be a favor), but also replaces the veil before his eyes and, indeed, with his innumerable laws builds a stone wall before him so that now neither Spirit nor letter is recognized or preached, only fables about human teaching, of which Christ says in Matthew 15 [:8-9], "In vain do they serve me with human laws and teachings; they honor me with their lips, but their heart is far from me."

Where does such a pope come from with his priesthood?

Indeed, he is not the heir to the apostolic see, for he surely destroys the apostles' office and teaching with his teaching. St. Paul stands firm here, saying, "We are servants or preachers of the Spirit and not of the letter." But what does the pope say? "We are preachers neither of the Spirit nor of the letter, but only of our own dream which is written down nowhere." Where then does he come from? I shall tell you: Christ names him in Matthew 24 [:15, 23-26], "When you see the desolating sacrilege in the holy place" (that is, the pope with his own teaching in the church, sitting in the chair of the apostles) "let the reader understand. For false prophets, teachers, and Christs will arise, saying, 'Lo, here is the Christ!' or 'There he is!' and they will lead many people astray." That is, they will present human teachings with which one looks for Christ here and there, thinking one could find him through works and ceremonies. Instead, he [Christ] lets himself be found only in the heart, Spirit, and faith, everywhere, every time, and by everyone. St. Paul [says], II Thessalonians [2:3, 9], "The man of sin and perdition will be revealed through the activity of Satan"; and in Daniel 7 [8:23-25] [we read], "At the end of the Roman Empire, a king will arise. His strength will consist of externals and appearance" (that is, of human teachings which teach only external ways and habits, as, for example, the lives of bishops, priests, and monks with their vestments and external works and ways). "He will cause fearful destruction, his cunning will be swift and geared to making human laws and increasing them," etc. More another time.

Now listen to what else God says about your idol and human teachings: St. Paul, Colossians 2 [:8], "Take care that no one deceives you through philosophy and empty deceit, human teachings, commandments concerning temporal, external things, which are not according to Christ's teaching."[73] What kind of teachings these are follows later when he says, " If you died with Christ, why do you live as though you still lived with human laws and submit to regulations, 'Do not eat, Do not drink, Do not handle, Do not touch'? These are nothing but temporal things which perish as they are used, on which human commandments and laws center—and yet they [human laws] have the appearance of being well and

[73] Luther added to the text, "commandments concerning temporal, external things."

wisely ordered. Yet they are nothing but superstition and false, foolish humility, intent only on hurting the body and perverting it. They [human laws and teachings] satisfy their animal-like mind, but they are of no value."[74] Where is the blade of the goatish spirit here? Did not St. Paul in a masterful manner here expose the lives of pope, bishops, clerics, and monks? Such lives consist only of not eating this, or not drinking that, of not touching money or not wearing a certain vestment or color and so on. Their spirituality is geared to temporal things which perish as they are used and represent nothing but an illusion and a shadow of holiness. But they thus deceive everyone and subjugate the world to themselves with their foolish humility. This is the king whose strength consists only of externals and not of armor, word, or word of God, Daniel 8 [:23-25].

Again, Christ says in Matthew 7 [:15], "Beware of false teachers, who come to you in sheep's clothing but inwardly are ravenous wolves." What else is sheep's clothing but such external holiness in vestments, shoes, tonsures, eating, drinking, days, and places? These are temporal things, and inwardly, in faith, which grants eternal holiness and rests on eternal goods, they are nothing. Indeed, they are only destroyers of such faith and ravenous wolves, as St. Paul confesses too, I Timothy 2 [II Tim. 3:5, 7], saying, "They have a form of piety without substance. They always teach and learn and can never arrive at a knowledge of the truth." If all of this were removed and changed, as it should be, where then would the papacy be, since it rests upon only this? Christ himself has to remove it on the Last Day; otherwise, nothing will come of it. Here we see clearly that we should flee sheep's clothing, namely, human laws and works.

Again, St. Paul [writes], Galatians 1 [:8], "If anyone, even an angel from heaven, should teach you differently than you learned, let him be accursed." And Colossians 2 [:7-8], "Beware of that which is not taught according to Christ."[75] Indeed, St. Paul wants nothing taught here except Scripture. What do you say to that, Emser? Perhaps you will introduce SS. Augustine, Benedict,[76]

[74] Col. 2:20-23. Luther translated very freely here.

[75] Luther summarized these two verses in this manner.

[76] Benedict of Nursia (*ca.* 480-*ca.* 547), founder of the Benedictine Order.

Francis,[77] Dominic, and other fathers, all of whom taught and maintained holy but human teachings. I answer that this is not enough to satisfy Scripture. God's word is more than all the angels, saints, and creatures. Therefore, no one can say that these same saints never erred. Who will guarantee, then, that they did not err in this either, since Aaron and all the elect could err here, and since Scripture is clearly before me? I want to be and must be defeated with Scripture, not with the uncertain teachings and lives of men, no matter how holy they may be.

Moreover, these same saints kept their teachings free and open, without making commandments out of them. Thus he who wanted to live accordingly could do so, and, if he desired, could also give up doing so. And even if they had erred so much as to make a commandment and law out of them, which I do not believe, I would judge them according to the words of Ezekiel [14:9], "If the prophet be deceived, I, the Lord, have deceived that prophet." I would count them among those of whom Christ says, Matthew 24 [:24], that the rule of the Antichrist will be so brilliant, with such erroneous teachings, and will perform so many signs and wonders, that, if possible, even the elect will be led astray. Accordingly, these holy fathers with the Spirit they had in faith may have miraculously escaped from the dangers of human teaching, and yet, their successors may all be lost, for they hold only to their works and human teachings at the expense of their faith and Spirit. But your pope, who should allow these teachings to be as free as the saints had them, makes necessary eternal commandments and laws out of them with his confirming, just as he does with his own laws.

Furthermore, I think you know that in the Old Testament the people were as much obliged to listen to their priests as we are obliged to listen to ours. Nor did God permit them to teach their own teachings and he forbade their doing so. That is why Moses and all the prophets so often preferred the little word, "My voice." He commands in Deuteronomy 4 [:2], "You shall not add to the words I command you, nor take from them." And in Zechariah 2 [Mal. 2:7], "The people should seek God's commandments and

[77] Francis of Assisi (*ca.* 1182-1226), founder of the Franciscan Order.

teaching from the mouth of the priest for he is the messenger of God." And Christ says in Matthew 23 [:2-3] that one should listen to the scribes because they sit in the chair of Moses, that is, because they teach the law of Moses. On the other hand, Scripture calls all those who teach their own laws false prophets, false priests, deceivers, seducers, wolves, ravenous animals, of whom He says in Jeremiah 23 [:32], "They have led my people astray when I did not send them or charge them to teach such things." Indeed, all the priests were sent and, on the basis of their office, charged with teaching the law; but they were not charged with teaching their own law. Again, [He says in] Jeremiah 25 [23:21-22], "I did not send the prophets, yet they preached. I did not command anything to them, yet they taught. If they had remained in my teaching, then they would have proclaimed my words to the people, and I could have turned them from their evil lives."

How will you survive in the face of such passages, pope? Where are you, Emser, you who pretend that one must have more than God's word? You invent dagger and spear. God says here one should teach nothing but his word. Otherwise, he would not convert anyone. Thereby he teaches us this: if something more than God's word is presented to us, it is certainly erroneous, seductive, un-Christian, lying, and deceiving. It only hinders God's work and grace within us. For this reason St. Paul calls the Antichrist the "man of lawlessness and son of perdition" [II Thess. 2:3-4], because he will turn the whole world away from God through his own law and teaching and thus prevent its encounter with God. Thus he will be a master of all sin and of all perdition, and yet he will use the name and image of Christ, calling himself "most holy" [*Sanctissimum*], "vicar of God" [*Vicarium dei*], and "head of the church" [*caput Ecclesiae*]. He will persecute all those who do not obey him in this regard, as is more than evident and obvious in the example of the pope.

Is there any greater labor on the part of all prophets than that of fighting against human teaching and keeping only God's word in a people? All idolatry is nothing but human teaching—for example, the cows of Bethaven [Hos. 4:15-16], Aaron's calf, the idol Baal, and the like. Who can safeguard himself enough against such teachings? Aaron, the highest priest, worshiped the golden calf, and Christ himself says, Matthew 24 [:24], that such deceit and imagery could even lead the elect astray. If the pope did not have such a great following and so much deceit, he could never be the Antichrist. There has to be deceit and a following among all the bishops, priests, monks, universities, princes, and all authorities. There is but one item God does not permit him to cover up—here the ears of the ass still stick out—and that is his disregard for the word of God, which he does not preach either. He is content to preach his own teaching. His singing betrays the kind of bird he is.[78] Just as John envisaged in Revelation 13 [:11] an animal with two horns, looking like a lamb yet speaking like a dragon, so too the crowd of papists has to be viewed; they appear to be Christians yet preach like the devil. Daniel 11 [:37-38] said regarding this that the Antichrist will give no heed to the god of his fathers, will not propagate his teaching, and will not be married; instead he will honor his god *Maozim*[79]—that is, he prohibits marriage only for the sake of his appearance and that of his papists. In place of God and his gospel he erects the idol *Maozim,* his decretals and his teachings, and binds spirituality to external places, as Christ says, "They will say, 'Here is Christ!' and, 'There is Christ!' " [Matt. 24:23].

Again, Jeremiah 19 [:5] says regarding the great Baal worship that they even sacrificed and burned their children, thinking they thereby did a great service to God. But God said, "I have not commanded it, and it never entered my heart," etc. From this it also becomes clear that nothing should be preached or presented to the people that God has neither commanded nor desired. Now we are certain that the pope with his papists has no commandment from God to propagate his own teaching in Christendom. It is nothing but a trick of the devil to hinder God and his commandment and the salvation of all men. Therefore, my goat should first prove and

[78] From the German proverb, *den Vogel erkennt man an seinen Federn,* meaning, "the bird is recognized by his feathers."

[79] Hebrew for "god of fortresses." The Vulgate, which Luther quoted, made a proper noun of the Hebrew word. In a letter concerning secret masses in 1534, Luther related the word to "mass": "He [the Antichrist] calls the idol *Maozim,* using the very letters of the word mass. Obviously he would have preferred to call it mass if he had not been constrained to use words of concealment. But he portrays the idol in such a way that we can certainly see he has the abominable mass in mind." Cf. *EA* 31, 390, and 41, 302.

make clear that God approves of his spear and dagger. He thinks it is sufficient when the spear is long and the dagger is short. It should be sufficient to call the one usage and the other human teaching, and [he thinks] that I should drop Scripture and make my judgment according to his mind instead.

So that you may also see the extravagance of your cleverness, listen to me: I certainly know about human teaching and usage with which you fight against me. How could I not know them, since I fight against them? What are you doing, you great philosopher, by bringing up against me the very thing that I am attacking? You should instead protect it by other means. If I besieged a city with an army and shot against its walls and gates until they collapsed, and you, from inside, became very angry at me and determined to get up and fight me, and yet if you did no more than to point out with your hand precisely these same walls and gates which I had shot down, shouted menacingly that I should look at them, and then pretended you had defeated me in this manner—what should I think of you? I would summon a cooper to have him put one or two hoops around your head so that it would not burst from too much nonsense. But even though you have heard how I make use of Scripture and attack human teaching and usage and will not accept their validity unless they have Scripture on their side, you are so smart that you do not protect them with Scripture but only carry them around, showing them to me as if I had never seen them. You claim you have won and have broken open the cuirassier, but everyone can see how desperate you are.[80] St. Augustine, in *Against the Donatist Petilian,*[81] considered it a great joke that when Ticonius introduced the thunder of Scripture against him [i.e., Petilian], he could answer only with the human teachings of his ancestors. He [Augustine] thought it was the most foolish

[80] Proverbial German, *wie dich die hunds tage reytten,* literally, "how the dog days plague you."

[81] Cf. *MPL* 43, 246-383; *PNF* 4, 519-628. Actually, Augustine's argument on this particular issue of Donatism (a schismatic movement in North Africa emphasizing the morality of the person over against the office of the ministry) is found in his tract *Against the Epistle of Parmenian. MPL* 43, 34-107. Ticonius (*ca.* 380), founder of a reformatory Donatist group, opposed the strict Donatists led by Petilian and Parmenian on the basis of Scripture. Augustine praised him for this, but at the same time denounced him for maintaining membership in schismatic Donatism.

answer. And I, who also introduce only Scripture, should regard goat Emser's answer as dear and precious wisdom when it is but human fancy and imagination presented without scriptural foundation! Nevertheless, he immediately threatens with it, calling it dagger and usage. It would therefore be good to advise you to stay home with your spear and dagger and to fight with Scripture against me, just as I do against you. What has become of your philosophy now which teaches "not to beg the question" (*petere principium*)? I think it is idiotic and your Aristotle is an arch-fool.[82] The same fate awaits a verse-maker[83] who wants to be a philosopher and theologian as awaited the ass with the bagpipes.

If the Manichaean heresy were to arise today and men pretended that Scripture did not give us enough, but that the Holy Spirit had awakened them and one should follow them, how would you, with all your papists, fend them off? In this case would you also not do any more than point with your finger to your teaching? Or would you say, "Oh, you are too slow; we ourselves have already discovered that one should believe and obey more than Scripture offers"? How nicely you papists would stand if you strengthened your enemy with your own example and admitted teaching and living outside Scripture! Now, is it not foolish and shameful that we ourselves not only confess freely but also boast that our cause is not founded upon Scripture? We go so far as to follow the example of the cuckoo[84] and sing our own praises as good Christians, berating everyone else as heretics, even though they have all of Scripture on their side, as we well know. This should be so intolerable to us, if we were not completely mad, that if our enemy accused us of doing it, we would risk life and limb [to deny] it. Is there anyone who would not rightfully mock us, if we ourselves confess that our foe has Scripture but our cause does not? How could we sing about ourselves more disgracefully and about our

[82] *Ertzstultus,* a pun on Aristotle.

[83] *Versifex.* Luther repeatedly used this expression against Emser, who composed a Latin poem in his tract *Answer to the Raging Bull in Wittenberg.* Enders, *op. cit.,* II, 43-44. One of Emser's poems dealt with the disputation at Leipzig in 1519. Cf. the German translation in *St. L.* 18, 1488-1489.

[84] From the German proverb, *Der Kuckuc ruft sein eigen namen aus,* which literally says, "The cuckoo calls out his own name." Cf. Thiele, *Luthers Sprichwörtersammlung,* No. 210.

enemies more honestly? Nor should we present such crude folly to the whole world as wisdom. Indeed, it is time that we used the scabbards of these brave war heroes for latrines!

Moreover, what I wanted [to show] in all my books was precisely what Emser confesses here. Yet he complains about me with a great, earnest, and murderous noise! Did I not also say that the affairs of the pope and of all papists are nothing but human teaching and usage, without any Scripture—something Emser wants to extort from me at all cost? What else am I fighting about but precisely this? I do it so that everyone may understand the true difference between divine Scripture and human teaching or usage and so that a Christian heart does not buy the one for the other—straw for gold, hay for silver, and wood for jewels—as St. Paul teaches, I Corinthians 2 [3:12], and St. Augustine too in many places, as well as the holy carnal law, if the hyperlearned "licentiate of holy canon law" had looked at it soberly. Why does this goat accuse me so fiercely when we both are of one mind and agree on the matter? Perhaps it was my sin to have spoken impolitely when I did not call human teaching a short dagger and usage a long spear? The reason is that I am not a rhymester. Moreover, since he has no other reason to write books than to show off his masterly skill in inventing names, to call human teaching a short dagger and usage a long spear, it would not have helped me at all to call it that. He might still, just to teach us, have called human teaching "goat horn" and usage "goat beard" and thereby knocked me down and confused me. Such wise and intelligent masters do philosophy and the arch-fool Aristotle create through the sophists!

If, then, goat Emser makes a murderous noise about me throughout the whole book for the sake of his anti-Christian head in Rome and thus gains great honor, it is only proper for me to make a noise about him for the sake of my head in heaven, whom he slanders and blasphemes. He may pretend that the Holy Spirit and Christ did not teach us enough, that Scripture is not enough, and that God's word must have an addition; and that whoever has nothing more than God's word, Scripture, and teaching is poison, a heretic, an apostate, and the worst man on earth and that all those who live with such words of God and such teaching and do not keep human teaching are condemned, cursed, and to be burned.

Thus Christ and the Holy Spirit too must be guilty and responsible; indeed, they deserve such blasphemy, since they produced and daily preserve such blasphemous, accursed, and condemned people through their word and teaching.

Look here! Is he not the greatest blasphemer ever known? Who indeed has ever heard more blasphemous, poisonous, hellish, heretical, raging, and nonsensical words than those Emser here pours from his poisonous and hellish mouth and lets stink to heaven? This poor creature spits and sprays his spit at God his Creator so terribly and gruesomely that it is abominable to listen to or speak of. If he could at least show where the Holy Spirit teaches too little and where Scripture needs the additions of men, there would be some appearance of reason. But now he himself admits that Scripture is on our side and he is unable to criticize us on the basis of Scripture; he also freely admits that his human work is not in Scripture, yet he nevertheless pours out such blasphemy upon us—that is, upon Scripture, as he himself admits—that I would not have thought even a devil in hell would be permitted to do such things. I say this only so that you, dear goat, may see that if sheer murderous noise and raging amplification could strengthen your cause, I could strengthen my cause even more with them. My cause does not need them. It is well grounded in Scripture. Yours certainly does, because it is built upon human dreams and upon the chamber of his [the pope's] heart.[85]

I trust that from all this everyone may see what Emser's spear and dagger are and what kind of bout he has fought with the famous fencer. I shall improve things for him when he returns for another round. But I do not swear to it either by my priesthood or by my holiness.[86] I shall satisfy him in other ways. Here I shall conclude with the three main parts of his book, the sword, the spear, and the dagger. They are so overcome that the whole book built upon them is also overcome. But to explain my view again: since

[85] *Scrinium pectoris.* A reference to the habit of storing official documents in a "chest" *(scrinium)* during the days of the Holy Roman Empire. Pope Boniface VIII (1294-1303), who added his own collection to existing canon law, claimed authority over canon law by saying, "The Roman pontiff has all laws in the chamber [*scrinium*] of his heart." Cf. *LW* 44, 202, n. 215; and below p. 281, n. 34.

[86] Cf. above, p. 131, n. 29.

Emser concedes that I have opposed neither the articles of faith nor Scripture—whereby he becomes my unwilling, unfavorable, but therefore all the more convincing witness to the fact that I am a truly devout Christian and have falsely been called a heretic by him for no reason—I shall wrest one more thing from him which he never expected and which he does not like to let go.

He should grant us freedom from human laws so that it is up to us whether or not we obey them. And if we are indeed to live under them, as I have taught and still teach, he should nevertheless grant us permission to state that they are neither necessary nor good for us and that we do not have to obey them; that moreover the pope is a tyrant, without any right to make these laws and that he thus commits an injustice; that we may obey them, not because it is our duty or the pope's due, but because it is our own free will to do so to serve him, just as Christ says in Matthew 6 [5:25] that we should make friends with the accuser; and that those who do not obey them [laws] should rightly not be called heretics. All this should be granted to us, and we shall prove it in the following manner.

When we have Scripture and Scripture has us, as Emser admits—which is undoubtedly satisfactory to God—we are more than sufficiently praised as devout Christians; those who slander us have to give the lie to themselves. What more do you people want from us? When you call us heretics, whom do you call heretics, since you yourselves admit that we are in agreement with Scripture? Can you condemn those whom God justifies? Does not truth punish you through your own Caiaphian and Baalian mouths? For you are only put in office to lead us to God and to God's word and to tend us with God's word, as Christ says in Matthew 4 [:4], "Man shall live by every word that proceeds from the mouth of God." Why do you pretend to lead us further and indeed pull us away from God toward yourselves and drive us from his word to your teaching and usage? Is this the office of shepherds or of wolves?[87]

[87] Cf. Emser's statement in *Against the Un-Christian Book of the Augustinian Martin Luther:* "Help me, you true and living Son of God, Holy Lord Jesus Christ, against the raging wolf, who aims to lead astray your sheep which you have bought and redeemed with your rose-colored blood." Enders, *op. cit.*, I, 15.

Therefore I say: Let us be free, Emser, and admit, as your conscience implores you, that the pope is a tyrant who has no right to make laws which are neither good nor necessary for us anyway. And, so that conscience does not vanish from the pope and you papists, admit that you are thieves, robbers, wolves, seducers, and betraying Judases with your laws. Then we shall gladly obey and endure them, just as Christ endured his rope and cross, to which Judas, the ancestor of the pope, had brought him. Then they do not harm us, and we endure them in the same way we endure someone's taking clothes, money, property, even life from us. We will even endure you too, when you burden our Christian freedom with your insane, foolish, and useless laws. But our conscience remains free from you and unburdened. But if you were to insist (as you do) that it is your right to do so and that we should take it as proper and right—just as though a murderer forced me to say that he has a claim on my life and property—then, Emser, we shall cry No as long as there is breath in us. For you wish to imprison our conscience so that we should stand in fear as before the law—even when it is an unjust law. Thus you want to catch us and strangle us with innumerable ropes, just as you do with your unlawful ban, forcing people to obey your roguery.

We shall endure injustice from you, but we shall never approve of it. Therefore, tell your idol the pope that he may make laws over me—as many as he pleases. I shall obey them all. But also tell him that he has no right to do so and that I do not owe obedience to him. However, I shall gladly endure his injustice, as Christ teaches [Matt. 5:39-42], and I shall no longer oppose the pope. Everything might as well be bad! What more do you want from me? Did I not teach this in [the commentary on] Galatians[88] and in all my books? But when the pope drives the whole world as though he had a right to do so, he confuses innumerable souls and seduces them into hell. That is why he is the "man of lawlessness and the son of perdition" [II Thess. 2:3], because he has imprisoned consciences and forced them to sanction his injustice, thus filling the world with sin and destruction. For anyone who believes the

[88] Cf. *Lectures on Galatians*, 1519. *LW* 27, 151-410.

pope has the right and power to make laws soon thinks he has to obey them as good and necessary and he does not endure them as tyranny and injustice. He obeys them unwillingly; he would like to get rid of the law but is not able to, and so he finally suffocates in sins. For whoever dislikes doing something he must do or thinks he must do, sins in his heart. Accordingly, all the pope's commandments (which are innumerable) are nothing but a rope strangling souls. With these he causes only sin and destruction in the whole world and thus destroys all of Christendom, as Daniel prophesied [Dan. 8:24-25; 9:27]. Christ therefore calls him an "abomination" [Matt. 24:15]. Few people, if any, escape him, except those who die in the cradle.

Do you understand me now, Emser? I do not desire to be free of human laws and teachings. I only desire to have the conscience free and to have all Christians make the sign of the cross against a faith which believes that the pope is right in his rule. For such a faith destroys faith in Christ and drowns the whole world in nothing but sin and destruction. The pope and you papists are the pious heirs of this sort of thing. You, who do no more than propagate such superstition, seduce the world, destroy Christian faith, and lead all souls to the devil when you should believe only in Christ and preach freedom from human laws so as to remain "ministers of the Spirit" and not "of the letter." Likewise, I do not desire to be free of Emser's slandering, hatred, and envy; but I do desire to be free in conscience so that I am allowed to believe Emser is tyrannizing me and doing me an injustice. For if I should sanction this as right, my conscience would already be imprisoned and could not be free until Emser ceased to hate, which might never happen. For if I had to sanction it, which I would not do willingly (since I cannot), I would be sinning endlessly against my conscience. Thus the whole world is now sinning endlessly and is perishing if it believes that the pope is right with his rule, domination, and governance. Yet no one is doing so willingly, since everyone hates the papacy—except those who want to enjoy it—so that it is justifiably called an abomination. The pope has therefore imprisoned the whole world with false conscience and superstition. People have to sin endlessly and unwillingly and [finally] perish. Woe to you, you terrible abomination! Come, Lord Jesus Christ, and save us from the Antichrist! Push his see into the abyss of hell, as he deserves, so that sin and destruction may cease. Amen.

Concerning the Indolence of the Papists

Let this be enough for the time being. Now let us pursue Emser's and the papists' lies and indolence further, in regard to the writings of the fathers and the usages upon which they build.

Emser and all the papists say that St. Peter was in Rome and ruled as a bishop for twenty-five years. This crude lie has been in existence longer than a thousand years, so that a long spear would indeed have resulted if usage would suffice to base the truth upon, as Emser dreams. Even St. Jerome is led into this error.[89] The papists began to lie very early and have continued to inherit and to increase the lie so much from one to the other that the pope is now nothing but lies. But we shall make this lie about the twenty-five years of St. Peter in Rome so clear that even Emser is forced to grasp it.

St. Luke, Luke 3 [:1], writes that John the Baptist began to preach in the fifteenth year of the Emperor Tiberius' reign.[90] Then, although no one really knows how long Christ preached, we could let the common opinion prevail that it was for a duration of four and a half years, namely, until the nineteenth or twentieth year of Tiberius' reign, and that he was crucified, resurrected, and gave the Holy Spirit to the apostles in that same year. After that Tiberius ruled until the twenty-fourth year. After him Caius ruled[91] for four years, then Claudius[92] for fourteen years; and after that Nero[93] for fourteen years too. Thus there would be a total of thirty-six years from the twentieth year of Tiberius' reign until the last year of Nero's. This was the year in which they say that St. Peter was killed by Nero.

[89] In the chronology *(Chronicon)* which Luther used to establish his own chronology. Cf. *MPL* 27, 554, and *LW* 41, 23, n. 36.

[90] Tiberius (14-37).

[91] Caius, called Germanicus (37-41).

[92] Claudius (41-54).

[93] Nero (54-68).

Now if St. Peter had been in Rome for twenty-five years, beginning with the fourth year of Claudius' reign, as they say, he was in Jerusalem and Antioch for only eleven years after Christ's ascension. Again, they say that he was in Antioch for seven years, and therefore in Jerusalem for only six years. St. Paul falls among the liars here and misses the mark, for he writes in Galatians 1 [:18] that he saw St. Peter for the first time three years after his own conversion in Jerusalem, which took place in the fourth year after the ascension of our Lord at the earliest. Moreover, more than fourteen years later, Peter, James, and John are found in Jerusalem [Gal. 2:1-10]. This makes eighteen years altogether that St. Paul alone attributes to St. Peter in Jerusalem. Who knows how long he stayed there after that?

If you add to these eighteen or perhaps twenty years the seven years in Antioch and the twenty-five years in Rome, then St. Peter would have been crucified by Emperor Nero forty-six or forty-seven years after Christ's ascension. But Nero had already died ten years earlier, namely, in the thirty-sixth year! That, I think, is talking a little too foolishly.[94] This is what happens to people who build on human teaching and usage, do not look at Scripture, and swallow whatever they find in the writings of the fathers. What now, Emser? If someone had a good dagger and spear to illumine this obscure fog of Scripture, he could make six years of the eighteen years St. Paul says Peter spent in Jerusalem, so that there could be seven years for Antioch and twenty-five years for Rome—indeed, Scripture is an obscure fog here!

In addition to those who say that St. Peter came to Rome in the fourth year of Claudius' reign, there are others who say he came in the second year, and so they give Peter twenty-seven years in Rome and three years in Jerusalem. Here, too, St. Luke, in Acts 18 [:2], agrees with [the chronology] of Paul in Galatians 1 [:18], saying that Claudius drove all the Jews from Rome, among whom he names Aquila and Priscilla. How then could St. Peter have come to Rome under Claudius? In short, I have never read more inconsistent and more uncertain histories than those about

[94] A German proverb, *unter die tauben werffen,* which literally speaks of throwing something to the pigeons.

St. Peter's activities in Rome. As a result, there are many people who say freely and openly that St. Peter never went to Rome. You papists have brought this about with your lies and inconsistent writings. The one says that he was martyred together with St. Paul on the same day, the other says there is a difference of two years. Whatever is written about it is shaky.

Although I maintained that St. Peter was in Rome, and still do, I would not want to die for it as for an article of faith. Moreover, I do not know how it could be either maintained or proven; indeed, no one (as far as I know) can prove it. It is not an article of faith, and no one is a heretic if he does not believe St. Peter was in Rome. On the other hand, it is outrageous to deny it unless it is thoroughly refuted. The safest thing is to let it remain uncertain and doubtful. For we ought to believe only what God has commanded us to believe in Scripture, and no one should either add to it or retract from it, as Moses teaches [Deut. 12:32] and as Paul says, Galatians 4 [3:15], "No one changes a man's testament or adds to it." How much less, then, should anyone change or add to God's testament.

But it is my opinion that it was by God's special providence that St. Paul's journey to Rome rather than St. Peter's was recorded in Scripture. For he foresaw very well that the papists would build their papacy upon it. That is why he placed them in mire and sand before they began to build, not leaving them any stable foundation. For if it cannot be proven with certainty by Scripture that St. Peter was in Rome (which is not possible), the papacy already lies in mud and amounts to nothing. For just as unnecessary as it is to believe that St. Peter was in Rome, since Scripture does not say so, so is it equally unnecessary to believe that the pope is the heir to his see and [therefore] the pope. Now see what the pope is sitting on! All they do with their propaganda is enable us to find their false and unworthy foundation even earlier, and so we may see them unhorse themselves with their wild raging. That is why I come to the conclusion here that it is unnecessary to consider the pope either the pope or the heir to St. Peter's see until they verify with Scripture that St. Peter was in Rome. Hey now, you papists! Be clever and lively, and look for spear, dagger, and sword to drive away this fog of Scripture!

But in thinking about it, I ask myself whether there was not a mistake in regard to Peter's twenty-five years in Rome; perhaps someone either said or wrote that St. Peter only came to Rome after the twenty-fifth year, and some people then understood it in the sense of his having been in Rome for twenty-five years. For if he was in Jerusalem for eighteen years, as Paul says in Galatians 1 [:18], and in Antioch for seven years, as they say, this adds up to twenty-five years. Accordingly, he would have been in Rome eleven years and been crucified by Nero in his last year—that is, the thirty-sixth year after the Lord's ascension. Thus it could also be a mistake [when they say] that he came to Rome in the third or fourth year of Claudius' reign, since it occurred in Nero's third or fourth year; accordingly, he would have lived eleven years under Nero, until Nero's last year, namely, the fourteenth. Indeed, it could not have happened otherwise if he came to Rome at all. But I shall let it stand as it stands.

Concerning Clerical Marriage

Since I gave the advice[95] that if a godly minister were weak, burdened with a woman and a child, and wanted to marry, he should listen to me and go ahead with it, you, you chaste goat, make a murderous noise saying, "Well, let the raging devil follow you in my stead." You boast very much about your extraordinary and blameless chastity, and your goat smells like real balsam in your nose. I answer: Well, you holy, holy virgin St. Emser, why has your chastity become so steely and so hard and unmerciful toward poor sinners? Moreover, I did not give the advice in a way to make your dear chastity follow me, as you pervert my words and poison the people in accordance with the custom of your Christian love and divine priesthood. Instead, my advice was to a poor priest burdened with children who is otherwise godly and leading a decent life. Your Holiness knows all this very well, and it does not involve you at all. I have neither given to nor taken anything from canons, vicars, evil priests who keep whores, or Emsers. But you have made a firm decision and thought, "Well, we must curse this

[95] Cf. *To the Christian Nobility of the German Nation,* 1520. *LW* 44, 177-178.

monk and lie about him, even if I should have to make up the accusations myself."[96] Thus you rage against me only with human laws, just as though you had won from me the concession that human laws count with me; and you think it unnecessary first to ground them in Scripture.

Your lily-white chastity does not need to tell me what human law says about this. I knew that very well and, if challenged, would not need the instruction of either a goat or an ass, but would instead have answered that St. Paul, I Timothy 4 [:1-3], does not speak as a man but as God himself when he says very clearly that to prohibit marriage is devilish teaching. An "iron eater"[97] would show his teeth here and bite a hole into my armor. But you flee before such a passage as if your horns were on fire. You fall silent and disappear like a water bubble. Why do you not strike me for once with such a sword too? I shall stand up against you without any guard. How often do I have to yell at you, you crude and unlearned papists, before you come with Scripture at least once? Scripture, Scripture, Scripture! Don't you hear me, you dumb goat and crude ass? Hey goat, get angry and butt me once! But do not step back too far so that you will not exhaust yourself in the attack! Are you not ashamed, you great teachers of the world, to let yourselves be mocked so often in regard to Scripture, even though you should be using it to defy me most emphatically and to gain the advantage over me? Indeed, you cannot deny that there never was a teacher on earth except the pope who prohibited marriage, meat, eggs, milk, butter, and the like and then sold them again afterward—and did so throughout the whole world. There have certainly been heretics who rejected marriage; but there were not many. Moreover, no uniform law was ever made out of it. Thus you cannot find fault with St. Paul or deny that such commandments of the pope are commandments of the devil, as St. Paul clearly says. Here you

[96] From the German proverb, *ein sache von eim alten zaun brechen,* literally, "to break something out of an old fence." Cf. Thiele, *Luthers Sprichwörtersammlung,* No. 32.

[97] *Eyssenfresser,* a man who performs marvelous feats with his mouth. The iron biter *(eysenbeysser)* appears as one of the figures in Murner's *Guild of Fools (Schelmenzunft).* He typifies people who like to talk without saying anything. Cf. *WA* 7, 674, n. 3.

must allow the pope to be the apostle of the devil and the Antichrist. You cannot prevent it, in spite of all your efforts.

Tell me, then: Is it proper for Christian people, especially priests, to be obedient to the devil and to follow his apostle the pope? If the priesthood had followed him up to now, forced and seduced by tyranny or deceit, does it not have the power to send the devil and his apostle packing? Or must they remain knowingly, unnecessarily, without courage and against their wills, under the laws of the devil? Where are you, Emser? Are you not listening? Are you sleeping with Baal? Or did you go on a journey [I Kings 18:27]? There is no question here of whether or not your chastity should follow me. I do not ask whether or not the devil follows me in your stead. At this point nobody cares about your wanting and following, or that of all the devils. Want, rage, follow, and fume until you have had enough! This is the crux of the matter,[98] and you should look with both eyes to see, if you can, whether such commandments are proper or improper. You are so evil that you knock down the Apostle himself!

To make sure I speak to you in the appropriate manner, you hyperlearned scholar in grammar, logic, and philosophy, do not make "a mode of necessity" [*modalem de necesse*] out of "a proposition of particulars" [*proposition de inesse*],[99] you sharp logician; do not "turn a fact into law" [*ius ex facto*], you hyperlearned licentiate of the holy burned law. And do not make a general "obligation" [*debere*] out of your personal "doing" [*facere*], you fledgling poet and grammarian—unless you want to run to the arch-fool[100] to look for "what is simply secondary" [*secundum quid simpliciter*],[101] as

---

[98] Proverbial German, *Hie ligt der hass,* meaning literally, "This is where the rabbit lies."

[99] Both terms were widely used in medieval logic. The *propositio de inesse* is an attributive proposition referring to the accidental or particular. The *modalis de necesse* is a modal proposition referring to necessity as one of six modes under discussion. Luther accused Emser of regarding the tradition about the priesthood as more significant than its origins, thus confusing an attributive proposition with a mode of necessity. For a brief explanation of this feature of medieval logic, cf. Jacques Maritain, *Formal Logic* (London: Sheed and Ward, n.d.).

[100] A pun on Aristotle. Cf. above p. 197, n. 82.

[101] A term used in medieval logic, defined as "an argument in which a proposition is used as a premise, without attention given to some obvious condition which would affect the proposition's application." Cf. Paul Edwards (ed.), *The Encyclopedia of Philosophy* (8 vols.; New York: Macmillan Co., 1967), VIII, 64.

you do with the priesthood where you call the literal, external, deadly priesthood—indeed the null and void priesthood—"simply priesthood" [*sacerdotium simpliciter*] and the one, spiritual, true, and living priesthood the "secondary one" [*secundum quid*]. How well you know what *secundum quid et simpliciter* means! You are just as fine a logician as you are a theologian. If I did not know logic and philosophy, you crude asses might well dare to make a name for yourselves as logicians and philosophers, even though you know as much about these things as an ass knows about music.[102] And although you have learned to use the words—as nuns use the psalter and the parakeet uses language—you nevertheless know neither the use nor the application of them; the farmer is recognized by his work and not by his dress.

But let me give you a piece of advice here: take your short dagger, with which you kill the cuirassiers, and say that this passage is obscure fog; we cannot understand it without the interpretation of the fathers. Further, with your high mind persuade us that we cannot know the meaning of "prohibit," "marry," "doctrine," "demons," "abstain," "food," "God," "create"; change "prohibit" into "command," "marry" into "to be without marriage," "demons" into "church," "God" into "pope," "create" into "be obedient." For you took it upon yourself to change and to pervert everything according to your whim. You have a good example and teaching for all of this in St. Aristotle, who also calls "nonbeing" [*non ens*] what others call "being" [*ens*], and "being" what others call "nonbeing." In addition, he invented "act and power, in itself and accidentally" [*actum et potentiam per se et per accidens*], just as you have invented the spear and dagger, sheath and blade. Your canon law assists you too, which creates sin where there is none and law where there is none, as is quite evident in ceremonies. It is therefore very fitting that you need to explain such philosophy and canon law without obscure Scripture.

Since, with this prohibition [i.e., against the marriage of priests] the pope is clearly proven to be the apostle of the devil, let Your Humble Chastity listen to the consequences. First, the whole priesthood, for the salvation of its soul, must flee from the

[102] Cf. above, p. 197.

pope, cursing and opposing him as if he were the devil himself. It must break the vow forced on it in the act of consecration, which was made for the devil and not for God [I Tim. 4:1-3], as your own holy law itself says, "It is not expedient for faith to obey evil laws."[103] All this is not my advice but that of St. Paul, who here speaks up strongly and judges the whole matter by saying that such teaching is of the devil and not of God. Second, it follows that all bishops and priests who follow the pope in this matter are messengers and helpers of the devil too. Thus it is clear that the papacy with its priesthood is the kingdom of the devil and the rule of the Antichrist, and that Emser is the defender of the devil and of the Antichrist. For to accept the devil's teaching and to defend it can surely never be justified. Who, in spite of all you papists, will oppose me here? Look around for the cuirassier and strike with your blade, you miserable Emser! However, if you say that St. Paul's word is directed against Faustus[104] and Jovinian,[105] whom Jerome and Augustine have opposed, I will judge that you have run around in the carnival mask of the past.[106] St. Jerome reproves Jovinian for praising marriage, whereas you say he prohibited marriage. This is how well you read Jerome and history! Faustus was a Manichaean whom Augustine did not oppose on the grounds of marriage. You crude ass's head! Should you not be more careful what you write about such matters? Some people have been called "Tatians,"[107] but their cause is nothing compared with the pope's prohibition. And even if it were, it is enough for me that the pope is just as much a heretic as they are, since he collects almost every

[103] *Decreti Secunda Pars,* causa XXII, ques. 3. *CIC* 1, 875.

[104] Faustus of Mileve (*ca.* 400), one of Augustine's teachers. Cf. Augustine, *Reply to Faustus, the Manichaean. MPL* 42, 207-518; *PNF* 4, 155-345.

[105] Jovinian (*ca.* 400), who opposed the meritoriousness of asceticism, was called "the Epicurus of Christians" because he maintained the equality before God of virgins and wives. Jerome attacked him in *Against Jovinianus. MPL* 23, 222-354; *PNF*² 6, 346-416.

[106] That is, Emser hides behind references to past events. Cf. his statement in *Against the Un-Christian Book of the Augustinian Martin Luther:* "This saying of St. Paul [I Tim. 4:1-3] should not be dragged in here, as Luther does, pulling it in by the hair. Rather, it refers to the heretics Jovinian, Faustus, and others who wanted to condemn marriage altogether in the church. Their heresy was sufficiently exposed and proven by Augustine and Jerome." Enders, *op. cit.,* I, 80-81.

[107] Named after Tatian. Cf. below, p. 292, n. 48.

heresy like a pot of soup, just as the Romans did in earlier times with their Pantheon—but more on that another time.

How very nicely you also reject St. Ulrich's epistle,[108] even though I do not build upon it, since I want to checkmate you not with human teaching but with Scripture. But if he had been on your side he would have had to count, since Scotus, Gerson, Bede,[109] and whoever else you want must count. Is this not fine logic: St. Ulrich's epistle was not found in Augsburg, therefore it is not by St. Ulrich? Quintilian's book[110] is found neither in Rome nor in Italy, therefore it is not by Quintilian. Emser's book is not found in Dresden; is it therefore not by Emser? Did Malmsey wine or Rastrum beer[111] teach you your logic? And who told you that St. Ulrich's epistle was not found in Augsburg, except your logic which always infers from the individual to the universal?

Indeed, I think that you have written this book under the impression that the whole world consists only of Jerome Emser, Jerome Walther,[112] and other similar clods, so clumsily do you step along without caution or care. For example, you write that it is necessary to burn heretics today because printing easily increases books and error, which did not occur before. You do not even have enough brains in your crude head to remember that John Huss and Jerome [of Prague] were burned at Constance before printing was

[108] Bishop Ulrich of Augsburg (d. 973), a saint since 993, is associated with a letter criticizing the prohibition against clerical marriage by the pope. Pope Gregory VII condemned the contents of the letter during a synod in 1074. Emser's "rejection" reads: "I do not believe that St. Ulrich wrote the epistle, recently published in his name and discovered in Holland, as they say. These are my reasons: first, his holy and chaste life; second, the style and composition are closer to our own time than to the time of St. Ulrich; third, it undoubtedly would have been found long ago at his monastery in Augsburg rather than in Holland; and fourth, it sounds like a lie when the epistle reports that St. Gregory is said once to have found more than six thousand heads of children wrapped in a blanket. For how could priests have had so many children?" Enders, *op. cit.*, I, 85-86. On the problems of content and authorship of St. Ulrich's epistle, cf. Albert Hauck (ed.), *Realencyklopädie für protestantische Theologie und Kirche* (24 vols.; 3rd ed. rev.; Leipzig, 1896-1913), XX, 213.

[109] Bede the Venerable (674-735), the most eminent English church father.

[110] M. Fabius Quintilianus (A.D. 35-95), author of the famous textbook for Latin oratory, *De Institutio oratoria.*

[111] Cf. above, p. 76, nn. 38, 39.

[112] Jerome Walther, Emser's friend and mayor of Leipzig. When Emser died, Walther had a tombstone placed on his grave in Dresden.

invented. It is a similar [stupidity] when you compare me with the pharmacists who write fine titles on their boxes but put poison into them; for I write the name "Jesus" in my poisonous books—even though it is not I but the printers who do so throughout the book; I do it only on the first sheet. Where did you ever see such pharmacists? Or do the pharmacists, too, have to turn into murderers and betrayers on my account? Your raving hatred does not let you put down a single good word. Ecclesiasticus [21:26] said it well, "The fools' hearts are in their mouth, but the wise men's mouth is in their hearts." That is why fools just prattle whatever comes to their mind, but wise men think before they speak. Why should you write anything good if you spit out so carelessly and thoughtlessly whatever comes into your mouth? And why do you always strike your own cheeks?

Therefore my advice, as before, is not to the chaste Emsers or miraculously holy goats but to the poor crowd of fallen priests: whoever cannot hold out may get married and still live without sin. If he cannot live without lust, despite the pope with all his devilish prohibitions, he should not be thrown into turmoil because of the arbitrary promise forced from him by the bishop in the place of the devil. For it certainly was not made sincerely or voluntarily. If the pope had caused no other disaster than these prohibitions he would still be the Antichrist, and he could be called the "man of sin" and the "son of perdition and abomination" [II Thess. 2:3; Dan. 9:27], since so many sins and so much perdition have come from this one prohibition. If you, goat, would take yourself by the nose you too would have to admit that it did not bring you much holiness. If you are chaste, God be praised! Just watch out how long it will last! You are not over the hill yet! Do not despise your poor fallen neighbors, and, you great giant, do not devour all the tainted and sick children!

I want to say one more thing and then come to an end: you and Murner, together with many others, burden me with the charge that I criticize only the vices of the clergy and remain silent about the punishable vices of the nobility and worldly authorities. Since you see this great fault of mine, why do you not criticize them and thus rectify my fault? Why do you always pick on me regarding something you yourselves do not want to do? Indeed, why do you not censure the vices of the clergy? Do I have to deal with everything in one book? Even if I had done it, you certainly would have found a reason to say that I did not maintain my course,[113] that I wanted to address the nobility but scolded it instead—as you do when you say that I taught less than the mendicant orders did and accuse me of being a bird fouling my own nest.[114] What could I write that your raging hatred would not slander, since you blaspheme God's word and work and look only for ways to increase your slander and lies? But I shall give you an answer. I think I have censured the nobility and the world more than you clergy—for example, in my books on good works,[115] on the Ten Commandments,[116] and my address to the German nobility.[117] In these books I have never really touched on the clerical vices, such as unchastity, avarice, hatred, gluttony, pride, indolence—except in the one addressed to the German nobility. But in that one I showed not the vices of the clergy in general but the avarice of the pope and the Roman curia and a small portion of its abominable nature. My dear fellows, truth hurts you. That is why you want to find something against me. The sheep has muddied the water for the wolf.[118]

But to tell you still more: I have not yet reached the point of openly attacking the vices of the clergy and of the worldly estate. It is my duty to pass judgment on the vices you papists consider virtues. By means of them you have filled the world with deception and superstition—such as indulgence, mass, vigils, churches, vestments—in short, with all your human teaching, which you regard as something holy. I fight all of this for the sake of the pure faith and I simply want to tear off your carnival masks. I am still far from morals and works. If we had the faith again and were liberated from your devilish laws and sects, it would be easy for us to teach morals and to punish vices; and if the spiritual estate were first of

[113] Proverbial German, *Nit auff der ban blieben.* Cf. Thiele, *Luthers Sprichwörtersammlung,* No. 286.

[114] An allusion to the German proverb, *Ein schlechter Vogel der sein eigenes Nest beschmutzt,* meaning "a bad bird which fouls its own nest."

[115] Cf. *Treatise on Good Works,* 1520. *LW* 44, 15-114.

[116] Cf., for example, *The Ten Commandments, Preached to the People of Wittenberg,* 1518. *WA* 1, 398-521.

[117] Cf. *To the Christian Nobility of the German Nation,* 1520. *LW* 44, 115-217.

[118] An allusion to Aesop's fable about the wolf and the lamb. Cf. Reed (ed.), *Fables of Aesop,* p. 32.

all pure in faith and faithful in God's word, it would easily lead the nobility and worldly estates in the direction they should go. But since we ourselves are of no use, what good does it do to censure and to scold them much? Bad morals and works are but a small thing, compared with the false teachings and superstitions in which the spiritual estate has drowned. That is why I did not write a very skilled book addressed to the German nobility, but have shown only the crude practices they could certainly improve. But we clerics need to teach faith and the word of God against human law and superstition. This is a work which is higher than heaven is above earth, as Isaiah 55 [:9] says. You clerics are accustomed only to being praised in your work, to receiving honor and money for it. If a little criticism is thrown at you, you are afraid the whole sky might fall on you. In all your books you only want to have the people punished without mercy, but you want to be called "gracious squires," to have everything you do accepted, and to have the most charitable construction placed on it. This is what you call honoring the priesthood, and if one refuses to do it, it is called shaming the priesthood.

Here I shall leave Emser for the time being. For whatever he babbles about the mass, brotherhoods, ascension of saints, vows, and other things is now sufficiently answered. Meanwhile, his booklet is in my favor with regard to four points.

First, he flees Scripture just as the devil flees the holy cross,[119] and he wants to lead me away from Scripture. This he will not and cannot accomplish, God willing.

Second, he lies in such an un-Christian, shameful, and wilful manner; he imposes errors upon me which he himself invents and which he could invent in sufficient number to write about unto eternity. From this I notice that it was not his intention to write against my teaching. Instead, he only wanted to do penance for his lust by blaspheming and lying.

Third, he freely admits that I attack neither the articles of faith nor Scripture. I am very grateful for this since I have never asked for a greater honor and prize, even from my best friends or God himself, than this one given to me by my deadliest enemy himself.

---

[119] Cf. above, p. 168.

Fourth, he admits that his cause stands outside Scripture and depends only on human teaching and usage and that he wants to draw me into it. I have never in all my writings sought more, and still do not seek more, from the pope and all my enemies than their confession that their cause is not founded on Scripture. Thus one can easily see what kind of wise man goat Emser is: he writes against me, and everything he attacks he also confesses and praises as being in Scripture, that is, founded upon God's word. And yet he rages and foams against God's word, for God's sake, so that he certainly needs not a sneezing plant but rather to be led to St. Cyriacus in chains.[120] But if he comes again I can pay him whatever is still unpaid. For now it is enough, or the reader will be swamped.

To Fool Murner

You should not think, dear fool Murner, that I despise your good opinion, for I shall believe you this first time, despite all those who give me a different picture of you. And although you are full of bitter, malicious, and vicious words, I still welcome your kind (as you write) admonition.[121] What I say here is by far not enough to answer each one of you individually. But since you are Emser's comrade, in that you base your cause on human teaching and usage and do not attack me with Scripture, I shall have answered you with what I said to Emser, for I do not sense the same lies in you as I do in Emser.[122] You are indeed strange soldiers; you do not want to meet me on my battleground, you shoot off many blind and useless shots, and you shake in your skin before Scripture. When I bring in Scripture against your human teaching and usage, you come along as if you had won the argument that human teaching

[120] The sneeze plant (*Niesse wurtzel; helleborus* and *veratrum* in Latin) was regarded as a cure for mental illness. Since such a cure is not strong enough for Emser, Luther suggests the drastic means of chains. The martyred St. Cyriacus (*ca.* 300) was usually pictured leading a little devil or dragon on a chain and thus was revered as the saint for mental illness.

[121] A reference to Murner's first treatise against Luther, entitled *A Christian and Brotherly Admonition.* See the Introduction, above, p. 140.

[122] Cf. below, p. 224.

and usage are right; you urge me only to consider the consequences, and thus you want to tear me away from Scripture. For heaven's sake, can I not bring you to Scripture at all?

Why do you teach me so skilfully what the crudest peasant or child, or indeed even a born fool, could teach me? Indeed, no born fool is so insane, and no devil is so malicious, as not to know and to confess that one should follow what is right. Listen to me, you poor, superficially learned papists. I shall clearly put a syllogism before you: I concede the major premise, "One should do everything that is good." Why should you quarrel with me about this? Are you not smarter than that? Instead, you should confront me when I attack you and fight against your minor premise, "Every human teaching and usage which I have attacked is good." Here I go to war, dear fellows, and this castle I shall besiege. This is where you should defend yourselves and be lively. If you are able to rescue yourselves here and bring me down, you should not worry about the conclusion; I shall gladly accept it and say, "Therefore, human teaching and usage which I have attacked should be kept." But since you do not protect the minor premise and advance only the major one and a conclusion, you are doing exactly what the builders of Babylon did [Gen. 11:7]: when stones were called for they brought water. When I hit you on the head you treat your feet. When I set fire to the roof, you try to extinguish it in the cellar. Why? Do you want to make seriousness a carnival? You ask me to drink and when I knock at the jug to have you pour for me, dear brethren, you drink from empty jugs and count money out of empty pockets.[123] This skill I have not yet learned!

You also threaten to retort with many books and with a great surplus of your skill in order to frighten me.[124] You reckon victory on the length and quantity of writing. Because you are certainly unable to win with arguments, you hope to overcome me with length and quantity.[125] But I am already overloaded, and you, you

[123] An allusion to the German proverb, *Aus lerer tasschen ist bose gelt zalen,* "It is difficult to pay money out of empty pockets." Cf. Thiele, *Luthers Sprichwörtersammlung*, No. 174.

[124] Luther heard this threat from Petrus Franciscus, a friend who wrote to him on December 25, 1520. Cf. *WA*, Br 2, 240.

[125] Murner had written three treatises. Cf. the Introduction, above, p. 140.

lazy and miserable hero, want to belabor me, a hardworking and laboring man! Why do you not get some lazy and unburdened fellows like yourself, or an evil wife who would like to have the last word too? But, fool Murner, do you regard me as the kind of fool who would quarrel with you or with anyone else over who might be able to prattle longest or have the last word? You would win the prize without difficulty. For it is quite obvious which way the scale would tip if you were weighed according to the size of your tongue. The Rhine would run dry before you ran out of words. But is this advising and rightly teaching the people in a Christian way when you rely on many words, always seek your own advantage, and march about on the field but have no intention of coming to battle, so that the poor people are detained and stand there with their mouths uselessly hanging open?

Have you not read that "mere talk tends only to want" [Prov. 14:23]? I think if you would deal with Scripture you would soon lose your way of triplicating everything and there would be a lot of empty space left on a sheet of paper. You have not yet tried the kind of skill and work needed to deal with Scripture, dear Murner. Indeed, you do not cite any and talk only about your own opinion. You do not analyze my writing, and pretend to have some kind of unusual skill. It is just as though I did not have anything else to do but to write one book after another to you alone; and if I do not do so, I am supposed to concede victory to you.

You have my book and scriptural arguments. Take them, argue also with Scripture, and leave the talkative blabbermouth Thomas Murner at home. Refute my Scripture with better Scripture, show the foundations for your teaching, and step into the light. Why do you have to tease and to defy me so long? Just come on, ride against me and see to it that you hit the mark; I shall not disappoint you. You do not have to hide your skill before anyone. If it is true skill it will not flee the light. Otherwise, your writing looks as though you wanted to collect honor and publicity rather than seeking me out with true seriousness, as you pretend. If you are able to teach me differently with Scripture, you need not have any doubt that I shall follow you. Indeed, you know quite well that all the fathers have erred many times. Therefore, usage and long tradition have uncertain value before God. Moreover, his word demands from us not to have either human teaching or usage. That is why I want to have Scripture. Scripture, fool Murner! Fool Murner, Scripture! Otherwise, look for another fighter. I have more important things to do than to wait for your babbling without Scripture.

I do not want your mere reasoning either. It is too spoiled, and worth nothing. This I shall show you in regard to one argument which you thought the very best: since I had called the Christian church a "spiritual assembly,"[126] you mocked me as though I wanted to build a church just as Plato built a city which is nowhere. And you are very pleased with your idea, thinking you had hit the mark. You say, "Would it not be a nice city, with spiritual walls, spiritual towers, spiritual cannons, spiritual horses, and everything spiritual?" It is your final opinion that the Christian church cannot exist without a physical location, space, and goods. My answer, dear fool Murner, is: Should I deny Scripture for the sake of reason and put you above God? Why do you not respond to my passages? For example: "There is no partiality before God" [Rom. 2:11]; "The kingdom of God is in the midst of you" [Luke 17:21]; and "The kingdom of God is not coming with signs to be observed; nor will they say, 'Lo, here it is!' or 'There!' " [Luke 17:20-21]. And Christ says in John 1 [3:6], "That which is born of the Spirit is spirit." Indeed, I think you call the Christian church or us the kingdom of God in which God lives and reigns. How can I follow your reasoning and deny Christ who says clearly that the kingdom of God is not a city, a place, or anything external? It is neither here nor there, but a Spirit within us. But you say that it is here and there.

What do you say to St. Stephen, Acts 8 [7:48], "The Most High does not dwell in houses made with hands"? My dear, let your reasoning show itself here and make an "also" out of the "not," saying that God also dwells in houses made by hands! And Isaiah 66 [:1], which St. Stephen quotes, saying, "What is the place of my rest? What is the house which you would build for me?" [Acts 7:49]. Dear Isaiah, do you not know? Well, Murner will certainly tell you it is in Rome or wherever the pope and Christians are. "No," he says, "but my Spirit dwells in a poor and humble spirit which

---

[126] Cf. above, p. 75.

honors my word" [Isa. 66:2]. What do you think now, fool Murner? I think even now you come along with your church on physical horses, places, and towers. Look how the best part of your booklet agrees with Scripture! Therefore, let your reason sleep and show me a single letter of Scripture proving that temporal place, city, or building belong to the church. If you can, I shall make no more demands and shall soon follow you.

Here is a lesson for you: nothing can be so pointedly argued with reason which cannot also be refuted by reason. If the temporal place or city is "churchly"[127] because Christians cannot live on earth without temporal space, then wine and bread—indeed, even the stomach with all its contents—would also be "churchly." Do spittle, snot, and excrement belong to or are they a part of the nature of the body because it cannot exist without them? Perhaps your cowl is not without lice either; do the lice therefore have to be monks' cowls? Since the Christian church cannot exist without suffering, persecution, death, or indeed sin, do suffering, death, persecution, and sin therefore have to be church and life? You want to build the church half upon temporal things, to mix the physical and the spiritual, and to unite sin and grace. Yet St. Paul says, "Our commonwealth is in heaven" [Phil. 3:20], and Christianity lives only by fleeing and deserting temporal cities, places, goods, honor, body, and everything earthly, and goes through them to eternal life just as it goes through sin, suffering, and death. Do you see now, my fool Murner, what it means to do theology with mere reason and without Scripture? If you reply to this [argument] do you think I could not reply to you again? But where then is the final truth?

I therefore conclude that the Christian church is not bound to any one city, person, or time. And even though the unlearned mob—the pope with his cardinals, bishops, priests, and monks—does not want to understand this or let it be true, it is certainly true for me and for everyone else,[128] even for the children in the street and all of Christendom in all the world. They stand on my side against the painted and invented church of the pope and his

[127] Cf. above, p. 152.

[128] *Er omnes.* Luther's frequent designation of the common people, meaning literally, Mr. Everybody.

papists. But if you ask why this is so, I give you this brief answer: All Christians in the world pray, "I believe in the Holy Spirit, one holy Christian church, the community of saints." If this article is true, it follows that no one can either see or feel the holy Christian church, nor can anyone say, "See, here or there it is!" For what one believes one can neither see nor feel, as St. Paul teaches in Hebrews 11 [:1]. On the other hand, what one can see or feel one does not believe. Is this not clear enough, dear Murner and Emser? Let us see what you can say against that! Are not children and peasants here more learned than the pope, cardinals, bishops, priests, and monks? Where are you, you squires who dare to interpret Scripture, to explain faith, and to proclaim with certainty that the common man does not understand any of it? The case is different: it is the pope and his bishops, with their followers, who do not know as much by far as the crude peasants and children.

Compare, then, the holy church of Christ and the insane church of the pope. The holy church of Christ says, "I believe one holy Christian church." The insane church of the pope says, "I see a holy Christian church." The former says, "The church is neither here nor there." The latter says, "The church is here and there." The former says, "The church is not dependent on any person." The latter says, "The church is dependent on the pope." The former says, "The church is not built on anything temporal." The latter says, "The church is built on the pope." What do you think, Murner? Are you not fine fellows? How nicely you interpret Scripture! It is just as St. Peter said about you, II Peter 2 [:3], "In their greed they will exploit you with false words." Is it not true that the pope, with his papacy, does not seek anything other than the money and goods of the whole world, and does not care at all about the gospel and faith? Yet he still invents things, and you join him, pretending to interpret Scripture and to teach faith. But there are no more unlearned people on earth than popes, cardinals, bishops, priests, and monks so that it is a miracle if anyone learned is found among you.

The consequence of such blind blasphemy is that there is no other place in the world where there are so many sects, schisms, and errors as in the papal church. For the papacy, because it builds the church upon a city and person, has become the head and fountain of all sects which have followed it and have characterized Christian life in terms of eating and drinking, clothes and shoes, tonsures and hair, city and place, day and hour. For the spirituality and holiness of the papal church lives by such things, as was said above.[129] This order fasts at this time, another order fasts at another time; this one does not eat meat, the other one does not eat eggs; this one wears black, the other one white; this one is Carthusian,[130] the other Benedictine;[131] and so they continue to create innumerable sects and habits, while faith and true Christian life go to pieces. All this is the result of the blindness which desires to see rather than believe the Christian church and to seek devout Christian life not in faith but in works, of which St. Paul writes so much in Colossians [2]. These things have invaded the church and blindness has confirmed the government of the pope.

But when you quote, with big letters, the passage in Matthew 16 [:18], "You are Peter," etc., saying that this is the text by which the papacy has been proven up to now, you are not scaring me, dear Murner. Moreover, there was no need to show me that the papacy was proven up to now by this text. Our question is not whether it is proven by this text, but rather whether it is proven correctly and well. Here you should use big letters to let yourself be seen as the undefeatable Murner and give me the correct answer. For in all of Scripture I have no stronger text against the papacy than precisely this passage that you regard as the single, strongest foundation for the papacy. When I take it away from you and knock it down so clearly that you could even grasp it with your hands, I trust you will admit that I have won and will allow me to knock the papacy down before your very eyes and call all of you, including the pope, false and lying perverters of Scripture. Therefore listen to me, because no papist has ever cracked this little nut for me, and none shall ever crack it.

Christ says, Matthew 16 [:18], "The gates of hell shall not prevail against the rock and the church built on the rock." Is this

[129] Cf. above, pp. 191-192.

[130] The Carthusian Order was founded by Bruno of Cologne in 1084 in the mountainous region near Grenoble, France. Carthusians were known for their almost total seclusion from the world.

[131] Named after Benedict of Nursia. Cf. above, p. 192, n. 76.

not true, Murner? Now, you cannot deny that the gates of hell daily dominate the papists and that the papacy, including the pope, does much evil and errs. Can you deny this, too, Murner? Indeed, you can see that those who adhere to the pope most tenaciously live the most evil life, and thus the gates of hell certainly dominate them. Accordingly, Christ's saying that the gates of hell shall not prevail against the rock and the church agrees with the pope and his church just as light agrees with darkness and Christ with Belial [II Cor. 6:15]. If you want to prove the papacy with this passage, then I am quite right to demand from you that you show us such a pope and papacy in which there is no sin and over which the gates of hell cannot dominate at all. When do you want to do this, Murner? Hurry and build a physical city for the church—come along on your horse, but beware of falling. It is dangerous for you to ride here.

Since this passage then does not tolerate a sinful pope and a sinful papacy, and since no one knows which pope is without sin—besides, the majority is sinning publicly and there is therefore neither a single person nor a place not dominated by the gates of hell—it is clear enough, I trust, that the holy Christian church cannot be demonstrated physically but can only be believed. Contrary to Murner and all the papists, it will have to remain a spiritual place standing in the Spirit, invisibly built upon the rock of Christ. Herewith I hope the papacy is reduced to ashes, since the one basic passage opposes it. Moreover, the papacy's building is based upon this passage just as though a madman built a straw hat upon a fire. We do not want to be blind either, juggling and making out of the "rock" (*petra*) "Peter" (*Petrum*) and all the sinful popes whom the gates of hell dominate. But Christ does not tolerate it and must not be given the lie.

What good does it do you, then, Murner and all you papists, to cite many fathers in connection with this passage? They have erred as men. But you want to regard error as foundation and truth. To me the principal saying of Christ is worth more than all the teachers and fathers, no matter how holy and learned they may be. Christ's words are clear enough and do not need any glosses. Therefore, get busy with all your papists and restitute the papacy with this passage and make your word come true. Otherwise, I shall not answer anything you say. Since I have proven you to be wrong in the main point, you are no longer worth believing until this lie is extinguished.

Let this be my answer to your babbling without Scripture this time. I did not want you to think that I was overlooking you. But I shall indicate to you in the following verses what other people think of your booklet. Sent to me from the Rhine, they show how unnecessary it is to answer you. I am surprised that you babblers and scribblers are courageous enough to appear on the scene, since you can see how many intelligent and reasonable judges are on guard! I myself could not have answered you as well as this poet did.

A Poem About Dr. Murner

As I shall report, Dr. Murner
Did not sleep one night.
He was busy composing two new booklets;
He really outdid himself on these.
He attacks Dr. Luther's writings,
But manages to miss the mark completely;
Like a blind man, he lashes out in all directions,
Yet the target remains unscathed.
He beats around the bush,
Careful, lest he get too close.
He sees the fox and looks fierce;
However, he does not attack him.[132]
Scripture is twisted to agree with him;
Long usage is the cornerstone of his argument;
This does not satisfy his foes.
He puts many new laws into action
To which, however, Luther pays no attention.
The bright light he would like to darken,
But it will not let itself be hid.
For this reason, I think, it happens
That Martin Luther does not answer him.

[132] Cf. above, p. 129, n. 25.

What do you suppose, goat Emser, such people think of you, since you present nothing but lies and the crudest monkey business, dreamed up in your own head? Even though Murner is certainly in agreement with your cause, he stayed away from lying.[133] Lying, however, is your best deed in your booklet. Oh, better yourselves, dear brethren! Scripture will come to light, human eyes will be opened, and you will have to adorn your cause differently. Otherwise, the bright light will disgrace you. I warn you truly. May God help us all to the real truth. Amen.

---

[133] Michael Stiefel, one of Luther's friends and disciples, said in a tract against Murner's poetry, "Luther did not yet know you when he wrote that you did not lie as much as Emser." Cf. *WA* 7, 688, n. 1.

DR. LUTHER'S RETRACTION OF THE ERROR FORCED UPON HIM BY THE MOST HIGHLY LEARNED PRIEST OF GOD, SIR JEROME EMSER, VICAR IN MEISSEN

1521

Translated by

Eric W. and Ruth C. Gritsch

INTRODUCTION

As soon as Luther's treatise *Answer to the Hyperchristian, Hyperspiritual, and Hyperlearned Book by Goat Emser in Leipzig* had left the press, Emser countered with a long reply entitled *Quadruplica to Luther's Recent Answer, Concerning His Reformation.*[1] Attacking particularly Luther's assertion of the common priesthood of all believers, Emser restated at length his previous position that ecclesiastical tradition which teaches the superiority of the priestly estate is more authoritative than the "grammatical" meaning of Scripture. Accordingly, the passage in I Pet. 2:9, "You are a royal priesthood," is to be interpreted in terms of a twofold priesthood, a "spiritual" one (which includes the laymen) and a "physical" one (which consists of the priestly estate).

When Luther received the *Quadruplica*—probably from his friend Philip Melanchthon or George Spalatin sometime in early July, 1521[2]—he told his friends in Wittenberg that he had no intention of replying. His confrontation with the emperor at the Diet of Worms in April and his subsequent exile at the Wartburg (from May 2, 1521, to March 6, 1522) placed him in the center of international political and literary feuds which he regarded as more important than the "prattling of the Leipzig goat." When Melanchthon suggested to Luther[3] that their friend Nicholas Amsdorf should reply to Emser, Luther reluctantly agreed. Plagued by illness—a recurrence of his intestinal trouble—Luther jotted down a few basic ideas and sent them to Amsdorf, urging him, however, not to be too concerned with Emser, who was a "wicked spirit" rather than a man.[4]

---

[1] *Quadruplica auff Luthers Jungst gethane antwurt, sein reformation belangend.* Cf. Enders, *Luther und Emser,* II, 130-183.

[2] Both men had sent Luther a package of books, as evidenced by Spalatin's letter to Luther on July 6, 1521 (*CR* 1, 417-418), and Luther's answer to Melanchthon's letter, dated July 13, 1521 (*LW* 48, 257). They do not mention Emser's treatise, but the thesis is warranted that it could have been among the books sent. Cf. *WA* 8, 241-242.

[3] In the letter mentioned above (note 2), answered by Luther on July 13, 1521.

[4] Cf. Luther's letter to Amsdorf on July 15, 1521. *LW* 48, 265.

But soon afterward Luther must have changed his mind—probably because his physical troubles disappeared[5]—and he penned a reply to Emser entitled *Dr. Luther's Retraction of the Error Forced upon Him by the Most Highly Learned Priest of God, Sir Jerome Emser, Vicar in Meissen,* which appeared in print shortly before October 8.[6] It deals only with Emser's interpretation of I Pet. 2:9 and advances once again Luther's argument for a common priesthood of all believers while ironically agreeing with Emser's interpretation.

Emser, not realizing Luther's irony, felt obliged to expose Luther's "defeat" and "contradiction" in another pamphlet, entitled *Reservation to Luther's First Retraction.*[7] But Luther showed his disgust by remaining silent. Thus Emser had the final word in the controversy lasting more than two years. Until his sudden death in 1527 he conducted a literary campaign against Luther. In 1523 he attacked Luther's translation of the Greek New Testament and encouraged others at the court of Duke George of Saxony to write against the new "archbishop" of Wittenberg.[8] Shortly before his death Emser published his own translation of the New Testament, based on the Latin Vulgate text and adorned with a preface by Duke George.[9] Although Luther later occasionally referred to Emser's attacks,[10] he summarized his feelings in a remark made about Emser in the context of his interpretation of Psalm 37, "What else is there to do but to let such people rage and rave and to despise them!"[11]

The following translation is based on the first German edition of Luther's final treatise against Emser, entitled *Eyn widderspruch D. Luthersz seynis yrthumsz erczwungen durch den aller hochgelertisten priester gottis Herrn Hieronymu Emser, Vicarien tzu Meyssen* and printed by John Grünenberg in Wittenberg. The text is found in *WA* 8, 247-254.

---

[5] Cf. his letter addressed to Melanchthon on August 3, 1521. *LW* 48, 288.

[6] Cf. the evidence for this conjecture in Enders, *op. cit.*, II, x.

[7] *Bedingung auf Luters orsten widerspruch.* Enders, *op. cit.*, II, 199-221.

[8] Cf. *WA* 8, 245-246.

[9] Cf. Enders, *op. cit.*, I, vi.

[10] Cf. the evidence cited in *WA* 8, 245.

[11] Cf. *WA* 8, 235.

DR. LUTHER'S RETRACTION OF THE ERROR FORCED UPON HIM BY THE MOST HIGHLY LEARNED PRIEST OF GOD, SIR JEROME EMSER, VICAR IN MEISSEN

Jesus

Grace and peace from God to all Christian readers. Amen.

It is undoubtedly quite well known and obvious that a hard struggle has arisen between me, Martin Luther, and the most highly learned, excellent priest of God and licentiate of the holy canon law, Jerome Emser, about this passage in St. Peter:

"You are a royal priesthood."[1]

In this passage St. Peter calls all Christians priests. I insisted on this and said that all Christians are priests and that Scripture calls those who are now called priests not priests or *sacerdotes* but *ministri, presbyteri, episcopi,* that is, "servants," "elders," and "guardians."[2]

Thereupon the excellent man rose up and thought, "If we lose the priesthood all our power is lost." For the power associated with the priesthood, namely, preaching, celebrating mass, dispensing

[1] I Pet. 2:9. Cf. above, p. 227, and Emser's statement in *Quadruplica:* "He [Luther] applies this passage only to the common people and wants to exclude our priesthood from it because it is a dream. So I hope to show him that the 'dream' is real and to prove that in the passage from Peter which is now under consideration the word 'priesthood' [*sacerdotium*] is applied not only to the laity but also to us. Therefore there are two kinds of priesthood, a lay priesthood and a priestly one." Enders, *Luther und Emser,* II, 138.

[2] Cf. above, p. 154, and Emser's lengthy argument in *ibid,* pp. 144-151.

the sacraments, and using the keys of heaven, is well known. "If this business is stopped then the kitchen will certainly get cold and the cellar will be empty." It was as a result of this great despair that he determined to fight against me, as is fitting for a priest of God.[3]

First, he tried his skill to the extent of consigning me to the devil and writing many shameful lies about me—as if blaspheming and lying would be any help to him! Yet he became angry when I called him a liar and a knave—which is what one customarily calls a liar in German. After that he dealt excellently with the matter and invented two kinds of priesthood—one spiritual and one physical. That is, he conceded to me that all Christians are spiritual priests, but [said] that he and those like him are physical priests. He collected many passages from the fathers in which his assembly is called priests; and so he attributed two meanings to St. Peter's saying [I Pet. 2:9], a spiritual one and a physical one.[4]

But I could not be satisfied with the passages from the fathers because they do not constitute articles of faith and are not binding, except insofar as they are founded on Scripture.[5] Even though some fathers applied this saying of Peter to the Emserian priests,[6] they substantiate nothing since such an interpretation is only human and without any scriptural foundation.

Furthermore, it seemed foolish to me, before I recognized the man, that with a long spear and short dagger he should threaten to unseat and to demolish the cuirassier (as he called me), and that he should threaten to strike me with the sword although he never touched this weapon. I thought it even more foolish when he interpreted my spiritual understanding to be a sheath and his physical understanding to be a blade.[7] For at the time I had not been in that

---

[3] An ironic allusion to Emser's tract *Against the Un-Christian Book of the Augustinian Martin Luther*. Cf. *ibid.*, I, 1-145.

[4] Cf. above, p. 229, n. 1.

[5] Cf. above, pp. 196-197.

[6] Cf. above, p. 179, and Emser in *Quadruplica. Ibid*, II, 138-139. Emser cited a number of church fathers in support of his position.

[7] Cf. Emser's statement in *Against the Un-Christian Book of the Augustinian Martin Luther:* "I shall not leave the word [of Holy Scripture] in the sheath, as Luther does, namely, leave it stuck in the letter or literal sense. Rather, I shall draw it." *Ibid.*, I, 9.

strange Egypt where the sheaths are stuck in the blade and the physical is hidden under the spiritual.

But I thought it completely foolish when he took the passage from Paul, "The Spirit gives life and the letter kills" [II Cor. 3:6], to signify that "Spirit" should mean his understanding and "letter" should mean my understanding. For even devils and public sinners share his understanding yet do not live before God through such a spirit,[8] while all the saints share my understanding yet do not die before God through such a letter. What is even more peculiar is that the fulfilment and significance of his living understanding is for the most part dead. For his priesthood, interpreted through the living understanding, is for the most part dead in sin while still consisting of priests interpreted through the living understanding. This is unheard of, and it is impossible in every other word or matter. Moreover, I thought it no help at all when he used glosses and patchwork to write that the Spirit, that is, spiritual understanding, gives life if man lives in grace.[9] For this is the same as saying that man must first live in grace and that spiritual understanding does not give him life (as he had struck and stabbed about before with blade, spear, and dagger), but instead finds him alive. Therefore, either St. Paul must have lied when he said, "The Spirit gives life," or Emser must have lied when he said that Spirit means spiritual understanding which does not give life, as he confesses in his gloss.[10] Thus I thought Emser had unhorsed himself and granted me the victory when I wrote that Spirit could not mean spiritual understanding. If spiritual understanding meant "to give life," because those who first live in grace possess it, then the letter can give life too. Indeed, the tiled stove and the keg can give life too—

[8] Cf. above, p. 146, n. 8.

[9] Luther did not quote Emser correctly. Cf. Emser's statement in *Quadruplica:* "It does not follow that the letter kills the pious or makes them sinners. For they do not insist upon it as the heretics do; they also admit the spiritual sense. It follows even less that the spiritual sense makes sinners holy or gives them life. For even if someone knew how to interpret all of Scripture on earth, and yet did not have the grace, Spirit, and love of God, he would be nothing, as St. Paul says, or he would be like a clanging cymbal. I Corinthians 13 [:1]." *Ibid.*, II, 172.

[10] Emser felt misunderstood and replied to Luther's charge in his final tract *Reservation to Luther's First Retraction:* "Why do you not show me . . . where I have written that one must first live in a state of grace before one can have a spiritual or physical understanding?" *Ibid.*, p. 203.

that is, according to Emser's interpretation, they can be possessed by those who are alive. On the other hand, spiritual understanding can mean that which kills; that is, it can be possessed by those who are dead. Indeed, my ink bottle can kill in this way. Emser's glosses would therefore add a new dimension to St. Paul's saying that "the Spirit gives life," etc.; namely, the Spirit is possessed by the living and the dead, but the letter is possessed by the dead and the living.

Because these high and excellent things seemed so completely foolish and ridiculous to me, the excellent man became angry and said I ridiculed them because I could not refute them with good argument.[11] Certainly it would not be right, and it would be quite unnecessary, for anyone to ridicule the most subtle inventions of such an excellent man.

But since there was no other way open to him than fighting with Scripture, he really got started and quoted more fathers than before. He began, "Step forward, Cyril,[12] step forward, Ambrose, step forward, Origen."[13] I really thought he wanted to do a song and dance routine! But it was his intention to present Scripture, that is, passages from the fathers without Scripture. But I still did not understand all this and did not regard it as Scripture.

Finally, he hits the bottom of this disgrace and strikes at me one ell deep into hard rock. For once his razor-sharp sword is glinting as if he were Master Lawrence among the perspirers, and he says, "Step forward, Christ," etc.[14] He indicates how Christ called these people priests when he said, Matthew 5 [:13], "You are the salt of the earth."[15] There you have it, Luther! This is

[11] Cf. *Quadruplica:* "My brother Luther opposes me with a piece of new rhetoric. Since he is unable to overcome my book with good arguments and proofs, he ridicules it." *Ibid.*, p. 130.

[12] Probably Cyril of Alexandria (d. 444). Actually, Emser did not mention him.

[13] Cf. *ibid.*, pp. 138-141. Emser introduced each paragraph with the phrase, "Step forward, St. Jerome," etc.

[14] A reference to St. Lawrence, a Roman deacon who was martyred in 258. According to a legend, he was laid on a hot grill until he died. Cf. Emser's statement in *Quadruplica:* "Step forward, yourself, I humbly beg you, O dearest Lord Jesus, high priest, bishop, and pope, you mouth of truth!" *Ibid.*, p. 141.

[15] "Tell him, holy Lord Jesus Christ, that you did not speak to the laymen but only to your apostles. . . . Tell him that you did not speak to the common people but to them when you said, 'You are the salt of the earth.' " *Ibid.*

the Scripture which proves Emser's people are called priests. This is the interpretation of St. Peter's saying: "salt" means "priests," "incense" means "vicar," "water" means "sacristan," "fire" means "schoolmaster," and "straw" means "pupils." In this way, and only in this way, will the quarrel come to an end. Now I am satisfied. Now laughter must come to an end. May the hangman ridicule such seriousness. Who can with good argument refute the fact that "salt" means "priest"? Therefore, so that there is no more rain [from Emser's pen] I shall undertake my rebuttal with complete seriousness, and it shall be this:

I, Martin Luther, confess that I agree with the highly learned nobleman and priest of God, Sir Jerome Emser, that the saying of St. Peter applies not only to the spiritual priesthood but also to the physical priesthood or, to say it as clearly as possible, to the whole priesthood existing in Christendom. I say this with complete seriousness, for I did not really look at the truth of the matter before. Now I hope Luther is no longer a heretic, for I have even joined Emser.

But I do not want to start a fire on the other side, among my good friends, so I ask them not to be offended by this contradiction, in view of the fact that truth should be served before everything else. Moreover, we lose nothing in this matter and gain more than before. If you ask how this can be I will tell you: in all my writings I never wanted more than that all Christians should be priests; yet not all should be consecrated by bishops, not all should preach, celebrate mass, and exercise the priestly office unless they have been appointed and called to do so. This was my final intention.[16]

But Emser overshoots the mark and insists most powerfully and unequivocally, with his cutting "living" understanding, that all Christians must also be physical priests, consecrated by bishops, allowed to preach, to celebrate mass, and to exercise all priestly offices without further order or call.[17] That is the prize and thanks Emser sought, fought for, and captured with honors from Luther in this sand. I heartily grant them to him, will help him to protect

[16] Cf. above, p. 155.

[17] This is a summary of all the heresies with which Emser charged Luther in his *Quadruplica*. Cf. *ibid.*, pp. 133-134.

them, and I ask everyone who does not wish to be a heretic to do the same thing.

In case anyone thinks I am being facetious, I shall earnestly prove that this interpretation of Emser is indisputable. Is it not indeed true and sufficiently evident that Emser says St. Peter also speaks of the physical priesthood? That is why he has lied so abominably and slandered me until I was forced to grant it to him. Thus it is even more indeed true and evident that no man can deny that St. Peter's saying is addressed to all Christians, be they young or old, men or women. Clearly, therefore, everything that is comprehended in [the physical priesthood] must be understood as given to all these Christians. For since all Christians are called priests when he says, "You are a royal priesthood" [I Pet. 2:9], and since it is also to be understood in the sense of the physical priesthood, which is consecrated and tonsured, as swordsman Emser teaches and constructs, we have to confess that all Christians are undoubtedly such physical priests. Otherwise, we are heretics and the devil's property, as Emser threatens. Perhaps this is why women wear veils and young maidens wear braids—so that no one can see that they are consecrated and tonsured.

Well then, this is finished. But it still has one major fault. I shall be glad to humble myself and hear women and children preach. But how do we convince Emser, the cuirassier-eater, to do the same? He will not want to be in the common priesthood. Besides, he will not permit women to teach him—even if they were only pretty, smooth young maids—because he is too chaste. But I wish he could be persuaded to make his confession to such a confessor at a secret place and to wait most humbly for his absolution! So that he does not get angry and complain that his cause is tomfoolery and a joke—which is true, however—we ourselves shall have to reflect what should be done in this matter.

I shall give my advice. Since they boast and brag about a special, uncommon priesthood, and since all priesthood—spiritual, physical, whatever it may be or may be called—is ascribed to all Christians in St. Peter's words as the passage demands, it follows that the Emserian priestliness[18] is a strange un-Christian thing. Therefore I think it is best if from now on we no longer call this

[18] *Priesterey,* a sarcastic pun on "priesthood."

special and strange priesthood "priests" but rather "tonsure-bearers," and drive this useless crowd from the land. What good does such a tonsured crowd do us? They are neither spiritual nor physical priests. And why do we need them if we ourselves are all physical, spiritual, and all other kinds of priests? It is just as Emser himself teaches us with his blade: they eat our bread like strange and unnecessary guests. Therefore away, away with these knaves!

So that everyone may know that St. Peter's saying is addressed to all Christians—even though this need not be proven because Emser himself admits it—we shall include the text according to its order and logical arrangement. It is I Peter 2 [:1-5] and reads as follows: "Put away all malice and all guile and all insincerity and hatred and all slander. Like newborn babes, seek the reasonable pure milk, that by it you may grow up; for you have tasted the kindness of the Lord. You came to him as to the living stone, rejected by men but in God's sight precious and chosen; and like living stones be yourselves built into a spiritual house, into a holy priesthood, and offer spiritual sacrifices acceptable to God through Jesus Christ," etc.

What man is so dumb he does not see that these words are addressed to all people in common? Who are the people who should put away the enumerated vices and seek the reasonable pure milk? Indeed, can this be understood in terms of tonsure-bearers? He [Peter] speaks of seeking milk the way women customarily speak about their babies. A baby "seeks" when it desires its mother and milk. This is the way all Christians should seek their reasonable milk, namely, the evangelical teaching which is unadulterated by human teaching, which is pure and clean and comes from the true mother, the bride of Christ, the holy church. Now he [Peter] tells them they should themselves be built upon Christ into a holy priesthood. When is "tonsurehood" holy? When does it offer spiritual sacrifices? Christianity is holy at all times or it is not Christianity. For he is not talking here of laymen's sacrifices but of priests' sacrifices. This occurs in the New Testament in such a way that as Christ himself was a priest and sacrifice, so all of us too as Christians are truly a holy priesthood and the sacrifice itself, as Paul elucidates in Romans 12 [:1], where he teaches that we should sacrifice our bodies as a priestly sacrifice.

St. Peter Continues [I Pet. 2:6-10]

"For it stands in Scripture, 'Behold, I am laying in Zion an extraordinary cornerstone, chosen and precious, and he who believes in him will not be put to shame.' To you who believe, therefore, he is precious, but for those who do not believe, 'The very stone which the builders rejected has become a principal cornerstone,' and 'a stone that will make men stumble, a rock that will make them fall'; they are offended by the word and do not believe him upon whom they are to be built.

"But you are a chosen race, a royal priesthood, a holy nation, God's own people, that you may declare the wonderful deeds of him who called you out of darkness into his marvelous light. Once you were no people but now you are a people," etc.

Tell me, can anyone be so crude as not to understand to whom St. Peter speaks here? Or do the passages from the fathers have to step forward here and provide the interpretation? He [Peter] names the people and the congregation very clearly, and he calls them all together a royal priesthood and commands them to preach the deeds of God who has called them. Now if this is also said of the Emserian priesthood, as our Emser teaches, all of us are certainly such priests. He may interpret "priests" as he pleases, but all Christians are nevertheless such priests through this passage. If all of us should preach, then the tonsure-bearers must keep silent, since they have a different, special priesthood above all Christians.

The two following passages are also to be understood in the same way: the first one is, "You did ransom us by your blood, and have made us a kingdom of God and priests," Revelation 5 [:9-10], and the other one is Revelation 20 [:6], "Over such the second death has no power, but they shall be priests of God and of his Christ." Both are said of the whole congregation and are to be understood in that sense as the words demand, without the aid of glosses. Moreover, these three passages are the only ones about priests in the New Testament. All the others call Emser's priests not priests but servants, guardians, and elders.[19] Thereby the Holy

[19] Cf. above, pp. 154-155.

Spirit teaches us that ointments, consecrations, tonsures, chasubles, albs, chalices, masses, sermons, etc., do not make priests or give power.[20] Rather, priesthood and power have to be there first, brought from baptism and common to all Christians through the faith which builds them upon Christ the true high priest, as St. Peter says here.

But to exercise such power and to put it to work is not every man's business. Only he who is called by the common assembly, or the man representing the assembly's order and will, does this work in the stead of and as the representative of the common assembly and power. It is therefore not true that there is more than one simple priesthood in the church; and the tonsure-bearers are not called priests in accordance with Scripture, as Emser lies. The name "priest" belongs to all of us, with all its power, rights, and the respect these robbers and thieves of God would like to tear away from us and claim only for themselves. But just as they called themselves "church" and we have taken away from them what they stole, so too did they make themselves priests. But this is now also taken away from them. We shall leave them the tonsures so that they may be tonsure-bearers because they no longer want to bear the word of God, but only want to pervert it.

What good would it do if Emser quoted thousands of passages from the fathers, all of which uniformly call his crowd priests? There would still be no Scripture here, only the words of men who have erred—although they were not as stubborn as these tonsure-bearers. But St. Peter's words are God's word. They let nothing but the one, common priesthood remain. It pulverizes all the others, and no Emser can alter it, even if he lies and blasphemes himself to death.

However, I leave the usage now in force alone, namely, that in accordance with ancient human custom only the anointed and tonsured crowd are called priests—even though they no longer exercise that office. It suffices for us to resist them so that they cannot draw Scripture into their trifles, threaten us into false fear with the word of God, and force their arbitrary will upon us, as they have done up until now and would still like to do. Instead, we

[20] Cf. above, pp. 155-156.

have the power to make them afraid, and, if they hesitate, we can try the "guardian's rod"[21] on them. They should be subject to the common assembly as servants and should discard their tyranny. If they do not do this, we shall show them Scripture and teach them manners. Of this they are afraid, these tender tyrants! That is why they want so much to be called only "squire priests" with the aid of Scripture. No, Emser's sword does not cut. This is no way for his spear to stab; this is no way for his dagger to break [open the cuirassier]. Lying and blaspheming do not help. But God and his word remain forever. Amen.

We have thus recaptured two names from these church robbers; they are no more either "church" or "priests" than all other Christians. Moreover, they must unwillingly return the names "clergy" and "laymen"—indeed, they shall be even less than laymen, so that they sit between two chairs, being neither spiritual nor worldly. May God help me to achieve this, so that we truly recognize this strange Egyptian people. May this be enough for the first rebuttal.

[21] *Custos virgam.* A reference to medieval teaching methods, which included the "guardian's rod" *(virga custodis)*.

AGAINST THE SPIRITUAL ESTATE OF THE POPE AND THE BISHOPS FALSELY SO CALLED

1522

Translated by

Eric W. and Ruth C. Gritsch

INTRODUCTION

On September 15, 1521, Archbishop Albrecht of Mainz celebrated the annual festival of relics at his newly built cathedral, the Church of St. Moritz and Mary Magdalene in Halle, with the official announcement that indulgences would be granted to all visitors to the exhibition of relics. Anyone who prayed at a shrine and gave alms was promised an indulgence of four thousand years; anyone who confessed his sins to one of the priests hearing confessions in the cathedral during the ten days of the celebration would receive a plenary indulgence. Pope Leo X had issued a bull in 1519 granting the cathedral of Halle the same privileges granted to the Church of St. Peter in Rome: its confessors were authorized to absolve cases usually absolved only by the apostolic see in Rome; in addition, they could convert vows into financial contributions for the completion of the Halle cathedral—privileges not unusual in the established indulgence practice of the Roman curia.

When Luther heard of Albrecht's announcement—probably by the end of September, 1521—he viewed it as a revival of the indulgence traffic he had so sharply opposed in his *Ninety-five Theses* of 1517.[1] Other news from the episcopal court in Mainz had already aroused his anger: priests who intended to marry or had married had been arrested while at the same time other priests received special dispensations to keep women in the parsonage. In addition, the archbishop himself was said to live an immoral life at Moritz castle, where he supposedly kept his mistresses.[2] "I shall not let myself be restrained," Luther wrote angrily to George Spalatin on October 7, 1521, "from privately and publicly attacking the idol at Mainz with regard to his brothel in Halle."[3] By November 11, 1521, Luther had written his angry attack against Albrecht of Mainz entitled *Against the Idol at Halle* (*Wider den Abgott zu Halle*). No

[1] Cf. *LW* 31, 17-33.

[2] Cf. *MA*[3] 3, 371-372.

[3] Cf. *LW* 48, 316.

longer extant,[4] its contents were regarded a threat to public peace. Elector Frederick prohibited its publication when Luther sent it to Spalatin to have it printed. Moreover, Albrecht himself had sent a delegation to Wittenberg and Weimar to explain his position to Luther's friends and to the Saxon courts. On September 30, 1521, Wolfgang Capito, head priest at the Mainz cathedral and a friend of Luther's cause, had traveled to Wittenberg in the company of Henry Stromer von Auerbach, Albrecht's personal physician, to speak with Luther's friends, Philip Melanchthon and Justus Jonas. On October 1 they had seen Elector Frederick and, between October 8 and 12, they had explained Albrecht's position to the Weimar court. Sometime later Spalatin informed Luther at the Wartburg about the Elector's decision to prohibit the publication of Luther's treatise *Against the Idol at Halle*. Luther was even more infuriated. "I will not put up with your statement," he wrote back to Spalatin on November 11, 1521, "that the Sovereign will not allow anything to be written against Mainz [Albrecht of Mainz] or anything that could disturb the public peace. I would rather lose you, the Sovereign himself, and the whole world [than be quiet]. If I have resisted [the] creator, the pope, why should I yield to his creature? Your idea about not disturbing the public peace is beautiful, but will you allow the eternal peace of God to be disturbed by the wicked and sacrilegious actions of that son of perdition? Not so, Spalatin! Not so, Elector!"[5]

He agreed to let Melanchthon make changes—he trusted Melanchthon's diplomatic skill—but insisted on publication. "Do not dissuade him [Melanchthon] from publishing it," he told Spalatin in his reply. "This question is settled, and I will not listen to you."[6]

When Wittenberg remained silent after Luther's outburst, Luther could wait no longer. On December 1, 1521, he addressed a letter to Albrecht of Mainz which was written in a threatening tone and demanded a reply within two weeks. "Therefore be it

[4] On the origins and contents of the tract, cf. the Excursus of Gottfried Krodel in *LW* 48, 344-350. For the full argument, cf. Krodel's article in the *Lutherjahrbuch*, XXXIII (1966), 9-81. Krodel's conclusions are based on convincing evidence and are incorporated here, in contradistinction to the conclusions of the *WA* editors in *WA* 10^{II}, 93-95.

[5] Cf. *LW* 48, 326.

[6] Cf. *LW* 48, 326-327.

finally made known in writing to Your Electoral Grace: if the idol [the sale of indulgences] is not taken down, my duty toward divine doctrine and Christian salvation is a necessary, urgent, and unavoidable reason to attack publicly Your Electoral Grace (as I did the pope) . . . and to show to all the world the difference between a bishop and a wolf."[7] He closed with the ultimatum: "I beg and expect Your Electoral Grace's definite and speedy reply to this letter within fourteen days; if after this appointed fortnight no public answer should appear, my little book *Against the Idol at Halle* will be released."[8] On December 3, Luther secretly went to Wittenberg, arriving there after several hours of hard riding. Melanchthon told him that Spalatin held back the manuscript, obeying the Elector's orders. Two days later, on December 5, Luther was back at the Wartburg. "What I have written," he wrote to Spalatin after his return, "I want published, if not in Wittenberg then certainly somewhere else."[9] Spalatin's reply—the letter is no longer extant but can be guessed at from Luther's later correspondence—seems to have calmed Luther's fury; Capito had managed to persuade Albrecht to reform the situation in Mainz; arrested priests had been released and Albrecht himself had preached reform. On December 12, 1521, Luther, in a letter to Spalatin, agreed to wait with the publication of his treatise against Albrecht and advised Spalatin to give the manuscript to Melanchthon, who was authorized to edit it if he felt it necessary.[10] Capito wrote to Luther from Mainz that Albrecht had indeed reformed and would write a personal letter to Luther indicating his compliance with Luther's demands. Luther then received Albrecht's letter dated December 21, 1521, and seemed satisfied with Albrecht's good will. "I will act, God willing," Albrecht told Luther, "as becomes a pious, spiritual, and Christian prince, as far as God gives me grace and strength. . . . I am more than willing to show you grace and favor for Christ's sake, and I can well bear fraternal and Christian punishment."[11]

---

[7] Cf. *LW* 48, 341-342.
[8] Cf. *LW* 48, 343.
[9] Cf. *LW* 48, 351.
[10] Cf. *LW* 48, 353.
[11] Cf. *WA*, Br 2, 421; Smith (ed.), *Luther's Correspondence*, II, 80.

Thus Luther was completely victorious: Albrecht, his old foe, had humbled himself before the Reformer.

But Luther was not quite satisfied. He was more concerned with the evil of the indulgences than with the person of the archbishop of Mainz. "I wanted to put an end to ungodliness," he wrote to Melanchthon on January 13, 1522. Further on he wrote, "I shall restrain myself and not treat the man as he deserves. . . . But I shall show him that I am alive."[12] He instructed Melanchthon to keep the manuscript so that it might be published to "serve as a general censure, should others go insane like that."[13] There is no convincing evidence that it was ever published. Instead, Luther turned to a general attack on the "papistic" establishment, which appeared sometime before July 9, 1522, under the title *Against the Spiritual Estate of the Pope and the Bishops, Falsely So Called.*[14] Luther's highly polemical and satirical language, more evident in this treatise than in others, was prompted by the recurrence of the indulgence traffic in the territory of Albrecht of Mainz. The so-called "spiritual estate" was used, according to Luther, to cover up the sins of ecclesiastical princes who betrayed the gospel and perverted their calling. In arguing for the right of priests to marry, Luther tried to recover the evangelical morality imperative for any man, including a priest.

Luther's treatise was attacked by his old opponent from Leipzig, Jerome Emser, who countered with a pamphlet entitled *Against the Ecclesiastic, Falsely So Called, and True Arch-heretic Martin Luther (Wyder den falschgenanten Ecclesiasten und warhafftigen Ertzketzer Martinum Luter)*,[15] which was published on January 3, 1523. Luther left that one unanswered like the others.[16]

Against the Spiritual Estate of the Pope and the Bishops, Falsely So Called (Wider den falsch genantten geystlichen stand des Babst und der bischoffen) was printed by Nickel Schirlentz in

[12] Cf. *LW* 48, 365.

[13] Cf. *LW* 48, 372.

[14] It was probably finished July 4, 1522, since Luther mentioned his attack against the "bishop masks" to Spalatin on that date. For details, cf. *WA* 10^{II}, 95, and Krodel, *op. cit.*, pp. 52-59.

[15] The edition is listed in *WA* 10^{II}, 95.

[16] Cf. below, pp. 288-289.

Wittenberg. The section entitled *Dr. Luther's Bull and Reformation* appeared separately in 1523 in two editions, one published in Erfurt, the other in Augsburg, under the title *The Bull of the Ecclesiastic in Wittenberg Against the Papal Bishops, Granting God's Grace and Merit to All who Keep and Obey It (Die Bulle Des Ecclesiastenn zu Wittenbergk Wider die Bepstischen Bischoff, Die da gibt Gottes genade zu lon allen den, die sy haltenz, und in volgen).*[17] A fragment of Luther's original manuscript was discovered by the WA editors in the Bodleian Library at Oxford University.[18] Our translation is based on this manuscript and the Schirlentz edition printed in *WA* 10^{II}, 105-158. We have translated the significant portions of Luther's original treatise as they appear in the notes of the *WA* and *MA*^{3} editions. These portions clearly indicate Luther's concern for the real issue, namely, the proper understanding of the offices of priest and bishop, over against the attack on the person of Albrecht of Mainz.

[17] The editions are listed in *WA* 10^{II}, 98-99.

[18] For an exact description of the find, cf. *WA* 10^{II}, 94.

AGAINST THE SPIRITUAL ESTATE OF THE POPE AND THE BISHOPS FALSELY SO CALLED

Jesus

Martin Luther, ecclesiastic[1] in Wittenberg by the grace of God: To the papal bishops [I offer] my service and self-understanding in Christ.

Although I might be regarded as a fool by you, dear lords, because of the haughty title I call myself, an ecclesiastic by the grace of God, you should know that I am not at all surprised by this. You curse, slander, condemn, persecute, and possibly even burn me as a heretic for the sake of a high and noble cause. In this you act as you please, according to the pleasure of your idol. As a result of God's disfavor you have the virtue that you do not want to listen. Neither do you want to give an answer. Instead, like the hardened Jews you blasphemously and stubbornly want to condemn me without a hearing, without investigating the cause, without overcoming me. You are not even ashamed of letting a man defy you so frequently with such good reason. Very well then, since it is a question of lowering the horns and acting with brute force, I too have to lower my horns and risk my head for my Lord. In order to get things started, I call myself an ecclesiastic by the grace of God in defiance of you and the devil, although you call me a heretic with an abundance of slander. And even if I called myself an evangelist by the grace of God, I would still be more confident of proving it than that any one of you could prove his episcopal title or name. I am certain

[1] An ironic emphasis, since Luther had lost all his ecclesiastical titles through the bull *Exsurge, Domine* in 1520 and the imperial edict of Worms in 1521. That is why Jerome Emser entitled one of his polemical tracts against him *Against the Ecclesiastic, Falsely So Called, and True Arch-heretic Martin Luther*. Cf. the Introduction, above, p. 244.

that Christ himself, who is the master of my teaching, gives me this title and regards me as one. Moreover, he will be my witness on the Last Day that it is not my pure gospel but his. Thus your raging and raving is not going to help you at all. Rather, the more you rage and rave, the haughtier we shall be toward you, with God's help, and [the more we] shall despise your disgrace. Even though you might take my life, since you are murderers, you will annihilate neither my name nor my teaching. For you too will have to die at last and put an end to murder.

Now that I am deprived of my titles through papal and imperial disfavor and my bestial character[2] is washed away with so many bulls that I need never be called either Doctor of Holy Scripture or some kind of papal creature, I am almost as shocked as an ass who has lost its bag. For these masks[3] were my greatest shame before God. I too was once in error (which I learned from your crowd at great price and with great effort), a liar, a cheater, a seducer, and a blasphemer against God's pure teaching, as you are now. But the Father of all mercy did not look at my vice, blasphemy, and my very sinful, evil life; instead, out of the infinite richness of his grace, he permitted me to know his Son, Jesus Christ, and to teach [him] to others, until we were certain of his truth. However, I need not have any title and name to praise highly the word, office, and work which I have from God and which you blind blasphemers defile and persecute beyond measure. I trust my praise will overcome your defiling, just as my justice will overcome your injustice. It does not matter if, with your blasphemy, you are on top for the moment.

Therefore, I now let you know that from now on I shall no longer do you the honor of allowing you—or even an angel from heaven—to judge my teaching or to examine it. For there has been enough foolish humility now for the third time at Worms,[4] and it has not helped. Instead, I shall let myself be heard and, as St. Peter

[2] A reference to the bull *Exsurge, Domine,* which called Luther a "wild boar." Cf. *LW* 32, x.

[3] *Larven,* "masks" used particularly during the carnival season.

[4] The first time was the hearing before Cajetan at Augsburg in October, 1518 (*LW* 31, 253-292); the second time was during the meeting with Miltitz at Altenburg in January, 1521 (Schwiebert, *Luther and His Times,* pp. 374-378); and the third time was at the Diet of Worms in 1521 (*LW* 32, 101-131).

teaches, give an explanation and defense of my teaching to all the world [I Pet. 3:15]. I shall not have it judged by any man, not even by any angel. For since I am certain of it, I shall be your judge and even the angels' judge through this teaching (as St. Paul says [I Cor. 6:3]) so that whoever does not accept my teaching may not be saved—for it is God's and not mine. Therefore, my judgment is also not mine but God's.

Finally, dear lords, let this be the conclusion: If I live you shall have no peace from me, and if you kill me you shall have ten times less peace, for I shall be, as Hosea says, a bear on the road and a lion in the street [Hos. 13:8]. No matter how you handle me, you shall not have your will until your iron head and stiff neck are broken with either grace or disgrace. If you do not improve as I would like to see you do, then it is agreed that you threaten with hostility and I do not care. May God grant that you know yourselves. Amen.

Preface

So that some well-meaning hearts do not get the impression that I go too far when I attack the great lords—or that I might create rebellion and unrest, as the tyrants themselves interpret it—I must first present defense and explanation with scriptural proof that it is not only right but also necessary to reprove the high officials.

The pope, to be sure, in his canon law forbade punishing the prelates.[5] These dear squires and painted bishops count on it. They do not study, they know nothing, they are not engaged in any bishop's work, and they enjoy peaceful, quiet, and good days. Yet they act as though they were bishops while in reality they are nothing but carnival masks and dummies[6] who ruin the whole world in the name of bishop. But let us hear what God says about it.

[5] A reference to the "privileges of the clergy," that is, the canon laws protecting the priesthood. The "privilege of the canon" *(privilegium canonis)*, for example, defined malice against a cleric as "sacrilege." Cf. *Decreti Secunda Pars*, causa XVII, ques. 4, C. XXI-XXIV. *CIC* 1, 820-821. The "privilege of the forum" *(privilegium fori)* exempted a cleric from trials before secular courts. Cf. *Decreti Secunda Pars*, causa XI, ques. 1, C. XLIII, XLVI. *CIC* 1, 639, 640-641. For a detailed discussion of clerical privileges, cf. *NCE* 3, 949-950.

[6] *Putzen, Popanz* in High German.

He says in Ezekiel 4 [3:17-19], "Son of man, I have made you a watchman over the house of Israel, and you shall hear what I tell you and proclaim it to them from me. If I say to the wicked, 'You shall surely die,' and you do not proclaim it to him, nor tell him that he should turn away from his evil way and live, that evil man shall die in his sins. But his blood I will require from you. But if you proclaim it to the wicked, and he does not turn from his sins or from his evil way, he shall die in his sins; but you will have saved your soul."

Tell me, is this not a severe commandment from the High Majesty, that a preacher must reprove the wicked if he would save his soul? For he speaks here of public reproval, since he commands someone to exercise an office, to preach his word. Why does he command it so severely? Undoubtedly because the preacher would commit the greatest sin against love if he were silent and disregarded the greatest good, the salvation of his neighbor's soul, to whom he certainly also owes the smallest good, food and clothing. He [God] says: He should hear God's word and not propagate his own words. We have no other word than Scripture. That is why all the wicked should be reproved with it.

Moreover, it does no good to put up the excuse that this saying does not speak of prelates, but of the wicked in general, etc. For it forces the conclusion that it is also to be understood to mean prelates since it does not exclude anyone but names the wicked in general, be they great or small or whatever. For God's word does not regard the person; it is above all persons and concerns everyone. Thus Ezekiel, although he was of a poor and low estate, was nevertheless sent to preach to the whole people of Israel, which included princes, priests, and great people.

Micah 6 [:1-2] says, "Hear what God says: Arise and plead your case before the mountains, and let the hills hear your voice, so that the mountains and the enduring foundations of the earth hear the judgment of God; for God must judge his people and reprove Israel," etc. Who are the mountains, the hills, and the enduring foundations of the earth to which one should preach, according to his commandment? Here he commands the proclamation of God's judgment and punishment to the leaders, not to the people.

Finally, the proclamation of all prophets was generally addressed mostly to the high officials such as kings, princes, priests, scribes, and leaders of the people, as all prophetic writings prove abundantly. Thus God spoke to Jeremiah, "See, I have set you this day over nations and kingdoms" [Jer. 1:10]; and again, "I have made you today a fortified city, an iron pillar, and a bronze wall, over the whole land, against the kings of Judah, against princes, priests, the common people. They will fight against you; but they shall not prevail against you, for I am with you, says God, to deliver you" [Jer. 1:18-19]. Now Jeremiah was certainly far below kings, princes, and priests, an unimportant person from the small town of Anathoth, but he had to preach God's word to, and against, all high estates and had to reprove them.

Third, Christ in the gospel was a completely low and unimportant person; he belonged to no high estate or order. But with whom does he enter into controversy? He reproves none but the high priests, the scribes, the religious outsiders,[7] and whoever was of high degree. Thus he certainly gave an example to all preachers to attack the great leaders without hesitation, since both the destruction and health of a people depend most upon the leaders. Why should we obey the foolish law of the nonsensical pope, which is against the example of Christ and of all prophets, and not punish the big shots and spiritual tyrants? What good would it do to leave the leaders alone and punish only the people? One could never throw out as much with good teaching as the evil leaders throw in with false teaching. It would be as Solomon says in Ecclesiasticus [34:23], "When one builds and another tears down, what do they gain but toil?" If, then, one builds up the people one must first oppose the harmful leaders and destroyers.

Therefore, we should hold fast here to the free teaching of St. Paul, I Timothy 5 [:20], when he says, "As for those who sin, rebuke them in the presence of all, so that the rest may stand in fear." Here St. Paul excludes no one, be he high or low. Although he says that you should not accuse a presbyter (that is, an elder; at that time the elders also ruled in the church) without two or

---

[7] *Sonderlinge*, often used by Luther in connection with *Rottengeyster*, "rebellious spirits." Luther probably thought that some of Christ's enemies were similar to the "radicals" *(Schwärmer)* of his own time.

three witnesses, he did not thus annul chastisement; rather, he confirmed it. Such is the opinion of this text when it says, "Those who sin, rebuke them in the presence of all." Our squires are wrong in their canon unlawfulness when they interpret the little word "presbyter" to mean "priests," that is, themselves. St. Paul speaks of the old men whom one should not allow to be accused frivolously. He also says in chapter 4 [I Tim. 5:1], "Do not rebuke an older man but exhort him as you would a father." St. Paul does not speak here of the bishops and priests—who are usually young people now, not without great damage to Christendom—but of old men. These should be honored, and if they did something wrong one should exhort them and not bite them, so that they stop.

Thus we should punish bishops and spiritual dominion harder and more severely than worldly dominion for two reasons: first, because this spiritual dominion does not derive from God, for God does not know these masked people and St. Nicholas bishops,[8] because they neither teach nor perform any episcopal duties. Nor did they derive from men. They have imposed themselves on others and placed themselves into this rule against [the wish of] God and men, as is the custom of tyrants who rule only out of God's wrath. Worldly dominion derives from God's gracious order to suppress the evil and protect the godly, Romans 13 [:4]. Second, worldly rule, even though it commits violence and injustice, hurts only the body and property. But spiritual dominion, whenever it is unholy and does not support God's word, is like a wolf and murderer of the soul, and it is just as though the devil himself were ruling there. That is why one should beware as much of the bishop who does not teach God's word as of the devil himself. For wherever God's word is missing, there we certainly find only the devil's teaching and the murder of souls. For without God's word the soul can neither live nor be delivered from the devil.

But if they say that one should beware of rebelling against spiritual authority, I answer: Should God's word be dispensed with and the whole world perish? Is it right that all souls should be

[8] Luther referred to the popular game played by students on St. Nicholas Day, December 6. They would elect a fellow student to be "bishop" to rule over them that day in accordance with existing episcopal ceremonies. Even though this masquerade had been prohibited in a bull of Pope Gregory XII in 1407, it was quite widespread and was frequently permitted in schools, probably to provide an emotional outlet for medieval youth who were usually disciplined severely.

killed eternally so that the temporal show of these masks is left in peace? It would be better to kill all bishops and to annihilate all religious foundations and monasteries than to let a single soul perish, not to mention losing all souls for the sake of these useless dummies and idols. What good are they, except to live in lust from the sweat and labor of others and to impede the word of God? They are afraid of physical rebellion and do not care about spiritual destruction. Are they not intelligent, honest people! If they accepted God's word and sought the life of the soul, God would be with them, since he is a God of peace. Then there would be no fear of rebellion. But if they refuse to hear God's word and rather rage and rave with banning, burning, killing, and all evil, what could be better for them than to encounter a strong rebellion which exterminates them from the world? One could only laugh if it did happen, as the divine wisdom says, Proverbs 1 [:25-27], "You have hated my punishment and misused my teaching; therefore I will laugh at your calamity and I will mock you when disaster strikes you."

Not God's word but stubborn disobedience [to God's word] creates rebellion. Whoever rebels against it shall get his due reward. Whoever accepts God's word does not start unrest, although he is no longer afraid of the masks and does not worship the dummies. He lets them go and awaits whatever comes to him. This is what the dear masks fear most, for until now they have let themselves be feared and worshiped as if they were bishops and spiritual rulers. But whoever starts unrest misuses God's word arbitrarily. Christ's word does not rage physically at anyone but proclaims rage physically to the tyrants and quietly frees souls from their bonds. So the tyrants are despised and this is the best kind of rage; for whatever is despised does not need much raging against, and can no longer maintain itself, as Psalm 10 [:15] says, "Lord, break the power of the wicked." With what? Just seek out his malice and he will disappear. These masks need no other disturbance than to be discovered and recognized as masks. Then everyone will immediately be their enemy and they will be deserted.

Take an example: in earlier times the mitre was a holy and definite symbol. The two points signified the two testaments—the old and the new—which a bishop carried on the head of his soul, that is, in his understanding. He was learned in Holy Scripture, as

St. Paul commanded, Titus 1 [:9]. The two ribbons hanging free in the back signified his preaching office by which he let this same New and Old Testament Scripture freely make its way to the people; and he taught them to obey it, he himself leading the way.[9] But what does it signify when a bishop puts on his mitre now? Some people think the two points signify that he should certainly know the Scripture of both testaments, but the two ribbons mean that he neither knows nor cares to know either of them. For it is almost the highest virtue of our present-day bishops and cardinals that they are particularly unlearned minds. As a matter of fact, it has become shameful for a bishop to study the Bible. Why should a prince study when it racks his brain? There are certainly enough mendicants[10] and monks to do so. Well then! What else are they but mere masks and child-bishops, able only to sprinkle and cense stone and wood (God be praised), one piece of wood after the other and one stone after the other, just as though they wanted to dedicate a church or an altar to God? Where else would God live? Or where could he retreat from the devil if the holy bishops did not sprinkle and cense the stones? It is just like during carnival when someone is made a king, yet remains no more than a peasant.

But St. Paul, I Timothy 3 [:1-7], describes what a true bishop is like: "This is indeed sure: Whoever desires a bishopric seeks a noble task. Now a bishop must be above reproach, the husband of one wife, temperate, sensible, dignified, hospitable, an apt preacher, no drunkard, one who does not curse, not violent but gentle, not quarrelsome, no lover of money. He must manage his own household well, keeping his children submissive and respectful in every way; for if a man does not know how to manage his own household, how can he care for God's church, or the common good? He must not be a recent convert, or he may be puffed up with conceit and fall into the condemnation of the slanderer. Moreover he must be well thought of by unbelievers, or he may fall into reproach and the snare of the slanderer." Now see whether it is not

[9] On the sources of Luther's allegorical interpretation of episcopal vestments, cf. F. Bock, *Geschichte der liturgisechen Gewänder des Mittelalters* (Bonn, 1859-1871), and J. Braun, *Die priesterlichen Gewänder des Abendlandes und ihre geschichtliche Entwicklung* (Freiburg im Breisgau, 1897).

[10] *Terminarii,* a Latin technical term for "begging monks."

a noble task to be a bishop in whose office are so many noble virtues! St. Paul does not want him to be a recent convert who has just come to the faith or one who is young in the faith, so that the slanderer may not have good cause and reason to judge him and to say, "See how they put a fool over the eggs."[11] Instead, he should be an experienced and brave man so that the slanderer must be ashamed to speak evil of him. Moreover, he should be praised and honored by the unbelievers; otherwise, he would be mocked by them and immediately ensnared, so that he would be unable to say anything when something dishonest is attributed to him which would then appear dishonest to the whole assembly and offensive to the unbelievers, for at that time Christians were mixed with unbelievers. That is why all their affairs had to be dignified, praiseworthy, and blameless in public.

Again, Titus 1 [:5-9], "This is why I left you in Crete, that you might amend what was defective when I left, and appoint elders in every town as I directed you. Someone who is blameless, the husband of one wife, whose children are believers and not open to the charge of being profligate or insubordinate. For a bishop, as God's steward, must be blameless; he must not be arrogant or quick-tempered or a drunkard or one who curses, or violent or greedy for gain, but hospitable, a lover of goodness, master of himself, upright, holy, and self-controlled; he must hold firm to the sure word as taught, so that he may be able to give instruction in sound doctrine and also to confute those who contradict it." See, these are the attributes and character of Christian bishops of whom there should be one in every town or congregation. But what is the purpose of such attributes now? The papal bishops certainly have noble attributes which cost less effort. What are they? They are: to be ignorant; to avoid marriage and instead to have little whores, as many as they need; to have a silver cane carried after themselves; to put on a precious hat; to have a big tonsure; to grab many towns and much land within the diocese; to ride fine horses; to hold princely court; to keep "episcopal officials,"[12] that is, sup-

[11] From the German proverb, *Wenn er die eyer zu brechen will, so setzt er narren druber*. It says, "He who wants to break eggs will put a fool over them." Cf. *WA* 10^{II}, 113, n. 1.

[12] *Officiales,* a Latin technical term for episcopal officers who were frequently used by the bishop to enforce his laws in the bishopric.

pressers of the common people; to kill souls with bans and with tyranny; and, before I forget, to paint and to attach their coats-of-arms everywhere with rods and crosses; to wear precious rings and gloves; to sprinkle the stone and wood of the churches with holy water; to confirm children and to give a friendly slap on the cheeks to the sponsors (especially if they happen to be pretty, smooth maidens—but without frivolity, of course, so that not everyone is laughing), and many more delicate attributes like these. St. Paul forgot or did not know them. They had to be invented by the Most Holy Father, the pope. Oh, idols of the earth and masks of the world!

On the other hand, St. Paul did not forget the kind of life these fellows would lead with such nice pointed red hats, coats, rods, tonsures, crosses, and other attributes mentioned above, for he said, II Timothy 3 [:1-5], "But understand this, that in the last days there will come times of stress. For men will be lovers of self, lovers of money, proud, arrogant, blasphemous, disobedient to their parents, ungrateful, unholy, inhuman, implacable slanderers, profligates, haters of good, treacherous, reckless, swollen with conceit, blind, lovers of pleasure rather than lovers of God, having the appearance of a divine life but denying the power of it. Avoid such people," etc. See here, this is a true picture of our bishops and spiritual squires!

St. Peter also, in II Peter 2 [:1-3], diligently portrays them and says, "But false prophets also arose among the people, just as there will be false teachers among you, who will secretly bring in dectructive heresies and situations, even denying the Lord who bought them. They will bring themselves swift destruction. And many will follow their licentiousness, and because of them the way of the truth will be reviled. And in their greed they will exploit you with false words." These words certainly refer only to the bishops and spiritual rulers among the people. Thus we see how, alongside Christ's teaching, they also erected human teaching, sects, orders, and various estates and brought them into the world. All of them pretend to be special tasks and ways emerging out of the common way of Christian faith. Thus Christ who bought us is denied; for they teach that we become godly and are saved through works whereas Christ alone bought our salvation through his blood. They even slander and condemn this way of truth. They refuse to admit that their deeds are wrong and that Christ alone is our salvation. We also see how filled with greed they are and how they aim all their preaching and teaching at the receiving of gifts and the building of churches and monasteries so that they can become rich and satisfied. They use these false, invented words to give the appearance of a good life, and yet they deny the foundation of truth. Everybody then considers them people who live and teach a fine and holy life, whereas it is nothing but appearance and faithless glitter, so that St. Peter rightly says, "Many will follow their licentiousness" [II Pet. 2:2].

St. Peter continues, "Their condemnation has not been idle, and their destruction has not been asleep. For if God did not spare the angels when they sinned but chained them with chains of darkness in hell to be kept until the last judgment; if he did not spare the whole world, when it was still new, but preserved Noah, a preacher of righteousness, with seven other persons, when he brought a flood upon the ungodly in all the world; if by turning the cities of Sodom and Gomorrah to ashes he condemned them to extinction and made them an example to all those who were to be ungodly; and if he rescued righteous Lot, greatly distressed by the licentiousness of the wicked (for by what that righteous man saw and heard as he lived among them, he was vexed in his righteous soul day after day with their lawless deeds), then God knows how to rescue the godly from trial and to keep the unrighteous under punishment until the day of judgment, and especially those who follow the flesh and live in the lusts of impurity, despise authorities, are lustful and love themselves, and do not fear to disobey the rulers" [II Pet. 2:3-10].

He [Peter] holds three terrible examples, strongly worded, before these tyrants: the angels, the world, Sodom. But it does no good; our squires do not believe what is said about them. They neither read it nor listen to it. But see how nicely he agrees with St. Paul when he describes their unchaste, impure, and licentious life. He says, "They are impertinent and malicious, they love themselves so much that they even despise worldly authorities and everything high and majestic on earth, and indeed curse it." For the pope has already dared for a long time to crush kings and princes underfoot, to depose them, to ban them, to curse them to the fourth and ninth generations, etc., and to practice all his impertinent wantonness on them, as if they were swine or dogs. Scripture, however, wants everyone to be subject to them [kings and princes], to honor and bless them, and to pray for them for the sake of peace in this life, since they are instituted by God's order to serve with the sword.

One finds timid kings and princes who are afraid of such execration and let themselves be blessed by the pope so that his impertinent wantonness, of which St. Peter speaks here, is strengthened and the whole world is defrauded. The bishops and all the clerics help to this end. They are the real despisers of authority and blasphemers of majesty; they do not want to be subject to any authority either physically or materially. Instead, they are impertinent, malicious, and most eager to execrate all majesties and to ban them. Tell me, did not St. Peter describe our squires well here? Of whom in all the world might this be said, that they are not subject to authorities, that they execrate kings and princes, that they are impertinent, malicious, and foolhardy enough to fear no one? Does not the whole world see who they are who do this?

St. Peter continues, "The angels, though greater in might and power, are unable to bear the judgment of God upon themselves, and they curse it. But these people are like irrational animals, creatures of instinct born to catch and kill; they curse matters of which they are ignorant. They will be destroyed for the sake of their abominable nature and thus will receive the reward for unrighteousness. They count it a pleasure to revel in having a good time now. But they are only blots and blemishes on the world, reveling in their dissipation and carousing with your goods. They have eyes full of adultery; they will not be rebuked or kept from sinning. Thus they entice unsteady souls. They have hearts trained in greed" [II Pet. 2:11-14].

Do you see how angry and upset holy St. Peter is? My dear, who are they who carouse with the goods of others? Who are they who think it is enough to revel in good times? Who are they who live as if they were irrational animals? Who are they whom no one is allowed to rebuke or oppose? Does this text need glosses too?

Is it not known that dioceses, religious foundations, monasteries, and schools of higher learning are nothing but warehouses where the goods of princes and of the whole world are collected and where they have none of their own goods? They think they are really the most precious stones of Christianity, yet St. Peter calls them "blots and blemishes." They revile and condemn the truth they do not know. As a result they are drowned in their nature, truly animal-like and sensual men who have never tasted the Spirit. Nevertheless they entice unsteady souls. For everyone wants to become a bishop, a priest, or a monk, especially the best young boys. They are encouraged in this, not for God's sake but rather so that they can live well with the property of others and revel in good days, without having to live on the basis of their own efforts and to eat their bread in the sweat of their own face, as all men ought to do, Genesis 3 [:19]. But everyone knows very well that they have hearts trained in greed. For they invent endless ruses to grab the properties of the whole world. To do so they even use God, the sacraments, the mass, and all spiritual things—this is apart from what they bring together through false usury, lying, and cheating. But what might the full eyes of the adulteress be? Undoubtedly a shameless and crude life; just as a daring adulteress stares, turning her eyes in all directions to be ready for every man, so they, like the adulteress, are a daring people ready for unchastity, in which they live freely, without punishment, and securely.

He [Peter] continues, "They are accursed children. Forsaking the right way they have gone astray; they have followed the way of Beor's son Balaam, who loved gain from wrongdoing but was rebuked for his own transgression. For the dumb subjugated animal spoke with human voice and prohibited the prophet's foolishness. These are waterless springs, clouds driven by the wind; for them is reserved the gloom of darkness in eternity" [II Pet. 2:14-17].

Just as Balaam was rebuked by the ass, so we can see now how greed rules so unashamedly among them that the common man coins a proverb out of it. There is no one who does not condemn it. But how terribly hard it is when he calls them accursed children! Who would be so brave as to call pope and bishops, with their whole crowd, an accursed people? Peter—indeed, the Holy Spirit through St. Peter—curses them. Who can avoid feeling sorry and anxious that he became a cleric in these accursed times? Oh, whoever can flee, let him flee the spiritual estate in these times! Moreover, he applies the true titles to the bishops. What is a waterless spring and a rainless cloud but a bishop without preaching? He holds the office of preaching but does not exercise it, just like a spring which occupies the place of a spring but yields no water, and clouds driven by the whirling wind which take the place of rain clouds but do not yield even a drop of rain. Likewise, our bishops rise in place of the apostles, but let themselves be driven by the pleasures and honors of this world, in accordance to the will of the devil. They preach nothing and are of no use to anyone. That is why eternal hellish darkness is reserved for them.

But if you say, "How can they be called waterless springs and rainless clouds since they fill all the world with their preaching and pretend to do great things?" St. Peter answers and confesses that they unfortunately preach much too much. He continues, "They boast of great things but without substance, and entice with licentious passions of the flesh men who have barely escaped and must now live in error. They promise them freedom, but they themselves are slaves of corruption" [II Pet. 2:18-19].

Here he gives reasons for comparing them with Balaam and describes the manner of their teaching. That is why we have to take a good look at this. Moses writes, Numbers 24 [:13] and 31 [:16], that Balaam gave the bad advice to King Balak to make the people of Israel sin and thus bring God's wrath upon them so that he could destroy them. For he could neither curse them nor overcome them with force. Balak did this and erected the idol Baal-Peor beside the people of Israel [and surrounded it] with beautiful women who attracted the children of Israel. They sacrificed to the idol, ate, drank, and sinned with it. Then God became angry; he had all the princes of the people hanged on the gallows and twenty-four thousand men slain [Num. 25:2-9]. You see, this is what Balaam brought about, the great prophet who had previously preached so many precious things and who took money for it from King Balak. Since St. Peter thus relates all these things to our bishops, we shall seek the same interpretation.

Scripture does not indicate clearly what kind of idol Baal-Peor was, although Ezekiel 23 [:19-20] refers to something similar when it rebukes the insatiable unchastity of the spiritual adulteress who desired the likes of asses and horses. But the teachers say it was Priapus. For the sake of my chaste hearers I would prefer not to speak about him. But St. Peter's words force me to do so in order that I may honor our clerical squires by portraying their virtues. Therefore, I ask all decent listeners to forgive me if I do speak of it a little, so that God's terrible wrath and the devil's malice may be recognized, and so that we may see what misery, despair, and blindness human nature produces when left to itself.

Priapus was the statue of a naked young man, done in the crudest, most shameful, and most indecent manner, with uncovered genitals as though he were a god of unchastity. St. Augustine writes in *The City of God*[13] that as a part of worshiping him the most reputable matron in town had to put a wreath on the abomination and unchastity of this statue, and, as we today lead brides to the church first, so then all brides had to place themselves upon this shameful unchastity. There you can see the result of God's wrath and of human blindness—there is nothing that can be thought up which is so shameful that people cannot be persuaded to do it, if only the most blessed name of God is attached to it. Is it not a miserable thing that the blessed name of God should be ascribed to such an inhuman abomination and that so many souls are thus seduced? God keeps silent about this and allows his name to be blasphemed so that those who are ungrateful to his grace and goodness may be led astray as they deserve.

We do the same thing. Everything the miserable pope and the accursed children, our bishops, invent and present, we accept and fall for. We think it suffices when they attach God's name to it and say it is good, divine, holy, blessed, Christian; we tramp along like stupid cattle without first thinking about whether it is commanded in God's Scripture. Thus the proverb, "All misery begins in the name of God,"[14] comes true. But He repeatedly forbade us to accept everything coming in his name, saying especially about the pope and our bishops, Matthew 24 [:5], "Many will come in my

[13] *The City of God (De Civitate Dei)*, VII, 24. *MPL* 41, 215; *PNF* 2, 137.

[14] From the German proverb, *In gottis namen hebt sich all unglück an*. *WA* 10^{II}, 119, n. 2.

name, saying, 'I am the Christ,' and they will lead many astray." That is why he also commanded us so strictly not to use his name in vain and taught us to pray, "Hallowed be your name." The divine name must remain holy and be attached only to those things that are truly divine, so that we are not led astray through God's name but rather are preserved.

Moses shows, first of all, that all this refers to the miserable plague of human teaching which God inflicts on the world today through pope and bishops. When he commanded, Deuteronomy 4 [:2], that they should neither add to his commandments nor take anything from them but instead obey them, he continued immediately and said, "For your eyes have seen what the Lord did at Baal-peor, and how he destroyed all those who worshiped it," etc. [Deut. 4:3]. Why should Moses make such an example of Baal-Peor—that they should neither add nor take anything from God's commandments—if he did not want to show that this idol is human teaching? Human teaching always takes away from God's commandments and adds its own commandments—just as the pope has now taken away all of God's commandments and substituted his own. As one can hear, the papists teach that it is not necessary to love God with all one's heart, and so the first commandment is taken away. Again, [one hears] that faith is not necessary for justification and that works save, and so the second and third commandments are struck down. Again, they teach children to be disobedient to their parents, just as they themselves are, as was said above, and so the fourth commandment is struck down. Again, they teach that it is not necessary to love one's enemy, and so they teach one to hold on to one's wrath, contrary to the fifth commandment. Again, he [the pope] has many ways to break up marriages and to make them, and so the sixth commandment is taken away. Again, they teach one how to attain and keep ill-gotten goods, usury, and interest, contrary to the seventh commandment. Again, all their teaching is false witness, which is contrary to the eighth commandment. Thus under the pope there are no divine commandments any longer; they have all been taken away. On the other hand, he adds some on how one can serve God and do good works through tonsures, cowls, orders, fasting, begging, eating milk, eggs, meat, butter, singing, organs, censing, bell-ringing, celebrating, buying indulgences, and the like, all of which God does not know. That is why his [the pope's] teaching is the true Baal-Peor.

Moreover, Moses agrees with this when he describes, Numbers 25 [:1-2], the worship of Baal-Peor as eating, drinking, and being unchaste. For the heathen were so blinded that they offered their best women and daughters to the unchastity of this idol. It went so far that neighbors were involved with each other's wives, just like dogs among themselves. Moses writes [Num. 25:6-15] that the daughter of a noble prince named Cozbi sinned with a prince of Israel and was therefore slain, together with her lover, by the priest Phinehas. Consequently, the miserable blind people had thought it a good idea to offer only their best child to the idol to ravish, just as the pope today with his teaching ravishes the world's best people, such as queens and princesses, and the most devout people, who think it is good for them and a right thing to do.

Now all of Scripture calls the keeping of human teaching "committing unchastity." Through all the prophets, God punishes the synagogue for having left him and for committing unchastity with human teaching. Therefore, this physical unchastity of Baal-Peor cannot mean anything but the spiritual unchastity through which souls are perverted and defiled and led from faith to works. For the soul is called a spiritual virgin and a bride of God only on the basis of faith, by which it receives the word of God and becomes pregnant with the Holy Spirit. The holy seed of the divine word fertilizes it and makes it a mother of truth. This is the true good work and the real divine life.

Third, even the names fit: Baal means "man" in Hebrew, in the sense in which a woman says, "This is my man, whether he is married to me or not." And it is said of an evil woman that she has many men. Thus Baal means the man who lives with a woman and includes the concepts of coitus and man's work. Otherwise, man is called *isch* or *enosch*, etc., that is, someone who serves in government, council, war, or any other brave enterprise. Thus the Jews called the idol of Ekron Baalzebub [II Kings 1:2], "man of flies," to shame him; it meant a man who was very weak, one who was hardly worthy to have a fly as a wife. Moreover, angry women curse this way, saying, "You are the husband of a rascally woman," etc., or in German, "You do not sleep with a pious woman." Such a man is called *maritus* or *coniunx* in Latin and not *vir* or *mas*. This is Baal in Hebrew. Peor or *phegor* means breath and really pertains to the mouth: "to gape with the mouth." That is why Baal-Peor is a man whose mouth is gaping, whom we call in German a "gaping fool."[15] Such people are just like fools or persons who are negligent and clumsy in everything; they have no other manly characteristic than their ability to sleep with women. That is why this unchaste and shameful idol has been rightly named, for his statue produces only this virtue that on all sides unchastity is manifested and nothing more. What else should a statue of a nude and shameful young man signify but a gaping fool and indecent woman-chaser? A portrait in armor signifies a warrior, etc. And even though our clerical squires do all this spiritually, as we shall hear, they are nevertheless bold enough to realize it physically as well. Tell me, what is such a tender crowd good for? Are they not true gaping fools? What are they able to do except ride fine horses and delicate maidens? All gaping fools can do this. They are and will remain Baal-Peor, and yet they pretend to be nothing less than spiritual rulers of Christendom who lead souls into heaven and drive away all error and heresy.

Spiritually, therefore, this idol is nothing but the holy canon law, the teaching of the pope and papists in Christendom. For it is a shameless portrait of spiritual unchastity. From it souls learn to build upon works, and it perverts the virginal chastity of the pure Christian faith. Thus one should really call the pope not "pope" but "Priapus," and the papists not "papists" but "Priapists." As shameful and un-Christian as it was for the heathen to erect such a shameless image, to provoke themselves into unchastity with it, and to worship this same god with physical unchastity, so shameless and even more un-Christian is it for the papists to erect their teachings and bulls, provoking souls to do human works such as indulgences and merit, etc. They think that with this spiritual unchastity they now serve God even better than before, just as though God had become a Priapus—whereas true service to him is offered only by faith and by God's work brought about by his grace, and spiritual chastity is only maintained by his divine word. Thus we see now

[15] *Maullaffe.*

that in all the world the Priapists lead souls to Priapus and fill the world with spiritual unchastity and idolatry because they erect nothing but human teachings and works in the holy place where God's word should stand alone.

And just as the shameless image of Priapus shows an indecent, insatiable, and raging young man intent upon dishonoring women, so the idol of the papists, human teaching, is also an insatiable raging [which seeks] to dishonor souls and to pervert faith. For we see how very diligently they propagate their teaching among the poor people, how nonsensical they are, and how they rage when their teaching is rebuked. They regret any soul which remains pure, unperverted, and decent in faith before them. The name Baal, "woman-chaser," demonstrates that such teaching is only capable of sleeping with souls and dishonoring them and can do nothing else. And Peor, the "gaping fool," [means] that they do not open their ears to hear God's word and to learn it—but only their mouth, which is always open. They alone want to teach and to preach. Just listen to them: they make great claims and are nothing but gaping fools and useless gossips. As St. Paul says, I Timothy 1 [:7], "They desire to be teachers of the law, but are useless gossips without understanding either what they say or the things about which they make assertions."

The foregoing helps us to understand St. Peter's words [II Pet. 2:14-19]—why he compares the pope and bishops to the prophet Balaam. For just as Balaam for the sake of money gave advice to erect the idol Baal-Peor and caused the people of Israel to fall, so he [Peter] says that they [the papists] follow the same path of Balaam and also erect a Baal-Peor for the sake of money. For as we see, all human things yield money, but God's word bears nothing but the cross, which no one wants. St. Peter could not have found a more fitting example in all of Scripture than this Balaam to indicate the nature of the papists. For basically the whole spiritual government is nothing but money, money, money. Everything is geared to making money. We feel only too well how they have drained the world and still drain it. Yet this would be the least harmful thing, if only they did not erect the idol of their teaching, bring the whole world to ruin, and lead it into idolatry for the sake of accursed greed and money. Here Balaam is doing the greatest harm and is teaching spiritual unchastity in all the world. This angers God and deprives us all of his grace and teaching so that not just twenty-four thousand but innumerable souls are slain and condemned.

He says, "They boast of great things but without substance" [II Pet. 2:18]. What does he mean by this? Undoubtedly he is attacking the dummy and gaping fool: their human teaching. It is as if he wanted to say that their teaching is the true Baal-Peor, the gaping fool who opens his mouth and preaches great things without substance. Is it not the case now that only the spiritual estate is elevated as if it alone were the path to heaven? No one trusts in his salvation now unless he is a cleric or buys salvation from the clerics. And the clerics are really daring; they sell their masses, vigils, prayers, fasting, and good works, and lead the people to heaven through their great spirituality. Are these not great things? But what is behind them? Nothing but cheating and glitter, indeed, perversion and destruction. There is no faith. Instead, they rely on tonsures, vestments, singing, the eating of eggs, fish, and butter; the sound of bells, and incense. They let themselves be called holy orders and spiritual estates which mediate between God and the people, so that there is no further need for Christ. Oh, Balaam, you rogue, with your shameless, harmful Priapus! How you take money and kill souls!

He [Peter] says further that through such great pretending they only entice the desires of the flesh into unchastity so that those who first escaped it must now live in error. I am afraid he uncovers here more than one misery hidden under the nice, glittering life. We see how big and widespread the spiritual estate is; all its members are totally bound to chastity. Yet Scripture and daily experience teach that chastity is a supernatural gift, very special and uncommon, and given only to a few great saints. But they come along and make it as common as daily bread; with their loud noise they entice many young people to join their estate. Afterward, however, they live in life-long impurity and some of them openly maintain common-law wives. Those who have no opportunity to get involved with women or men do worse, and at the very least live with evil lusts and indecent desires if they have no opportunity to express them. Among them there is either plain harlotry in the name of clerical and chaste life, or an impure, involuntary, miserable, lost chastity. So the misery is greater than anyone can believe or tell. St. Peter touches this point here when he says, "Through their great pretenses they entice the desires of the flesh into unchastity" [II Pet. 2:18], as if he wanted to say, "They give high praise to the spiritual estate in their preaching, and they elevate chastity, but in this way they only entice and draw the poor people more than ever into the middle of the unchastity in which they themselves live."

Moreover, they get these same people to the point—even if they [the people] had truly fled from all sins through baptism and made a beginning in the Christian faith—of now falling for the clerical life and thinking that baptism means nothing and is of no more use. They also let faith go as something bad, insignificant, and common, and begin a harder, higher, and more severe life. This proves to be impossible, and so they are caught in misery. It may very well be that the devil keeps peace (although rarely) for one, two, three, or even ten years, but he leaves no one alone forever unless that person becomes a believer. He has the unbelieving man so securely in the net of unchastity that he can have no doubts about it. That is why he plays with him and leaves him undisturbed at times, for he knows very well that without faith no one can escape him. For even those who live in noble faith are hard pressed enough. In short, take this as a general rule: disregard the great claim of chastity by clerics who are not vigorous in faith, which is the case now with almost all of them. They lead a life that only appears to be chaste for the sake of enticing many young people, but there is nothing behind it. Would to God that a hundred religious foundations and monasteries were but one religious foundation and one monastery! You may be sure that St. Peter does not talk to deaf ears[16] here. That is why I have often said, and still say: Do not get involved with clerics, monkery, and nunning where Holy Scripture and pure faith are not studied and practiced among them day and night. Religious foundations and monasteries are gates of hell if faith is not valiantly and vigorously exercised in them, and they

[16] Proverbial German, *auss keynem topffen reden*, meaning literally, "not speaking out of a pot." Cf. Thiele, *Luthers Sprichwörtersammlung*, No. 137.

can be neither advised nor helped. I warn you, beware of the clerical life which is carried on without Scripture.

To observe constant chastity one needs strong and fine faith which powerfully elevates the Spirit above the flesh and dries out its streams like a fire, so that a man even hates this life and is almost like an angel, as Isaiah 5 [11:5] says of Christ, "Righteousness shall be the girdle of his loins and faith the girdle of his waist." Faith must gird and hold up the waist; otherwise it is not held up. But they come along, knowing nothing about faith, and want to help matters with works, eating fish, and woolen vestments. They are just as wise as the man who wanted to stop the Rhine with a straw dam yet left its spring and source unchecked. He will drown the land without, however, damming the Rhine. In the same way they have left nature's natural source open because they have no faith. And yet, with vestments and eating fish, they want to prevent nature from overflowing or breaking through. Nature does not permit this and acts in its own manner. Thus their chastity does not remain purer than if they had wives and husbands. What St. Peter says here is indeed true: with their great pretenses they entice the poor common people to think that through the spiritual estate and works they become holy and chaste, and that they serve God in the spiritual estate. You see, this is the error lived in by those who were once saved from all error through Christ. Does not St. Peter give glorious praise to the spiritual life here, [saying] that it is loud boasting without substance, an unchaste, impure, and seductive life which leads true Christians away from the right path and keeps them in error? I would be a heretic a thousand times over if I portrayed our bishops, priests, and monks in this manner. They use St. Francis, St. Dominic,[17] St. Augustine, St. Bernard,[18] and other saints in the religious orders to defend themselves. But they do not see that these same saints were saved through faith and not through their orders (as they [the papists] claim). They did not regard the orders as paths to salvation.

It is enough for the time being to have these two apostles, Peter and Paul, on our side. They show us the papists with their un-Christian and pernicious spiritual nature and teaching. [They

[17] St. Dominic (1170-1221), founder of the Order of Friars Preachers.
[18] Bernard of Clairvaux (1090-1153), Benedictine abbot and mystic.

also show us] that with all their pretensions they are accursed children and should be avoided. We shall save what Christ, Isaiah, Jeremiah, Ezekiel, and other prophets say about it until the pope, the bishops, and their followers[19] get angry at this booklet and blow the fire into a full flame.

No one should blame me for not treating the bishops as bishops. They do not consider themselves bishops, and I go too far when I call them bishops, which is an ancient, holy, and honorable title. I should only call them wolves and murderers of souls. A bishop should be learned in the Bible; he should study day and night; he himself should preach to his people; he should visit the poor, the sick, and the needy; he should provide for them and help them. But like thieves they rob the godly people of their property by lying and cheating. That is why I shall scream at the wolves here, indicate some of their virtues, and warn everyone against them. I shall not attack their person nor shall I attack them because of their worldly estate and nature; rather, I shall attack them because of their wolfish rule.

I have a good example for all this in St. Paul, Acts 23 [:3], who rebuked the high priest Ananias publicly in the council, saying, "God shall strike you, you whitewashed wall! You are sitting to judge me according to the law, and yet contrary to the law you order me to be struck!" He calls the high priest a wall washed with chalk, that is, a mask, someone who pretends to be what he is not. He wishes punishment on him and pays no respect at all to him as a high priest. But when several people criticized him for it, saying, "Would you revile God's high priest?" he answered, "I did not know, dear brethren, that he was the high priest" [Acts 23:4-5]. His meaning is quite clear. If he had really believed that it was wrong to wish punishment on him he certainly would have asked the high priest for grace and forgiveness and would have recanted it. But he did not do it. Therefore, it should not be assumed that he did not know that it was the high priest. Is it possible that he could

[19] At this point Luther's original version (cf. the Introduction, p. 242) contained an attack on Archbishop Albrecht of Mainz. The following quotation shows how sharp Luther's attack was: "No one should blame me for not treating the bishop of Mainz as a bishop. He does not consider himself a bishop. I go too far when I call him a bishop, which is an ancient, holy, and honorable title. I should call him only a wolf and murderer of souls." Cf. *WA* 10^{II}, 131-132, and *MA*[3] 3, 375.

be brought to court without anyone telling him, "Dear Paul, you will be brought before the high priest," or, "Look, the high priest is sitting there"? For one certainly makes sure of introducing the people participating in such public affairs. Even if he had not known that it was the high priest, he could still see him sitting there in the judge's place, giving the order to strike him. He really must have denied the authority which he himself acknowledged. Therefore, his words must mean, "I did not know, dear brethren, that he was the high priest," that is, "He should be high priest but is not and I do not consider him such," as St. Augustine interpreted it.[20] So if St. Paul attacks the priest who was instituted on the basis of Mosaic law, why should I be afraid to attack the painted bishops and masks who come from the pope without any commandment of God or men?

The First Virtue of the Bishops

They have the pope's bulls and indulgences preached instead of the word of God. What an un-Christian, wolfish, and seductive thing this is, is proven by the fact that it is against God's first commandment. He commanded there that only his divine word is to be preached and he alone is to be honored, so that he might be our God, Teacher, and Master, as he says through Isaiah, "I am your God, and teach you what is good for you" [Isa. 48:17]; and Christ says in Matthew 23 [:8], "You are not to be called teachers on earth . . . for you have only one master, Christ." He also says, Matthew 15 [:9], "In vain do they worship me with their human teachings and commandments." Therefore, all human teaching is certainly nothing but mummery and idolatry which is put in place of God and leads the people into damnation. No one can deny that bulls and indulgences are not the word of God or that there is nothing written of them in Scripture. Everyone must admit that these and many more passages clearly condemn everything which is not the word of God. God himself judges all of this as vain,

[20] *Our Lord's Sermon on the Mount (De sermone Dei in Monte),* I, 19, 58. *MPL* 54, 1259-1260; *PNF* 6, 25-26.

seductive, and idolatrous, to be avoided as much as possible on pain of his divine disfavor and eternal death.

But since our squires have iron heads and brass necks they refuse to hear this. They listen to no one and continue in their ways instead of risking life and limb against human teachings or willingly shedding their blood for the pure word of God and for the salvation of poor souls, over whom they falsely boast that they are bishops. They are concerned only with their wolfish fury, with murdering souls, driving them into God's disfavor and into hell, and leading them away from God's word to human lies. Thus we have to open our eyes really to avoid the wolves beneath the bishops' hats. That is why I ask and admonish all devout Christians to take to heart God's grace and disfavor. Just as you would deal with a physical Priapus or idol, so you should also deal with the bulls of Balaam and the soul-murderers in Rome. Just think what a great service you render to God when you destroy the idols and sanctify his divine name by cleansing it of idolatry. Therefore, anyone who has the desire and the opportunity may tear up and destroy such bulls, if he is able to do so with a good conscience and understanding. To destroy idols, as Moses commands so often in Deuteronomy, is the best service one can render to God. Gideon smashed Baal, Judges 8 [6:27], and King Asa smashed Priapus, I Kings 5 [15:13]. They were highly praised and honored for it by God. But in these days the sheep have to beware of the shepherd more than of the wolves.

The Second Virtue

Christ says, "You received without pay, give without pay." My wolves attack this clear saying of Christ as though a fool had said it. They not only preach lies and human teaching, they even ask money for doing so without any shame at all, even though they themselves should be giving all the spiritual goods for nothing on pain of Christ's disfavor. Even if indulgences were worth anything and were good, they should still be given to everyone for nothing, in accordance with Christ's words. It is even greater vice to take money in return for lies and wrongs. St. Paul also says, "If we have food and clothing we shall be content with these." But does this Balaam not have enough goods in Rome alone—not to mention what he takes in from his oppression of all Christendom—to make him a mighty king? Why does he set such great store by money and nothing by the salvation of souls? Both St. Peter and St. Paul teach that among other virtues a bishop should have the virtue of not being shamelessly dissipated; they want him to earn his livelihood honestly and with honorable work, setting a good example for others. Paul himself was a craftsman, a weaver of rugs. He earned his livelihood with his hands and was not ashamed of being an apostle higher than any bishop; and yet he worked at his trade wherever he went. But is it not shameless pleasure-seeking to seek money with bulls and indulgences and to offer lies for the sweat and labor of the poor? Beyond this there are many even more shameful ways by which the bishops obtain money; but [we shall deal] with that another time, when they get angry.

They say, "A prince must have more than food and clothing so that he may exercise his princely estate in a princely manner." I am willing to grant that. St. Paul speaks not of princes but of bishops and he does not know from where these princely bishops come. They are princes, not bishops, fooling the world with their bishops' masks and titles. St. Paul will neither change nor rearrange his words to accord with the princes; instead, the princes will have to be guided by him or they will remain masks not bishops eternally. Here I must tell the story[21] of how a great bishop rode across the land in a princely manner, as they do more frequently than worldly princes. A shepherd was standing on the road, open-mouthed, looking at all the elegance. The bishop asked him why he was so astonished and why he had his mouth open. The shepherd spoke, "I wonder whether St. Martin rode along in this manner too." The bishop replied, "Well, St. Martin was a lowly man, but I am a prince." The shepherd said, "Am I permitted to ask a question?" "You may ask," the bishop replied. The shepherd said, "Well, if the devil leads the prince away, where will the bishop be?" Then the princely bishop was ashamed of himself and rode away. Paul, too,

[21] The story is told about St. Gillian, an Irish missionary who was killed in Würzburg, Germany, in 688. Cf. *RGG* 3, 1272.

was a lowly craftsman; therefore he went around and preached. He was able to be an apostle, but he could never have been a bishop. Oh, the anger of God's raving!

The Third Virtue

They permit the indulgence bulls,[22] which originate in Rome, to preach that people may keep their ill-gotten goods if they give them a portion of them and also let them have the profits from them.

I do not know what I should say to this. Should I regard the pope and his followers as big, crude asses' heads or even as mad and senseless when they are allowed to present such shameless knavery publicly and have it preached? God commanded, "You shall not steal," that is, you shall neither possess nor keep ill-gotten goods. They openly defy this commandment, trample on it, teach and say that one may keep ill-gotten goods if the pope allows it. What else does this mean but, "You certainly may steal; God lied or fooled us when he said, 'You shall not steal' "? You see, our gracious God must therefore be a liar and a fool to these accursed children and damned masks. They stuff his own commandment back down his throat and teach the people to be thieves, robbers, usurers, cheaters, and destroyers.

Tell me, pope, from where do you have the power to claim ill-gotten goods? God himself, the creator of everything, will neither accept nor approve this. And you, God's greatest slanderer, want to be more than God. You assume a higher power than God himself. You teach the people to destroy God's commandment and to engage in theft, robbery, usury, and all unnatural works. The people who condemn the gospel, burn books which have not been condemned, break the imperial promise of safe-conduct, and run head-on against God, attacking all his works, should be overthrown by God in such a way that their minds are perverted enough to preach in public the violation of divine commandments. Oh, how abundantly the gospel has been revenged, and how well God has rewarded them with

[22] For example, the bull of indulgences issued by Pope Leo X on March 31, 1515. Cf. *LW* 31, 21-22, and Walther Köhler, *Dokumente zum Ablassstreit von 1517* (2nd ed. rev.; Tübingen, 1934), p. 86.

their own senseless, blind, perverted, and hardened hearts! Now would be the time to pulverize not only all papal bulls but also the doors and places on which they hang, because of their great blasphemy. Dear man, do not be confused by these crude, poor heads with their mad and senseless preaching. Keep in mind that God not only commanded that you should not steal, but also that you should not covet your neighbor's goods. You may be sure that he will not recant his words. How is it possible for someone to help you have and own your neighbor's goods? He says in Isaiah 61 [:8], "I am a God who loves justice, and I hate burnt offerings resulting from robbery." Yet your wolves teach you not only to offer burnt offerings resulting from robbery but also to keep the [spoils of] robbery. Do you see how, with their blasphemy, they lead you into God's wrath and into the abyss of hell? And yet they let themselves be called bishops and spiritual rulers of the soul. Beware, beware of them, dear man!

What a poor man I am. When I see this excessive, unspeakable blindness of our bishop masks I often get the notion that I should also keep quiet and let things take their course. For it often appears to me to be a desperate situation which can no longer be helped. These accursed masks have so ruined the situation and have so swamped the whole world that the Last Day and its wrath are forced to come. But on the other hand, the miserable corruption of the poor souls so gruesomely strangled by the masks does not give me rest or let me remain silent, because I might be able to help and advise a few. If you possess ill-gotten goods, just remember that you should not keep them. You will not change God's commandment. How nice it would be if you could add to it your neighbor's thanks and agreement! For to be sure, everyone owes it to his neighbor to cancel his debt if he has some of his goods he could not very well return.[23] Of this you can read more elsewhere.[24]

Now look, is it not necessary for the pope, the bishops, and the priests to be taken to school like young children and to be taught the Ten Commandments, how they should not steal or desire their neighbor's property, to say nothing of teaching other people

[23] It is difficult to ascertain Luther's intention or meaning in this sentence. He probably refers to the freedom of the conscience from legal obligations.

[24] Cf. *Receiving Both Kinds in the Sacrament*, 1522. *LW* 36, 241-242.

how to steal, rob, and be usurers? They are bishops, but not bishops of Christians; rather, they are bishops of thieves, robbers, and usurers, indeed, arch-thieves, arch-robbers, and arch-usurers—as everyone must clearly recognize and confess from what was said above. It is a miraculous sign of God's wrath that human reason lets itself be persuaded not to regard such thieving, robbing, and destroying of God's word by the pope as wrong. It would be unbelievable for anyone to suffer and be silent about it if experience did not force us to see it happen daily. Who can sanction the making of ill-gotten goods into honest goods? Pigs, horses, indeed, stone and wood are not as insane as we have become under the pope.

They say, "The pope is the supreme head of Christendom. That is why he should obtain all ill-gotten goods, the owners of which are not known." My answer is, where is this written? In the flue in Rome! Why should not each man do with ill-gotten goods as he himself pleases, if he cannot find the proper owner? Why does he need anyone else—especially the pope—to do it for him? This is a subtle lie to make the pope the head over thieves, robbers, and usurers and to allow him to steal and to rob more than any other man on earth. Thus he becomes the supreme head of theft, robbery, and oppression. If he were the highest authority in Christendom he should stop dealing even in honest goods, as the apostles did, and cling to prayer and preaching above all else, Acts 5 [:42]. But now he even burdens himself with thieving, robbery, and all ill-gotten goods. Is he not a fine follower of the apostles? Why does he not also take the honest goods of all Christians, since he is their supreme head, and obtain these too, so that they can enjoy their leisure and be cared for by the Most Holy Father? Such monkey business should be presented to fools and not to reasonable men—especially not to Christians.

The Fourth Virtue of the Pope

In all the indulgence bulls[25] he promises forgiveness of sins to all those who have repented and confessed. This is the worst poison and most harmful seduction emanating from that supreme seducer, the pope, and from his masks. Christ, Matthew 9 [:2], did

[25] Cf. for example, Köhler, *op. cit.*, pp. 18, 21-22.

not say to the paralytic, "If you put money in the box your sins are forgiven." Rather, he said, "Be of good courage," or, "Trust firmly and your sins are forgiven." These wolves and damned masks tear people away from this blessed faith and trust in God's sheer grace which alone grants forgiveness of sins. Instead, they lead people to put their trust in bulls, paper, and money so that simple minds learn to rely on their own works and not on God's grace. The accursed pretension of such bulls is abominable beyond imagining, because it condemns and destroys God's first and foremost commandment, namely, the commandment which teaches trust in God's grace alone. They teach trust in paper and wax, that is, in their invalid and accursed lies.

Naturally our ungracious lords themselves would no doubt teach such Christian faith and have it taught if they were bishops. But since they are unlearned papal masks, unable to do anything but destroy truth, just like their creator [the pope], they have no choice but to have masks, tomfoolery, and poison preached for the sake of money, whether they want to or not.

Thus I ask once again that for God's sake no one should think that I overstate the case. I am just as hurt as all devout Christians are when we have to see and to hear such shameless, public, raging blasphemy and destruction of God's commandments. In this matter alone they deserve to be treated much worse, for what I do is a thousand times too little. St. Paul condemned himself and all angels if they preached anything besides the gospel [Gal. 1:8]. What would he do with these senseless creatures of the pope and with these bishop masks who do not preach something besides the gospel but impudently and maliciously teach things contrary to God's word? No one should think even for a moment that what is said here is said against bishops or the spiritual estate; nor should anyone think that what happens to them should happen to spiritual authority. For they are not bishops. They are unlearned idols and dummies, masks and gaping fools who do not even know what "bishop" means, to say nothing of the duty of a bishop. They are nothing but wolves, tyrants, soul-murderers, and apostles of the Antichrist who want to destroy the world.

I might as well pour it out and let everyone know that the bishops who now rule over many territories are not Christian bishops according to divine order. They are bishops according to the order of the devil and of human abomination. They certainly are also messengers and governors for the devil. This I shall prove honestly and well so that neither they themselves nor anyone else can refute it. First, St. Paul writes, Titus 1 [:5-7], "Appoint an elder in every town, a blameless man, the husband of one wife. For a bishop must be blameless since he is God's steward." Here, I think, no one can deny that bishop and elder are one and the same for St. Paul, since he says Titus should appoint an elder in every town, a blameless man because a bishop must be blameless. He calls this same elder "bishop." Thus it is clear from this text that Paul means this man to be a bishop, a brave, old, and honest man who has a chaste wife and devout children. He should provide the church with preaching and sacraments. That is why he must be learned and completely blameless. My dear, is there anyone so crude or mischievous that he could misunderstand or deny anything in this text?

Furthermore, I ask whether or not St. Paul's word and order are derived from God's word and order? I think that the pope himself, with all his devils, even though he suppresses every word of God, cannot deny that St. Paul's word is God's word and that his order is the order of the Holy Spirit. For he [the pope] does not deny God's word; rather, he simply does everything that is contrary to it, under the pretext and cover of God's word. If, then, everything Paul says and institutes is God's word and the order of the Holy Spirit, we conclude, first, that everything contrary to his word and order is certainly contrary to God and the Holy Spirit. If it is contrary to God and his Spirit, it is certainly of the devil. I think all this is clear enough. Or does anyone doubt it? How can God be against himself when Christ says that even Satan is not against himself [Luke 11:18]? Second, it follows that all Christians must on pain of God's disfavor and for the salvation of their souls, keep God's word and order as taught and instituted by St. Paul. On the other hand, they must tear down and destroy and eradicate all of the devil's order, which is established contrary to God's word and order, even if they should lose body, life, property, honor, friends, and everything else. And if they cannot destroy it, they must still avoid it and flee from it as though it were the devil himself. Is that not clear enough too? For with regard to God's word and commandment, one must either do or leave everything, so that his will may be done in heaven and on earth above all things. But one should either destroy or avoid the devil's order above all things. Now listen, you bishops—indeed, you masks of the devil—Dr. Luther will read you a bull and a reformation which you will dislike.

Doctor Luther's Bull and Reformation[26]

All those who work toward this end and who risk body, property, and honor that the bishoprics may be destroyed and the episcopal government rooted out are God's dear children and true Christians. They keep God's commandment and fight against the devil's order. Or, if they cannot do this, at least they condemn and avoid such a government. On the other hand, all those who obey the government of the bishops and subject themselves to it in willing obedience are the devil's own servants and fight against God's order and law.

I shall prove this thoroughly and surely as follows: St. Paul said to Titus that he should appoint a married and blameless bishop in every town [Titus 1:5-7]. That is undoubtedly God's order, will, and opinion. Our papal bishops fight against this; they removed the bishops from every town and made themselves bishops over many towns. But St. Paul stands here—indeed, the Holy Spirit stands here firmly and strongly—saying that every town should have a bishop and that they must all be equals. St. Paul speaks of every town and considers all bishops to be equal. Well, come on, you masks! Be cheerful and brave! Here you stand against St. Paul, against the Holy Spirit; and the Holy Spirit stands against you. What will you say now? Or have you become dumb? Here you have your verdict: all the world must destroy you and your government. Whoever stands on your side falls under God's disfavor; whoever destroys you stands in God's favor.

By no means do I want such destruction and extinction to be understood in the sense of using the fist and the sword, for they are not worthy of such punishment—and nothing is achieved in this

[26] This piece appeared in two special editions in 1523. Cf. *WA* 10^{II}, 99-100, and the Introduction, above, p. 245.

way. Rather, as Daniel 8 [:25] teaches, "by no human hand" shall the Antichrist be destroyed. Everyone should speak, teach, and stand against him with God's word until he is put to shame and collapses, completely alone and even despising himself. This is true Christian destruction and every effort should be made to this end.

But, you dear masks, I shall give you some good advice. Why do you not, my dear, hire a real liar to write a small book about two kinds of bishops, for example, just as someone[27] did about two kinds of priests? For if St. Peter's saying, which he spoke to all Christians, "You are a royal priesthood" [I Pet. 2:9], can mean physically shorn and anointed priests, so that all Christians to whom this is addressed are priests—husband, wife, child, young and old, tonsured and anointed—why could not someone also thumb his nose at St. Paul's saying [Titus 1:5-7] (if someone could lie and blaspheme as well as he [Emser]) and interpret it too in terms of two kinds of bishops? Then all pastors or preachers in towns and cities would be spiritual bishops even though they bought neither coat nor cloak from Rome. On the other hand, you would be the physical bishops, gracious princes and lords riding on pretty horses with pointed hats and nice gloves.

Even though St. Paul might not tolerate such a delicate gloss since he appoints one or more bishops in every town, one should strike him with the blade and not the sheath of the spiritual sword.[28] One should just attack him with it and strike him on the mouth as Ananias did [Acts 23:2] and say, "Well, with the word 'town' St. Paul means a territory extending as far as the diocese." For since the pope has the power to change reason, why should he not have even greater power to interpret the words as he pleases? They interpret the names as they please; therefore, if such a splendid pope would wish it, "town" would have to mean "garden," and "ass" would have to mean "man."

If someone said to me at this point, "Previously you have rejected the pope; will you now also reject bishops and the spiritual estate? Is everything to be turned around?" my answer would be:

[27] A reference to Jerome Emser, who engaged Luther in a literary controversy regarding the doctrine of the priesthood. On the two kinds of priests, cf. above, pp. 152-154.

[28] Cf. above, pp. 151-152.

Judge for yourself and decide whether I turn things around by preferring divine word and order, or whether they turn things around by preferring their order and destroying God's. Tell me, which is right: for them to turn God's order around, or for me to turn their blasphemous devil's order around? Do not look at the work itself but at the basis and reason for the work. Nobody should look at that which opposes God's word, nor should one care what the consequences may or may not be. Instead, one should look at God's word alone and not worry—even if angels were involved—about who will get hurt, what will happen, or what the result will be.

But, if you reply, "The people whom you are attacking are too great, too important, and too learned," I answer that Christ, Peter, Paul, and the prophets proclaimed that there would be no greater disaster on earth than the advent of the Antichrist and of the final evil. Do you think such words are said about goose feathers and tree leaves? God's word always speaks of great things, against great leaders, and against many people. It is great in every way, as he says. Most certainly, therefore, the people who are doing evil now must be even greater. He speaks very harshly and terribly about this when he thinks that no human being would be saved if those days were not shortened [Matt. 24:22]; he expects to find almost no faith when he comes [Luke 18:8]; and even the elect will be seduced. My dear, consider these words. They are not empty words. You will find that it must be the great people who will work this evil. The pope, bishops, and all their followers are now such people. To sum it up: What does it matter how great, how many, and how learned they are as long as it is obvious that they are against God? Is God not greater and higher than all things? The Turks, too, are great and mighty—yet they are against God.

If you continue, "Well, there have been numerous holy bishops in charge of many towns," I answer that all ordained and holy bishops were usually only bishops in one town, such as Cyprian, Hilary,[29] Ambrose,[30] Augustine, Irenaeus,[31] etc. They kept the order of the Apostle. One can certainly find some, like Titus, who

[29] Hilary of Poitiers (*ca.* 315-367).
[30] Ambrose (*ca.* 340-397), bishop of Milan.
[31] Irenaeus, bishop of Lyons, *ca.* 177.

appointed other bishops in towns, as St. Boniface[32] did, who was [to other bishops] what Titus was to St. Paul. But this does not mean that they were in charge of many towns. And even if they had been, is their example higher than God's word? Is not God more than his saints? How often did the saints err and sin? God protected Daniel among the lions and the three men Hananiah, Azariah, Mishael[33] in the furnace of Babylon [Dan. 3:26]. Why should he not also protect his elect in the midst of the devil's order, even if they had been seduced, as Christ says [Luke 18:7]? One must build not upon the deed, example, and words of the saints but rather on God's word alone. God is the only one who can neither lie nor err.

Second, let us hear more from St. Paul about these divine orders. St. Luke says, Acts 20 [:17, 28], "From Miletus Paul sent to Ephesus and called to him the elders of the church. And when they came to him, he said to them: 'Take heed to yourselves and to all the flock, in which the Holy Spirit has made you bishops, to feed the church of God which he obtained with his own blood.'" What does this mean? Ephesus was only one town and St. Paul calls all its elders bishops! He must have overlooked the papists' little book of defense and the decretals as well.[34] How else could he be so brave as to give one town many bishops and to call each of the elders "bishop" when they were not princes but walked on foot? How could anyone be a bishop if he does not ride a high horse and does not let himself be called gracious lord, which is enough by itself to create a bishop? But here one can see that St.

[32] Boniface, whose real name was Wynfrith (672/75-754), was consecrated bishop by Pope Gregory II in 719 to supervise the mission among the Germanic tribes. In 752 he consecrated his disciple Lullus bishop.

[33] Luther used the Hebrew names, probably on the basis of the Greek translation of the Old Testament. Modern translations (the R.S.V., for example) use the Babylonian names Shadrach, Abednego, and Meshach.

[34] A reference to the two parts of canon law, the collection of conciliar decrees *(canones)* and papal decisions *(decretales).* In Luther's time canon law consisted of three parts: (1) the *Decretum Gratiani,* named after the monk Gratian who issued a collection in Bologna in 1150; (2) the *Decretalium Gregorii IX. libri quinque,* five books named after Pope Gregory IX, who continued the first collection between 1230 and 1234; and (3) the *Liber sextus,* the "sixth book" issued by Pope Boniface VIII in 1298 as a supplement to the five books. Finally, the *extravagantes,* and appendix, were added to the whole collection by Clement V in 1313. This addition was also called the "seventh book" *(liber septimus)* or "Clementine constitutions" *(constitutiones Clementinae).*

Paul calls all those who offer the word and sacrament to the people "bishop," just as ministers and curates do now. That is why I think that they possess the estate of the bishop every time they go into the villages to preach or are pastors in a village. On the other hand, the high riders and gracious lords have no more of the bishop's estate than the mere name and the clothes. It is as though a painter painted the picture of a bishop with the caption, "Here is an episcopal god, the crude clod." They are exactly that kind of bishop —not to mention the fact that they oppressed pastors and curates, forbade them to marry, plundered the gospel, and brought the poor people nowhere but into hell—these children of perdition and hopeless masks!

Thus we can see that nothing Christian ever comes from a bishop's court. The courts of worldly princes might as well be considered monasteries when compared to the bishops' courts. What comes forth from them is not the gospel but only bats, citations, letters of interdict, torture-letters, money-letters, bulls, and lies. They abuse and oppress everyone with them. Their teaching is like their being bishops. Even if one dressed an ass with a lion's hide, he still would remain an ass; his ears and his song betray him.

Third, St. Paul writes to the Philippians, "Paul and Timothy, servants of Jesus Christ, to all the saints in Christ who are in Philippi with the bishops and deacons: grace to you and peace from God our Father and the Lord Jesus Christ," etc. [Phil. 1:1-2]. Look here: Philippi was only one town too, and he [Paul] greets all the faithful and their bishops. These are surely the elders, the same as those he used to appoint in all the other towns. This is now St. Paul's third passage about the divine order, accordingly to which only those who tend the people with preaching and sacraments, such as the pastors with their curates do, should be and should be called bishops—provided they have a chance to do so in the face of bishops' horses and riders. The name *episcopus* also proves this. It derives from *epi* and *scopein* [in Greek], *attendere, superintendere* [in Latin], "to tend" and "to be a guardian" of the people, just like a guardian or watchman in a town. Thus *episcopus* or "bishop" in Greek really means "guardian, watchman, overseer" in German. In Hebrew it means *visitator a visitando,* a visitor who goes to the people to see what is afflicting them, as Christ says,

Luke 19 [:44], "You did not want to know the time of your visitation." Or as we would say, of your episcopacy, *episcopes*. But the "bishop god"[35] has invented a different way; he sits on a silk pillow, summons people to appear before his officials and his butcher's stall some ten miles away, and there he tortures them[36] just as he pleases. Oh, this lost people and mob of eternal wrath!

Since it is clear, then, from these three passages that the bishops are not only masks and idols but also an accursed people before God—rising up against God's order to destroy the gospel and ruin souls—every Christian should help with his body and property to put an end to their tyranny. One should cheerfully do everything possible against them, just as though they were the devil himself. One should trample obedience to them just as though it were obedience to the devil; and one should see to it that one or more devout married men become pastors or bishops in every town. Moreover, those who are pastors now should recant such obedience, because with their promises of chastity they were obedient to the devil and not to God. They should do so in the same way someone recants his allegiance to the devil. They should marry in defiance of the devil and for the sake of hurting these "bishop gods," so that the divine order instituted by St. Paul against these accursed masks might be re-established. Let this be Dr. Luther's bull which grants God's grace as a reward to all who heed it and obey it. Amen.[37]

But so that St. Paul's order does not stand alone (for I have heard it said that the dean and canon in Magdeburg said to the dismissed preacher,[38] "Who is Paul, Paul? The pope has received more power from Christ than St. Paul!"), we want to hear, for the sake of such honest Christian people, what St. Peter himself and Christ have to say about it. In I Peter 5 [:1-4], St. Peter addresses all Christians in this fashion, "So I exhort the elders among you as a fellow elder: tend the flock of Christ who is among you, and be

[35] *Bischoff goetz,* literally, "bishop idol."

[36] *Fleyschbanck ubirtzehen,* literally, "to treat them like oxen in a butcher stall" or "to skin them."

[37] Luther ends his bull with these words.

[38] Andreas Raugsdorf, who was expelled from Magdeburg in 1521 by the cathedral chapter.

its bishops, not by constraint but willingly, not for shameful gain but eagerly, not as domineering over them as if they were your inherited property,[39] but being examples to the flock. And when the chief shepherd is manifested you will obtain the unfading crown of glory." Here you can see that St. Peter calls elders and bishops one and the same thing, just as St. Paul does. They are the ones who teach the people, and this makes all of them equals. He says they should not strive to be domineering as if they were lords over property. He calls himself a fellow elder and wants all pastors and preachers to be his equals and to be equals among themselves. What do our idols have to say to this, since they are not only lords but also tyrants over our body, soul, and property, elevating themselves and refusing to be the equal of anyone?

In conclusion, hear what Christ himself says, Luke 22 [:25-26], "The kings of the Gentiles exercise lordship over them; and those in authority over them are called benefactors. But not so with you; rather let the greatest among you become as the youngest." Listen to this, you masks! You cannot deny that your external and worldly government is much higher than that of any king or prince. For you rule over body, soul, and property, not through God's word as does even the lowest preacher—as was said above about Jeremiah[40]—but through external things and works, just like worldly princes. Tell me then: How does your business agree with this saying, "But not so with you"? What does "not so" mean? It means that the episcopal estate as we know it now should not be so, if it is to be Christian. No matter what it is, Christ himself tells you "not so." Let us see what you say to this "not so"! Perhaps you will say "not so" means "it is so" and teach that the pope has more power than Christ himself.

Therefore, just as you would avoid your enemy, if he appeared in the mask of your dear brother, so avoid these murderers of the soul who appear in the mask of bishop and in the name of shepherd. St. Paul prophesied that just as the devil appears in the mask of an angel of light, so these devil's apostles appear in the mask and in the name of the apostles and servants of Christ. But we shall recognize them by their works and teachings [II Cor. 11:13-15]. For

[39] Luther added this phrase to the biblical text.

[40] Cf. above, p. 251.

they preach without any shame or hesitation about investing money, rather than about the gospel.

The Fifth Virtue of the Bulls in Rome

He [the pope] pretends to change vows for the sake of money, except the vows of St. James,[41] Rome, Jerusalem, and the vow of chastity. I have written much about vows previously,[42] so there is no need to repeat it now. When I ask that blind head the pope what his explanation is for being able to dissolve some but not all vows, he answers only that some vowed things are great, such as chastity, and some are small, such as eating bread and water on Friday. Thus he may change small vows but not large ones.

What a blind and crude brain these masked people have that they judge and differentiate vows not according to God's commandments but according to works! Tell me, is it not just as much an oath to swear about three pennies as to swear about a thousand guilders? If the vow is the same, why should it not be as valid in small as in great matters? Would it be invalid if someone paid a thousand guilders too much? This masked people is insane and senseless. Therefore stand fast and do not make a difference in the vows because of a difference in matter or works. One vow is like the other, whether it concerns something great or something small. For God's commandment does not differentiate; it simply says you shall keep everything you vowed. It does not say that you may break the great vows and keep the small vows, or vice versa. Therefore, do not believe these seducers when they change the vows. They may change none of them; and if they can change any, then you and everyone else can do the same and change all the vows. To change vows is the same as annulling this commandment of God: "Keep what you vow." If one of its parts is annulled, all of them are annulled. There is one simple commandment governing all vows.

For if it were true that the pope has power to change things with regard to small works in one of God's commandments, he could

[41] A reference to Compostella, cf. p. 43, n. 32.

[42] Cf. *The Judgment of Martin Luther on Monastic Vows*, 1521, *LW* 44, 243-400.

do it as well in all the others. Thus it would follow that with regard to the first commandment, he might give permission not to love God with all one's heart in small works such as eating and drinking, walking or standing still. He might also give permission to worship an idol with external works; or permit committing adultery with a worthless woman. Many more such abominations would follow if one could change or tear up one part of one of God's commandments. Thus you can see that these masks do nothing but tear up God's commandments for the sake of money. So beware of Balaam. He can change no vows for you; but if he can change even one, then you can change them all without spending any money.

Much more could be said here, but time does not permit it. We shall say more about it another time. For the time being, let this very brief statement suffice: first, some vows are vowed to men and should be kept as long as the one to whom they are vowed demands it or demands it justly. We do not speak of these vows here. Second, there are vows vowed to God or to his saints; they are of two kinds: those that are against God and his commandment, which should not be kept at all; and those that are not against his commandment, which are to be kept. Now the greatest problem is to know those vows which are vowed against God and his commandments. Here one must look at the Ten Commandments. Let us begin with the last ones. If you vow to desire your neighbor's property, his wife, to bear false witness against him, to steal his property or damage it, to ravish his wife and to kill his body, and finally if you vow to show neither love nor goodness to him—in all this you can see clearly that such vows are sin and are to be avoided on pain of God's disfavor. Indeed, everyone has to acknowledge this. Furthermore, if you vow to be disobedient to father and mother and not to do what they want, is not this, too, against God's commandment? Why are we so blind that we keep such vows of disobedience? Is it not contrary to this commandment for a daughter to get engaged to a young man against the will of her father and mother? Is it not contrary to this commandment for daughters or sons to vow to become priests, monks, or nuns against the will of father and mother? Did not God himself in Numbers 30 [:2-8] annul such vows and interpret this commandment in this way? For example, if either a husband or a wife vows to make a pilgrimage to St. James, or to do this or that, but the wife does not want to stay without her husband, tell me, is it not against God's commandment which has obligated the man to care for his wife and children and not desert them? Yet this mask of a pope makes these vows so strict that he emphasizes them in his bulls,[43] when he should instead tear up all of them and destroy them. But it is proper for the pope to prohibit what God commands and to destroy what God creates. How else could he be pope? My God, if these masquerading masks only erred and did evil to themselves, we certainly would be only too glad to endure them and to bear them with all honor. But since they do nothing but murder souls and destroy God's word, there can be no excuse either for silence or for enduring them. No one should tell me about patience and honor here. Accursed be silent patience here! Accursed be honor which retreats here and leaves room for these murderous masks to dominate poor souls!

To continue, let us talk about monks and monastic vows. Here, more than ever, the ears of these masks will ring and their teeth will gnash. Tell me, if a priest, a monk, or a nun vowed to obey the spiritual estate or order in unbelief or on the basis of the Jewish faith, how much better would he or she be than a man who vowed to sleep with his neighbor's wife? Would it not be a denial of the Christian faith and a worse sin than three adulteries? But how many people are there now, do you think, who become priests, monks, and nuns without denying the Christian faith but at the same time being spiritually in the Jewish faith? Does this appear strange to you? Listen a bit: this is the Christian faith that one believes that we are justified and saved not through any works but solely through Christ our mediator and through mercy, bestowed on us quite freely—Galatians 1 [:4]. Thus man despairs of himself and of all his deeds and clings to Christ's merit alone. Jewish faith means receiving God's grace through works and through one's own doing, and thus doing penance and being saved, Romans 10 [:3]. Christ has to be excluded as unnecessary or at least as not very necessary. Now see whether the majority of priests, monks, and nuns do not begin their spiritual lives in such Jewish faith; for they say they want to do penance and to be saved through the strict life, and they attribute to works and to the spiritual estate what belongs to Christ and to faith alone. What is this other than denying Christ

[43] Cf. for example, the bull of indulgences issued in 1515. Köhler, *op. cit.*, p. 86.

and becoming spiritual in unbelief—that is, that true Christians become Jews and pagans? It is just as St. Peter says, that those who already escaped error and sins are again entangled by them and have to live in error [II Pet. 2:20].

They themselves confess that they are Jews and pagans and they say, "Why should I become a priest, a monk, or a nun and torture myself in the order, if this did not save me and make me godly and pure?" Do you not see that these are the words of a Jewish faith in which Christ has neither room nor work? They expect from their orders and works what they should expect from Christ. That is why it is certain that all religious foundations and monasteries containing spiritual people who think their estate makes them godly and saves them are much worse than common brothels, taverns, and murderous pits. God also gives a sign that all of them are unchaste. For, because they eliminate the chastity of the Christian faith through such Jewish faith, they of necessity also have to eliminate physical chastity. As St. Peter says, they entice others to licentious passions through their great pretensions [II Pet. 2:18]. Thus all the orders and spiritual vows are contrary to God's first, second, and third commandments and they should be destroyed, stopped, and done away with. All clerics should be conscientiously advised either to denounce Jewish faith and begin their spiritual lives anew in Christian faith, or to give up tonsures and cowls, monasteries and altars in order to be free to do what they wish. This is no different from what they would do if they slept with women outside of marriage; for they would then either have to leave the women or to marry them.

You see, this is the spirituality of Baal. I have written my own booklet about it in which, God willing, I have refuted the spiritual vows with sufficient scriptural evidence and argumentation.[44] I hope this will do for a good conscience and honest mind so that they do not let themselves be so miserably entangled in the spiritual estates and be duped and destroyed by them. I do not care if I gratify these unlearned masks or make them angry by absolving priests, monks, and nuns from their vows and by destroying monasteries and reli-

[44] Cf. *To the Christian Nobility of the German Nation*, 1520. *LW* 44, 115-217. Luther here discussed spiritual authority in general and clerical marriage in particular.

gious foundations. Who can ever gratify these masks, who refuse to listen unless one tells them what is in their foolish hearts (as Solomon says [Prov. 18:2])? On the other hand, if one asks them for scriptural evidence and reasons for what they are doing, they only point to their red carnal [cardinals'] hats and bishops' masks and say, "Do you not see that I am a carnal [cardinal]? Should I be learned in addition and show you scriptural evidence and other reasons? Why is this necessary? We not only have the Holy Spirit, we have the Most Holy Spirit also, namely, the spirit of the pope. He is not only as holy as Christ but rather the most holy."[45]

I do not want to say any more about these mad, accursed papal bulls until these sensitive, pure people become more restless. For now it suffices for everyone to know that to save his soul and to prevent divine disfavor he must burn, disgrace, and destroy these Roman bulls of indulgence. In addition, these masks who erect them must not only be despised as unlearned and crude minds but must also be avoided as raving wolves and hellish soul-murderers, in accordance with the teachings of both St. Peter [II Pet. 2:1-3] and St. Paul [Acts 20:29].

Finally, is it not a shame that these bishops of God's disfavor, my ungracious lords, arrest the poor priests who get married? What will become of this? Burden yourselves more and more, dear masks! You have already lost the common prayer; you lead a knavish and whorish life; you fatten your lust and boast with the blood and sweat of the poor; you rob everyone of his property with lying and cheating; you torture the soul, body, and property of the world with bans and tyranny; you do not preach the gospel; and you not only refuse to exercise the spiritual office of the bishop but also prohibit and prevent others from preaching; you drive them away and persecute them. At the same time you are nothing but hateful, ugly, and hostile masks whom the world neither wishes to endure nor can endure because of your unbearable burdens, tyrannies, vices, outrages, and depravities. Dear masks, help us to get rid of you by increasing your merits and putting more on the scale! By no means ever consider how you might win the favor of the people with love, mildness, virtue, and goodness! Just carry on

[45] *Allerheyligst* in German, *sanctissimus* in Latin. A reference to the way the pope was addressed.

and on, dear masks. You are on the right track. For this is what your fathers the Jews did. When they had killed Christ, prohibited his word, and driven his apostles away, they could not sleep in peace; so they had to bring the Romans upon themselves, who annihilated and destroyed them. Why should you hesitate to do the same thing since you are the true children of such fathers?

If I were to ask why the poor priests are arrested and tormented because they married, where did God forbid them to do so, or how did they sin by doing so, I think they would step forward with their beautiful hats and long tails and say, "It is written in the most holy decretal."[46] These are the explanations these most learned and most reverend people will know to give for their action. May the Most Holy Father Pope and his most reverend bulls forgive me —I almost mocked these masks for their brave and spiritual intentions!

Adviser, advise well! Why do these whore-keepers dislike it when young men marry? No doubt because they lose their interest rates. For bishops receive the greater part of all their annual interest rates in almost all religious foundations from nothing but the priests' whores. Whoever wants to keep a little whore must give one guilder a year to the bishop. There is a proverb among them, "Chaste priests are not liked by the bishop—indeed, they are his enemies." Who else but a bishop could be a rich tradesman with women in this world? Who would blame the spiritual fathers for permitting whoredom for the sake of money, for selling living bodies of women and for prohibiting marriage which does not yield money? People make their living in many ways. A merchant sells spices and linen, bishops sell the flesh of whores. How else could they make a living? To top it all, if a priest's maid stumbles over a dishpan and breaks in two, so that one part of her must be carried to baptism, the interest rate increases beyond the annual guilder. The bishop now has a reason to show his mercy by selling a mother to the poor priest. Blessed are the bellies that carry babies! But let the father worry about whether the breasts that are sucked are blessed too. The spiritual bishop has twice received his share from the belly. Are these not noble and dear female bellies, which have

[46] Cf. *Decreti Prima Pars*, dist. LXXXI, C. XV. *CIC* 1, 284-285.

to be bought twice a year and which twice become pregnant with money for the spiritual lord!

My dear, do not think this a bad reason to motivate these holy spiritual people to forbid the poor priests to marry. Should they not prefer whores to pious wives? A married woman is a shameful and harmful thing; she does not produce a single penny for the most reverend fathers and lords in God. Forgive me this joke, my dear man; it comes not from a joking heart but rather from one made anxious by these very senseless and blind masks. They are completely deprived of all sense, wit, and reason by God's wrath so that pigs, oxen, and asses are smarter than they are. Yet they are spiritual rulers, which is really punishing the world with fools and babes, as Isaiah says [Isa. 3:4]! Do you think they can cite reasons and arguments other than those cited, which are only greed and money? Even if they were cruder than crude asses they still could not say that God has prohibited marriage to the priests. Indeed, St. Paul instituted it for the priests when he said, "A bishop should be the husband of one wife, keeping his children submissive and respectful," I Timothy 3 [:2, 4], and Titus 1 [:6]. Do you hear this, you masks and gaping fools? I mean you who are wolves and who subject innocent blood to tyranny. Answer me: what would you like to say or what could you say about St. Paul's statement that a priest should have no more than one wife? How are you going to interpret "one wife"? As a priest's whore whose belly you sell twice a year? St. Paul means only one wife, not two or more wives as was custom and law in the Old Testament. So if a priest wanted to obey this divine saying, who are you, you bloodthirsty masks, to prevent him? What is your argument? What do you say against it? Why do you elevate yourselves above God and his words? Should one worship you unlearned asses more than God?

The pope prohibited it. What shall I say? My dear asses, if the pope commanded you not to honor your father and mother (which he really does) and destroyed all of God's commandments, should you not be the ones to oppose him, risking life and limb for the sake of God's word? Did you not read St. Peter's saying, Acts 4 [5:29], "One must obey God rather than men"? Then you know that all human commandments, even if they were good and useful, are invalid and are no longer binding when they become unbearable.

Your own fleshly law teaches you that.[47] You can see that it is impossible for all priests to obey the accursed human law prohibiting marriage. Yet you great insatiable keepers of women still forcibly drive the poor souls into sin for the sake of your accursed greed. You can see and understand that they cannot obey the law, but [you say] they should obey it without any trouble. Oh, you murderers of souls! How shamefully you stain your hands with innocent blood! What an account you will have to render for such tyranny!

But now it is indeed clear that these human commandments regarding the prohibition of clerical marriage are not human commandments but rather commandments of the devil. Three passages from St. Paul prove it. Two of them are the passages to Titus [Titus 1:6] and to Timothy [I Tim. 3:2] mentioned above, that a priest shall have only one wife. This is God's word and order, [spoken] through St. Paul. That is why whatever is commanded contrary to this or what is commanded or ordered differently must be the devil's work. For God does not speak against himself or give the lie to his mouth, as all Scripture and all reason must confess. But all reason must also confess that these papal laws are indeed contrary to Paul's divine order. Is all this not clear enough, you silent and blind masks? How can you chafe against that? Are your iron heads and crude minds not ashamed publicly to command and force everyone to keep the commandments of the devil contrary to divine order? The third passage is I Timothy 4 [:1-3], "Teachers will come with pretensions, teaching devilish doctrines. They will forbid marriage and enjoin abstinence from foods which God created." See, he himself calls it devilish teaching to prohibit marriage. Nor does he speak here of the Tatians,[48] as the liar of Dresden says.[49] The Tatians did not prohibit marriage; rather, they condemned it as something sinful. But St. Peter speaks here of those who prohibit it rather than condemning it or regarding it as sinful, just as they

---

[47] *Decreti Prima Pars,* dist. IX, C. I. *CIC* 1, 16.

[48] Named after the Syrian apologist Tatian, who broke with the Roman congregation in 172. In Luther's time he was considered the founder of a very ascetic group called Encratites, who prohibited marriage, the eating of meat, and the drinking of wine. Recent research considers Tatian a supporter of the Encratites rather than their founder. Cf. *RGG* 2, 494.

[49] Jerome Emser. Cf. above, p. 210.

prohibit food without regarding it as sinful. The pope is doing just that: he does not, like the Tatians, say that marriage is an evil or a sin; again, he does not consider meat, eggs, milk evil or sin. Instead, he prohibits them in order to make a pretense of spirituality, as St. Paul says here. Thus they speak through pretensions based on the devil's teaching.

Since there are three powerful passages which irrefutably prove that the prohibition of marriage is something devilish commanded contrary to God's order, the priests should have a good conscience. They should cheerfully put their trust in these sayings and take them into consideration. And anyone who otherwise has no desire to take a wife should do so anyway, just to hurt the devil and to spite him and his teaching. You masks should assist in this, unless you wish to be the apostles of the devil and of his teaching.

But if someone is troubled by the fact that he vowed chastity at the time of his ordination, it suffices for him to know, as was said above,[50] that all vows contrary to God's commandments and order are invalid and are to be dissolved on pain of God's disfavor. Now these vows are indeed based on the teaching of the devil and opposed to God's commandments and order, as the foregoing argument clearly demonstrates. Accordingly, priests have dedicated their chastity not to God but to the pope who represents the devil and to human teaching. That is why men must dissolve their vows again, since such dedication does not lead to God. Therefore, it is not at all dangerous for a priest to take a wife. Only these masks regard it as dangerous; on the other hand, they sell whores for money, which is really dangerous, and punish no one for it. Are they not fine, lovely masks? They crucify Christ and let Barabbas go. Woe, woe, woe to them! I can but warn them and all those who support them to be on guard. God will not allow his word to be mocked.

Just look at the malice of the devil: just as he tricked people with his rattling and rumbling,[51] so that they thought the souls of the dead moved around the house to seek help, and thereby made a carnival out of the mass, so did he make up many abominable and false examples about priests' cooks, until he managed to create

[50] Cf. above, p. 286.

[51] A reference to poltergeists and similar phenomena. Cf. *LW* 54, 279-280.

the general rumor that a woman who has sinned once with a priest is beyond help and eternally lost. As a result, they fall into despair and lose all hope of becoming better, so that there are no worse women than the servants of the priests. That was his aim. No one paid attention to this devil's roguery; everyone let it go on, and these souls were permitted to despair and freely to expose themselves to danger.[52] The result was that his commandment of chastity was considered all the more holy, and God's commandment was all the more despised. O Lord God, how blind, how sure, how ignorant are the pope and the bishops! They really are and will remain masks, but unfortunately to the advantage of the devil and the disadvantage of the poor and miserable souls.

This will do for a beginning, until I see how the masks react. I hope they will try to defend themselves with blasphemy and blow on the embers.[53] May God help them to do this through the merit of their shameful, harmful, and mask-like nature and government. Amen.

I also ask those who wish to attack the masks in writing to do so publicly and honestly, in accordance with the gospel's rule and St. Paul's teaching. They should put their names on the title page and stand forth boldly for the right as I do. For we have the advantage that the masks are unlearned, in disrepute in all the world, and now disgraced before everyone as those who avoid the light, who cannot tolerate justice, and who will not come onto the field [to fight]. Thus their glitter is gone, and they are no longer ornamented with pretensions. For there is no better way to torture them than to defy them legitimately and to offer to hear their reasons and arguments. Then they are forced to be so ashamed in their hearts and consciences that they must keep silent and cannot find any support for their side. But if they proceed with their blasphemous power, which is all that is left to them for a brief time, their shame and disgrace are that much greater and they are despised and come to fall even sooner. Therefore, it only advances our cause if they continue as mad masks to blaspheme and rule without hesitation.

[52] Proverbial German, *sich frey ynn die schantz geben.* It is similar to *in die Schanze schlagen* and means literally to risk one's life for something or to take a chance.

[53] Proverbial German, *ynn die aschen blassen,* literally, "blow into the ashes."

In accordance with St. Paul's teaching, however, we should not only strike and punish consciences, but pour oil as well as wine into the wounds. In case these passages [from Scripture] have had an effect on some kindhearted bishops and have shocked their hearts, we have to anticipate their questions and tell them what they should do to be saved and to take the danger out of their estate.

Here, of course, there is no advice or consolation other than that a bishop should create learned men (if he himself is not gifted) who will preach the gospel clearly and purely in his stead all over his diocese. Moreover, he should watch over them and should stake everything on the gospel that Christ teaches us to stake on it. Thus we read that St. Valerius, bishop of Hippo, had St. Augustine preach for him before he became bishop and protected him.[54] Likewise, the custom in many Greek lands was to have priests preach for their bishops in their presence. In addition, by means of prayer, service, and assistance, such a bishop should do for the poor what he cannot achieve with preaching. A bishop refusing to do these things should by no means consider himself to be in the state of salvation.

If you say, "Well, what would such conduct do to the princely estate which the bishops now occupy?" I answer that we are not speaking of how one should be a prince but of how one should be a bishop and be saved. Who made bishops into princes? Christ forbade them to be princes when he separated them from princes and said, "The worldly princes are lords and exercise dominion over all their subjects, but you should not be like them."[55] The Prince of Princes will neither recant nor withdraw these words for the sake of your principality. Let diocese and principality go if you cannot be a bishop in them. Why do you want to destroy your soul eternally for the sake of temporal honor? Since it is so difficult to keep someone in a right, good, and holy state, how dare you remain in a state that is damnable? "For what will it profit you (says Christ [Matt. 16:26]) if you gain the whole world and forfeit your soul?"

But how could princes and nobles support their children and friends if there were no dioceses and religious foundations? Here

[54] Cf. Possidius, *Life of Augustine (Vita Augustini)*, IV, 8. *MPL* 32, 37.

[55] Luke 22:25-26. Luther here paraphrased the biblical quotation very freely.

you can see the blindness of us Germans. If a peasant strangled your son, beat him to death, or shamed your daughter or sister, there would be bloodshed and strife; you would rage and rave, and if you could ruin a territory you would do so, because you would think great injustice had been done to you. But my dear, open your eyes and see whether there could be a greater murderer or enemy of your child or of your friends than you yourself are. You help him get the diocese even though you are certain that he must give himself to the devil and carry on in such a way that he cannot be saved. You know this. Tell me then, do you not do him more harm than if you put a thousand swords through his heart?

If he had fallen into such a state by accident, you would pull him out with body and property, if you had any good in you at all, even if you only had a piece of bread to share with him. But what do you do? You push him into the abyss of hell so that your principality and your property will not be divided and diminished. You do not care if your flesh and blood is destroyed unto eternity, just as long as you can remain rich and great. You see, this is the custom now in all of Germany. All the bells should be tolled in the face of such abominable murder and strangulation of souls. The *Te Deum* should be sung, candles and flags should be paraded with full pomp, that it might be just as it was when the mad Israelite kings burned their children as sacrifices to the idol Molech [II Kings 23:10] with great noise and clangor to avoid hearing the children's cries and weeping.

This is also being done with daughters and sisters: they are enticed and indeed pushed into nunneries whether or not they want to go, only to avoid the destruction and impoverishment of families and estates. They should rather be in the same estate [in the world]. But it will not help anyway, for God still plagues us, so that principalities and nobles are being impoverished. Perhaps it would not happen if they had not been guilty of such abominable murder against their own flesh and blood. The innocent blood cries out against them and God hears it and avenges it.

Consider one side of this misery. The majority of young women in nunneries are robust and healthy, created by God to be wives and to bear children. But they are not strong enough to remain in this state, because chastity is a grace higher than nature, even if nature were pure. Moreover, God (when he created man and woman) did not want to have his law generally weakened or gradually annulled with miraculous signs. Instead, virginity should be a rare thing before him. So if you have a daughter or a friend who has fallen into such a state, you should help her out of it, if you are honest and devout, even if you had to risk all your property, life, and limb to do so.

But for the sake of your miserable property you push them into the mouth of the devil without consulting them. What are the consequences? Listen: I have never heard confession from a nun. Nevertheless, I will tell you on the basis of Holy Scripture what it is like for them, and I know that I am not lying. Unless she is in a high and unusual state of grace, a young woman can do without a man as little as she can do without eating, drinking, sleeping, or other natural requirements. Nor can a man do without a woman. The reason for this is that to conceive children is as deeply implanted in nature as eating and drinking are. That is why God gave us and implanted into our body genitals, blood vessels, fluids, and everything else necessary to accomplish it. The person who wants to prevent this and keep nature from doing what it wants to do and must do is simply preventing nature from being nature, fire from burning, water from wetting, and man from eating, drinking, or sleeping.

Thus I conclude that these nuns in the convents are forced to be chaste against their will; they dislike not having men. But if they are in convents against their will, they lose this life and the next; they are forced into hell on earth and hell in the other world. You see, you bring them to this point for the sake of your accursed property. This is the harvest of a few mad and senseless princes who so tyrannically watch over the locked monasteries. They want to hinder nature. And it is easy for them to talk, for they lie with women whenever they want to and give their own nature enough air and room. But the poor crowd of common people must die in their own hell because of it.

To continue, nature does not cease to do its work when there is involuntary chastity. The flesh goes on creating seed just as God created it to do. The blood vessels function according to their own nature, and thus the fluids rise—and with them the secret sin which

St. Paul calls impurity and softness [Gal. 5:19]. To put it bluntly for the sake of those who suffer miserably: if it does not flow into flesh it will flow into the shirt. But people are ashamed to complain about it and to confess it. The result is that in their heart they malign you and God, curse their own estate, and are hostile to all those who have helped them to become like this. Such people would rather marry a shepherd boy in their need, while they would otherwise hardly take a count. See, this is what the devil intended when he taught you to quench nature and subdue it even if it wants to be free.

But what shall we do in this matter, since goods cannot be distributed equally? Answer: Why do we not do what was done among the people of Israel, where only one man was kept as king? His brothers were given something and made equal to the rest of the people. Must all those who are born princes and nobles remain princes and nobles? Would it matter if a prince took a plain wife and was satisfied with a decent burgher's property? On the other hand, a young noblewoman could marry a burgher. In the long run it is not feasible for nobles to marry only nobles. Even though we are unequal before the world, before God we are all equally Adam's children and God's creatures, and one man is worth as much as another.

Now look, if your child or friend in a convent in her despair and need would like to take what is due to her so that she can enter a blessed estate, why do you not help her to achieve it before she falls into such despair? Why do you not give her what God gives, be it noble or not? O Lord God, how little we care for the poor souls, and how much we are drowned in greed!

I am therefore saying now that it is better to let the diocese and all honors go and to be a poor burgher or peasant than to fail to exercise the episcopal office or to see that it is exercised. For there is neither reason nor excuse for this. God's word must remain, and not only the episcopal estate but also heaven and earth must pass away. Judge yourself accordingly.

But if the pope and his followers do not like to see the gospel preached (which is the case now), you have even more reason to avoid the diocese or the episcopal estate. One must obey God rather than men [Acts 5:29]. You should not think you honor your episcopal estate and will be excused if you walk around preaching, as a bishop did recently.[56] These miserable people were silent about the gospel and wanted to offer their souls as pledges for the people, and thus lead the consciences. I say to such a bishop: Put your soul into an empty corner; if the devil takes it away, where would I be if I had counted on it? I want a bishop who does not offer me his soul as a foundation, for I do not know to whom it belongs. Rather, I want one to preach the pure gospel to me and to offer me Christ's soul as a foundation. Then I know for certain where I stand.

I am not speaking now of papal bishops and of what they should do. They would not tolerate it anyway. But I do ask whether somewhere there is someone who wishes to be a Christian bishop and who wants to protect his own soul together with those of his people. He should travel around and preach or have preached not human teachings but God's word in purity. Enough has been said above about the masks and bishop idols. May God give us his grace, and may he send again true laborers into his harvest; may he punish the murderers and burn their city, because they throw his servants and his Son out of the vineyard and kill without ceasing [Matt. 22:1-7]. Amen.

---

[56] Probably the bishop of Meissen. Cf. Luther's letter to Nicholas Hausmann on August 3, 1522. *WA*, Br 2, 584.

THAT A CHRISTIAN ASSEMBLY OR CONGREGATION HAS THE RIGHT AND POWER TO JUDGE ALL TEACHING AND TO CALL, APPOINT, AND DISMISS TEACHERS, ESTABLISHED AND PROVEN BY SCRIPTURE

1523

Translated by

Eric W. and Ruth C. Gritsch

INTRODUCTION

In the spring of 1522 the small town of Leisnig, located in electoral Saxony on the river Mulde, joined the Reformation and began to reorganize its parish along lines similar to those followed in the larger cities such as Wittenberg, Augsburg, Nürnberg, and others.[1] But Antoninus, the abbot of Buch, the nearby Cistercian monastery, who exercised the right of patronage over the city, was hostile to the Reformation. In the ensuing division between a large majority of townspeople, supported by peasants from surrounding villages, and the abbot, some influential citizens of Leisnig asked Luther to pay them a visit and to support their cause. Luther went to Leisnig on September 25, 1522, and presumably discussed two items with them: first, the right of the parish to select its own priests and preacher; and, second, the establishment of a "common chest" for the parish according to the practice in Wittenberg.[2] By the end of 1522, the Leisnig congregation elected Henry Kind, one of the Cistercian monks, as their priest, and Magister John Gruner, from the town of Oschatz, as their preacher—without the approval of Abbot Antoninus. Various attempts to reach a compromise between the congregation, the monastery, and the bishop failed.[3]

On January 25, 1523, a delegation from the Leisnig congregation visited Luther in Wittenberg to ask once more for support. Led by the feudal landlord of Leisnig, Sebastian von Kötteritzsch, and another representative of the town council, Hans Salbach, they presented Luther with a written request to provide a biblical rationale for their practice of calling their own priest and preacher and of reorganizing the financial structure and style of worship of the parish. Luther promised to do so and immediately went to work writing the treatise entitled *That a Christian Assembly or Congregation Has the Right and Power to Judge All Teaching and to Call, Appoint, and Dismiss Teachers, Established and Proven by Scripture.* Printed by Cranach and Döring in Wittenberg, it appeared

[1] For sources and details regarding the town of Leisnig, cf. *LW* 45, 161-168.

[2] Cf. Schwiebert, *Luther and His Times,* pp. 535-550.

[3] Cf. the description in *LW* 45, 164.

the beginning of May, 1523, perhaps on May 10.[4] Soon afterward Luther wrote *Concerning the Order of Public Worship*[5] and the Preface to *Fraternal Agreement on the Common Chest of the Entire Assembly at Leisnig*,[6] thus fulfilling his promise to present the Leisnig congregation with a rationale for their right to call their own preachers, to reform worship, and to reorganize the financial structure of the parish.

The treatise was written in such a way that everyone, not just the people of Leisnig, could obtain directives for a proper understanding of congregational authority. Luther clearly emphasized the word as the basis for ministry: since the congregation shares in the authority of the word on the basis of baptism, it may call its own preachers. Everyone who is baptized may exercise the office of the word, which belongs to the individual Christian as well as to the Christian community. In the later development of the Reformation, congregationalism, so strongly emphasized by Luther here, had to give way to the state church. But Luther emphasized in the treatise and throughout his life that the doctrine of the common priesthood of all believers should be the theological basis for a proper understanding of the role and authority of the pastor who is called to be the "priest of priests."

The translation of Albert T. W. Steinhaeuser in *PE* 4, 71-85, precedes ours. A revision by Theodore G. Tappert of Steinhaeuser's translation is available in *SW* 2, 321-334. Our translation is based upon the first German edition of the treatise, entitled *Das eyn Christliche versamlung odder gemeyne recht und macht habe, alle lere tzu urteylen und lerer zu beruffen, eyn und abzusetzen, Grund und ursach aus der schrifft,* in *WA* 11, 408-416.

---

[4] This is the conjecture in *WA* 11, 402.

[5] Cf. *LW* 53, 7-14.

[6] Cf. *LW* 45, 159-194.

THAT A CHRISTIAN ASSEMBLY OR CONGREGATION HAS THE RIGHT AND POWER TO JUDGE ALL TEACHING AND TO CALL, APPOINT, AND DISMISS TEACHERS, ESTABLISHED AND PROVEN BY SCRIPTURE

First, it is necessary to know where and what the Christian congregation[1] is, so that men do not engage in human affairs (as the non-Christians were accustomed to do) in the name of the Christian congregation. The sure mark by which the Christian congregation can be recognized is that the pure gospel is preached there. For just as the banner of an army is the sure sign by which one can know what kind of lord and army have taken to the field, so, too, the gospel is the sure sign by which one knows where Christ and his army are encamped. We have the sure promise of this from God in Isaiah 55 [:10-11], "My word" (says God) "that goes forth from my mouth shall not return empty to me; rather, as the rain falls from heaven to earth, making it fruitful, so shall my word also accomplish everything for which I sent it." Thus we are certain that there must be Christians wherever the gospel is, no matter how few and how sinful and weak they may be.[2] Likewise, where the gospel is absent and human teachings rule, there no Christians live but only pagans, no matter how numerous they are and how holy and upright their life may be.

Thus it undeniably follows that bishops, religious foundations, monasteries, and all who are associated with them have long since ceased to be Christians or Christian congregations, even though they have claimed they are more entitled to this name than anyone else. For whoever recognizes the gospel sees, hears, and understands

[1] *Gemeyne.* Luther here distinguished between "church" *(Kirche)* and "congregation" *(gemeyne).*

[2] Cf. *Concerning the Ministry,* 1523. *LW* 40, 42.

that even today they insist on their human teachings, have driven the gospel far away from themselves, and are still driving it away. That is why one should consider pagan and worldly what these people do and pretend.

Second, in this matter of judging teachings and appointing or dismissing teachers or pastors, one should not care at all about human statutes, law, old precedent, usage, custom, etc., even if they were instituted by pope or emperor, prince or bishop, if one half or the whole world accepted them, or if they lasted one year or a thousand years. For the soul of man is something eternal, and more important than every temporal thing. That is why it must be ruled and seized only by the eternal word; for it is very disgraceful to rule consciences before God with human law and old custom. That is why this matter must be dealt with according to Scripture and God's word; for God's word and human teaching inevitably oppose each other when the latter tries to rule the soul. This we shall prove clearly with regard to our present discussion, in this manner:

Human words and teaching instituted and decreed that only bishops, scholars, and councils should be allowed to judge doctrine. Whatever they decided should be regarded as correct and as articles of faith by the whole world, as is sufficiently proven by their daily boasting about the pope's spiritual law.[3] One hears almost nothing from them but such boasting that they have the power and right to judge what is Christian or what is heretical. The ordinary Christian is supposed to await their judgment and obey it. Do you see how shamelessly and foolishly this boasting, with which they intimidated the whole world and which is their highest stronghold and defense, rages against God's law and word?

Christ institutes the very opposite. He takes both the right and the power to judge teaching from the bishops, scholars, and councils and gives them to everyone and to all Christians equally when he says, John 10 [:4], "My sheep know my voice." Again, "My sheep do not follow strangers, but flee from them, for they do not know the voice of strangers" [John 10:5]. Again, "No matter how many of them have come, they are thieves and murderers. But the sheep did not listen to them" [John 10:8].

---

[3] Canon law.

Here you see clearly who has the right to judge doctrine: bishops, popes, scholars, and everyone else have the power to teach, but it is the sheep who are to judge whether they teach the voice [i.e., the words] of Christ or the voice of strangers. My dear, what can these water bubbles[4] say against it, with their feet scraping,[5] "Councils, councils! One must listen to the scholars, the bishops, the crowd; one must look at the old usage and custom"? Do you think the word of God should yield to your old usage, custom, and bishops? Never! That is why we let bishops and councils decide and institute whatever they please; when God's word is on our side we—and not they—shall judge what is right or wrong and they will have to yield to us and obey our word.[6]

Here I think you can indeed see clearly enough how much trust should be placed in those who deal with souls by means of human words. Who cannot see that all bishops, religious foundations, monasteries, universities, and everything belonging to them rage against this clear word of Christ? They shamelessly take away the judgment of teaching from the sheep and annex it to themselves through their own law and blasphemy. That is why they should certainly be regarded as murderers and thieves, as wolves and apostate Christians, for they are openly convicted here not only of denying God's word but also of opposing and acting against it. Such action was quite appropriate for the Antichrist and his kingdom, according to the prophecy of St. Paul, II Thessalonians 2 [:3-4].

Christ says again, Matthew 7 [:15], "Beware of the false prophets, who come to you in sheep's clothing but are inwardly ravenous wolves." You see, here Christ does not give the judgment to prophets and teachers but to pupils or sheep. For how could one beware of false prophets if one did not consider and judge their teaching? Thus there cannot be a false prophet among the listeners, only among the teachers. That is why all teachers and their teaching should and must be subject to the judgment of the listeners.

Again, the third passage is from St. Paul, I Thessalonians 5

---

[4] *Wasser blassen.* Luther frequently used this expression to indicate the futility and transience of his opponents' arguments. Cf. *WA* 10^{II}, 508.

[5] *Scharren*, an image to denote bragging and vainglorious behavior. The allusion may be to the provocative behavior of a rooster when he scrapes his claws on the ground.

[6] Cf. Luther's sixth sermon in Weimar, 1522. *WA* 10^{III}, 397-398.

[:21], "Test everything but hold fast to that which is good." You see, here he does not want to have any teaching or decree obeyed unless it is examined and recognized as good by the congregation hearing it. Indeed, this examination is not the concern of the teachers; rather, the teachers must first state what is to be examined. Thus here too the judgment is taken from the teachers and given to the Christian pupils. There is a radical difference between Christians and the world: in the world the rulers command whatever they please and their subjects accept it. "But among you," says Christ, "it should not be so." Instead, among Christians each person is the judge of the other person; on the other hand, he is also subject to the other person.[7] However, the spiritual tyrants have made a worldly power out of Christendom.

The fourth passage is again from Christ, Matthew 24 [:4-5], "Take heed that no one leads you astray. For many will come in my name, saying, 'I am the Christ,' and they will lead many astray." To sum up, do we really need to quote any more sayings? All of St. Paul's warnings, Romans 16 [:17-18], I Corinthians 10 [:14], Galatians 3, 4, and 5, Colossians 2 [:8], and elsewhere, and all the sayings of the prophets in which they teach us to avoid human teaching,[8] do nothing but take the right and power to judge all doctrine away from the teachers and with a stern decree impose it on the listeners instead, on pain of losing their soul. Accordingly, they not only have the power and the right to judge everything that is preached, they also have the duty to judge, on pain of [incurring] the disfavor of Divine Majesty. Thus we see in what an un-Christian way the tyrants treated us when they took this right and obligation from us and made it their own. For this alone they richly deserve to be driven out of Christendom and to be chased away as wolves, thieves, and murderers who rule over us and teach us things contrary to God's word and will.

Thus we conclude that wherever there is a Christian congregation in possession of the gospel, it not only has the right and power but also the duty—on pain of losing the salvation of its souls and in accordance with the promise made to Christ in baptism—to avoid, to flee, to depose, and to withdraw from the authority that our

[7] Cf. Luther's two theses in *The Freedom of a Christian,* 1520. *LW* 31, 344.
[8] Cf. *Avoiding the Doctrines of Men,* 1522. *LW* 35, 125-153.

bishops, abbots, monasteries, religious foundations, and the like are now exercising. For it is clearly evident that they teach and rule contrary to God and his word. This first point is established certainly and firmly enough, and one should depend upon it, that it is a divine right and a necessity for the salvation of souls to depose or to avoid such bishops, abbots, monasteries, and whatever is of their government.

Second, since a Christian congregation neither should nor could exist without God's word, it clearly follows from the previous [argument] that it nevertheless must have teachers and preachers who administer the word. And since in these last accursed times the bishops and the false spiritual government neither are nor wish to be teachers—moreover, they want neither to provide nor to tolerate any, and God should not be tempted to send new preachers from heaven—we must act according to Scripture and call and institute from among ourselves those who are found to be qualified and whom God has enlightened with reason and endowed with gifts to do so.

For no one can deny that every Christian possesses the word of God and is taught and anointed by God to be priest, as Christ says, John 6 [:45], "They shall all be taught by God," and Psalm 45 [:7], "God has anointed you with the oil of gladness on account of your fellows."[9] These fellows are the Christians, Christ's brethren, who with him are consecrated priests, as Peter says too, I Peter 2 [:9], "You are a royal priesthood so that you may declare the virtue of him who called you into his marvelous light."[10]

But if it is true that they have God's word and are anointed by him, then it is their duty to confess, to teach, and to spread [his word], as Paul says, I Corinthians 4 [II Cor. 4:13], "Since we have the same spirit of faith, so we speak," and the prophet says in Psalm 116 [:10], "I came to believe, therefore I speak." And in

[9] The R.S.V. translated this verse as "God has anointed you . . . above your fellows." Luther was aware that this passage could be interpreted in two different ways. In his exposition of Psalm 45, he wrote, "I do not disapprove of the translation 'above Thy fellows' in order to indicate excellence, though it can also be rendered 'on account of Thy fellows.'" *LW* 12, 246.

[10] Cf. also Luther's previous discussion of spiritual priesthood in *To the Christian Nobility of the German Nation,* 1520. *LW* 44, 127-131; and *The Babylonian Captivity of the Church,* 1520. *LW* 36, 112-117.

Psalm 51 [:13], he [God] says of all Christians, "I will teach the ungodly your ways, and sinners will return to you." Here again it is certain that a Christian not only has the right and power to teach God's word but has the duty to do so on pain of losing his soul and of God's disfavor.

If you say, "How can this be? If he is not called to do so he may indeed not preach, as you yourself have frequently taught," I answer that here you should put the Christian into two places. First, if he is in a place where there are no Christians he needs no other call than to be a Christian, called and anointed by God from within. Here it is his duty to preach and to teach the gospel to erring heathen or non-Christians, because of the duty of brotherly love, even though no man calls him to do so. This is what Stephen did, Acts 6–7, even though he had not been ordered into any office by the apostles. Yet he still preached and did great signs among the people. Again, Philip, the deacon and Stephen's comrade, Acts 8 [:5], did the same thing even though the office of preaching was not commanded to him either. Again, Apollos did so too, Acts 18 [:25]. In such a case a Christian looks with brotherly love at the need of the poor and perishing souls and does not wait until he is given a command or letter from a prince or bishop. For need breaks all laws and has none. Thus it is the duty of love to help if there is no one else who could or should help.

Second, if he is at a place where there are Christians who have the same power and right as he, he should not draw attention to himself. Instead, he should let himself be called and chosen to preach and to teach in the place of and by the command of the others.[11] Indeed, a Christian has so much power that he may and even should make an appearance and teach among Christians—without a call from men—when he becomes aware that there is a lack of teachers, provided he does it in a decent and becoming manner. This was clearly described by St. Paul in I Corinthians 14 [:30], when he says, "If something is revealed to someone else sitting by, let the first be silent." Do you see what St. Paul does here? He tells the teacher to be silent and withdraw from the midst of the Christians; and he lets the listener appear, even without a call. All this is done because need knows no command.

[11] Cf. Luther's sixth sermon in Weimar, 1522. *WA* 10^{III}, 395-396.

If then St. Paul says here that anyone from the midst of the Christians may come forward if there is a need and calls him through such a word of God, and tells the other to withdraw and deposes him by the power of his word, how much more right does a whole congregation have to call someone into this office when there is a need, as there always is, especially now! For in the same passage St. Paul gives every Christian the power to teach among Christians if there is a need, saying, "You can all prophesy one by one, so that all may learn and all be admonished" [I Cor. 14:31]. Again, "You should earnestly desire to prophesy, and do not forbid speaking in tongues; but all things should be done decently and in order" [I Cor. 14:39-40].

Let this passage be your sure foundation, because it gives such an overwhelming power to the Christian congregation to preach, to permit preaching, and to call. Especially if there is a need, it [this passage] calls everyone with a special call—without a call from men—so that we should have no doubt that the congregation which has the gospel may and should elect and call from among its members someone to teach the word in its place.

But if you say, "Did not St. Paul command Timothy and Titus to institute priests[12] [I Tim. 4:13; Titus 1:5], and do we not read, Acts 14 [:23], that Paul and Barnabas instituted priests among the congregations? (Therefore, the congregation cannot call anyone, nor can anyone draw attention to himself and preach among Christians; rather, one must have permission and authorization from bishops, abbots, or other prelates who represent the apostles)" I answer that if our bishops, abbots, etc., did represent the apostles, as they boast, one opinion would certainly be to let them do what Titus, Timothy, Paul, and Barnabas did when they instituted priests, etc. But since they represent the devil and are wolves who neither want to teach the gospel nor suffer it to be taught, they are as little concerned with instituting the office of preaching or pastoral care among Christians as the Turks or the Jews are. They should drive asses and lead dogs.

Moreover, if they were really decent bishops who wanted to have the gospel and wanted to institute decent preachers, they still could not and should not do so without the will, the election, and

[12] Luther's translation of "elders."

the call of the congregation—except in those cases where need made it necessary so that souls would not perish for lack of the divine word. For in such a need, as you have heard, not only may anyone procure a preacher, be it through pleas or the power of worldly authority, but he should also hurry to the scene himself and make an appearance and teach if he can—for need is need and has no limits —just as everyone should hurry to the scene of a fire in town and not wait until asked to come.

Otherwise, if there is no such need and if there are those who have the right, power, and grace to teach, no bishop should institute anyone without the election, will, and call of the congregation. Rather, he should confirm the one whom the congregation chose and called; if he does not do it, he [the elected man] is confirmed anyway by virtue of the congregation's call. Neither Titus nor Timothy nor Paul ever instituted a priest without the congregation's election and call. This is clearly proven by the sayings in Titus 1 [:7] and I Timothy 3 [:10], "A bishop or priest should be blameless," and, "Let the deacon be tested first." Now Titus could not have known which ones were blameless; such a report must come from the congregation, which must name the man.

Again, we even read in Acts 4 [6:1-6] regarding an even lesser office, that the apostles were not permitted to institute persons as deacons without the knowledge and consent of the congregation. Rather, the congregation elected and called the seven deacons, and the apostles confirmed them. If, then, the apostles were not permitted to institute, on their own authority, an office having to do only with the distribution of temporal food, how could they have dared to impose the highest office of preaching on anyone by their own power without the knowledge, will, and call of the congregation?

But since in our times there is the need, but no bishop, to provide evangelical preachers, the examples from Titus and Timothy are invalid. Instead, one must call [a preacher] from among the congregation, regardless of whether or not he is confirmed by Titus. For those under Titus' care would and should have done the same thing if Titus had not wanted to confirm him, or if there had been no one else to institute preachers. That is why this time is very different from the time of Titus when the apostles ruled and wanted to have true preachers. Now our tyrants only want to have wolves and thieves.

Why do these raging tyrants condemn us for such electing and calling? They themselves do and must do the same thing. Not one of them is ever instituted pope or bishop by the power of someone; rather, he is elected and called by his chapter[13] and then confirmed by others—the bishops by the pope as their supreme head, and he, the pope himself, by the cardinal of Ostia[14] as by his inferior. And even if one of them were not confirmed, he would still be bishop and pope. Thus I ask the dear tyrants: if bishops are made by the election and call of their own congregation, and if the pope is pope without confirmation by any other authority and by election alone, why should not a Christian congregation, too, make a preacher by its call alone? For they [the tyrants] regard the episcopal and papal estate as higher than the office of preaching! Who gave them this right and took it from us, especially since our calling has Scripture on its side, but their calling is nothing but a mere human trifle without Scripture, with which they rob us of our rights? They are tyrants and knaves who deal with us just as the devil's apostles should.

That is why there is still a custom in some places of having worldly authorities such as councilmen and princes institute and pay preachers themselves in their towns and castles, just as they please and without the permission or authorization of the bishops and popes.[15] And no one interfered, even though (I fear) they did not do it out of a [correct] understanding of their Christian rights. Rather, they did it because the spiritual tyrants despised and underestimated the office of preaching and made a great separation between it and the spiritual government, even though it is the

[13] The cathedral chapter elected the bishops. This arrangement was decreed after the investiture controversy, in the Concordat of Worms in 1122.

[14] The cardinal of Ostia headed the college of cardinals as dean during the conclave, the process of election. After a candidate for the papacy had received the required two-thirds vote from the conclave, the dean asked him whether he would accept the office and what name he wanted to be known by. He then gave the pope-elect the "solemn benediction" *(benedictio)*, or, if the candidate was not yet a bishop, immediately consecrated him. Cf. *NCE* 4, 114.

[15] A reference to the common custom of having a town council create "preaching posts" *(praedicatores)*. Occasionally, a town council or a prince would supervise already existing preaching posts.

highest office, on which all others depend and from which they follow. On the other hand, where there is no office of preaching, none of the others can follow. For John says, John 4 [:2], that Jesus did not baptize, he only preached. And Paul boasts, I Corinthians 1 [:17], that he was not sent to baptize but to preach.

Therefore, whoever has the office of preaching imposed on him has the highest office in Christendom imposed on him. Afterward he may also baptize, celebrate mass, and exercise all pastoral care; or, if he does not wish to do so, he may confine himself to preaching and leave baptizing and other lower offices to others—as Christ and all the apostles did, Acts 4 [6:4]. Thus it becomes evident that our present-day bishops are spiritual idols and not bishops. For they leave the highest office of the word, which should be their own, in the hands of the very lowest [orders], namely, chaplains, monks, and mendicants.[16] They also leave the lower offices such as baptizing and other pastoral care to them. In the meantime, however, they administer confirmation, consecrate bells, altars, and churches which are neither Christian nor episcopal duties and which they themselves invented. They are perverted and blind masks and true child-bishops.[17]

[16] *Terminarien.* Cf. above, p. 254, n. 10

[17] *Kinder bisschoffe,* the same thing as St. Nicholas bishops. Cf. above, p. 252, n. 8.

INDEXES

INDEX OF NAMES AND SUBJECTS

INDEX TO SCRIPTURE PASSAGES